Living Language™

CONVERSATIONAL
JAPANESE

THE LIVING LANGUAGE COURSES®

Living Spanish
Living French
Living Italian
Living German
Living Japanese
Living Russian
Living Portuguese (South American)
Living Portuguese (Continental)
Living Hebrew
Living Swahili
Children's Living French
Children's Living Spanish
Advanced Living French
Advanced Living Spanish
Living English for Spanish-Speaking People
Living English for French-Speaking People
Living English for Italian-Speaking People
Living English for German-Speaking People
Living English for Portuguese-Speaking People
Living English for Chinese-Speaking People
Living Language™ Spanish Video
Living Language™ French Video

Conversation manuals and dictionaries for any of the
Living Language Courses may be purchased
separately.

CONVERSATIONAL
JAPANESE

A COMPLETE COURSE
IN EVERYDAY JAPANESE

By Ichiro Shirato

Assistant Professor of Japanese, Columbia University

BASED ON THE METHOD DEVISED BY
RALPH WEIMAN
FORMERLY CHIEF OF LANGUAGE SECTION
U.S. WAR DEPARTMENT

SPECIALLY PREPARED FOR USE WITH
THE LIVING LANGUAGE COURSE®
IN JAPANESE

Crown Publishers, Inc., New York

This work was previously published under the title
Conversation Manual Japanese.

Copyright © 1962, 1985 by Crown Publishers, Inc.
All rights reserved.

Manufactured in the United States of America

Library of Congress Catalog Card Number: 60-15399

ISBN 0-517-55877-7

1985 Updated Edition

CONTENTS

v

vii

x

INTRODUCTION to the COMPLETE LIVING LANGUAGE COURSE®

The Living Language Course® uses the natural method of language-learning. You learn Japanese the way you learned English—by hearing the language and repeating what you heard. You didn't begin by studying grammar; you first learned how to say things, how words are arranged, and only when you knew the language pretty well did you begin to study grammar. This course teaches you Japanese in the same way. Hear it, say it, absorb it through use and repetition. The only difference is that in this course the basic elements of the language have been carefully selected and condensed into 40 short lessons. When you have finished these lessons, you will have a good working knowledge of the language. If you apply yourself, you can master this course and learn to speak basic Japanese in a few weeks.

While *Living Language™ Conversational Japanese* is designed for use with the complete Living Language Course®, this book may be used without the cassettes. The first 5 lessons cover Japanese pronunciation, laying the foundation for learning the vocabulary, phrases, and grammar that are explained in the later chapters.

All the material is presented in order of importance. When you reach page 150, you will have already learned 300 of the most frequently used sentences and will be able to make yourself understood on many important topics. By the time you have finished this course, you will have a sufficient command of Japanese to get along in all ordinary situations.

The brief but complete summary of Japanese grammar is included in the back of this book to enable you to perfect your knowledge of Japanese. The special section on letter writing will show you how to answer an invitation, make a business inquiry, and address an envelope properly. Just as important is the *Living Language™ Common Usage Dictionary*. This is included in the course primarily for use as a reference book, but it is a good idea to do as much browsing in it as possible. It contains the most common Japanese words with their meanings illustrated by everyday sentences and idiomatic expressions. The basic words—those you should learn from the start—are capitalized to make them easy to find.

Keep practicing your Japanese as much as possible. Use your Japanese whenever you get a chance—with Japanese-speaking friends, with the waiter at a Japanese restaurant, with other students.

This course tries to make learning Japanese as easy and enjoyable as possible, but a certain amount of application is necessary. The cassettes and books that make up this course provide you with all the material you need; the instructions on the next page tell you what to do. The rest is up to you.

Course Material

The material of the complete Living Language Course® consists of the following:

1. *2 hour-long cassettes.* The label on each face indicates clearly which lessons are contained on that side. (Living Japanese is also available on 4 long-playing records.)

2. *Conversational Japanese book.* This book is designed for use with the recorded lessons, or it may be used alone. It contains the following sections:

   Basic Japanese Vocabulary and Grammar
   Summary of Japanese Grammar
   Letter Writing

3. *Japanese-English/English-Japanese Common Usage Dictionary.* A special kind of dictionary that gives you the literal translations of more than 15,000 Japanese words, plus idiomatic phrases and sentences illustrating the everyday use of the more important vocabulary and 1,000 essential words capitalized for ready reference.

How to Use Conversational Japanese with the Living Language™ Cassettes

TO BEGIN

There are 2 cassettes with 10 lessons per side. The beginning of each lesson is announced on the tape and each lesson takes approximately 3 minutes. If your cassette player has a digit indicator, you can locate any desired point precisely.

LEARNING THE LESSONS

1. Look at page 3. Note the words in **boldface** type. These are the words you will hear on the cassette. There are pauses to enable you to repeat each word and phrase right after you hear it.

2. Now read Lesson 1. (The ▭ ▭ symbols indicate the beginning of the recorded material. In some advanced lessons, information and instructions precede the recording.) Note the points to listen for when you play the cassette. Look at the first word: **Ákira,** and be prepared to follow the voice you will hear.

3. Play the cassette, listen carefully, and watch for the points mentioned. Then rewind, play the lesson again, and this time say the words aloud. Keep repeating until you are sure you know the lesson. The more times you listen and repeat, the longer you will remember the material.

4. Now go on to the next lesson. It's always good to quickly review the previous lesson before starting a new one.

5. There are 2 kinds of quizzes at the end of each section. One is the matching type, in which you must select the English translation of the Japanese sentence. In the other, you fill in the blanks with the correct Japanese word chosen from the 3 given directly below the sentence. Do these quizzes faithfully and, if you make any mistakes, reread the section.

6. When you get 100 percent on the Final Quiz, you may consider that you have mastered the course.

Living Language™

CONVERSATIONAL
JAPANESE

LESSON 1 DÁI ÍKKA

A PRELIMINARY NOTE

Japanese, as spoken by the majority of Japan's ninety-two million people, is the language you will be learning in this course. Not only can it be used throughout Japan, but also, to a limited extent, in Korea, Taiwan, and some parts of Southeast Asia.

Japanese is a language that is peculiarly original among the world's languages. Despite the fact that more than half the words in Japanese were borrowed from Chinese, the linguistic structure of Japanese is completely different from Chinese. And although the grammatical rules of Korean and Japanese are amazingly similar, these languages are also unlike each other except for the Chinese words which both have adopted.

There are several things you should know and remember to make your understanding of Japanese easier:

1. In Japanese, verbs, adjectives, copulas (linking words), and certain endings are inflected in a number of categories.

2. Japanese is rich in many small words called "particles." These are used very frequently to show the grammatical relationship within a sentence of one word to another. Mastery of these particles is a key to the rapid learning of Japanese.

3. Punctuation is used in Japanese much the same as in English. The use of punctuation marks in the Japanese writing system is relatively new, and rules governing punctuation usage have not yet been firmly established.

THE ALPHABET: THE LETTERS

All Japanese words and sentences in this course have been transcribed into English, and all the letters of the English alphabet (except for "l,"[1] "q," and "x") appear in their usual order and are called by their usual English names. Note, however, that the letter "c" appears only in combination with "h" and that these two letters together (ch) are *always treated as one letter.*

A comprehensive list of signs and instructions in Japanese characters (together with their English meanings) appears in Lesson 40, and an explanation of the Japanese traditional writing system as well as a description of Japanese characters appears in the Summary of Grammar. For a discussion of the Japanese Syllabary, see Lesson 5.

ACCENT

Regardless of their length, words *may* or *may not* be accented in Japanese. Consequently, it is possible for a word of one syllable to be accented or a word of several syllables to be unaccented. All words in this manual which do not carry an accent mark (´) are unaccented. In all cases, an accent mark denotes a drop in the pitch of the voice *directly after the accented syllable*. The degree of the drop does not matter, so long as it occurs. However, the more excited the speaker is, the greater may be the change in pitch.

Remember these points:

1. On an unaccented word, the tone (or pitch) of the voice is held even except on the first syllable

---

[1]The sound of *l* is sometimes heard in the pronunciation of Japanese by Japanese nationals. But since this sound is always interchangeable with the Japanese variety of *r*, for the sake of simplicity, all sounds that might sometimes be pronounced *l* are written throughout this course as *r*.

(where it is slightly lower), *no matter how long the word is.*

2. When a single-syllable word is accented, the drop in pitch occurs *after that word.*

3. In multisyllabic words having the accent on the first syllable, the pitch of the voice is dropped *directly after* that syllable and this lowered tone is maintained for all the other syllables in that word.

4. For multisyllabic words having the accent on the second or any subsequent syllable, the same tone is maintained for *all* the syllables *through the accented syllable* (with the exception of the first syllable, on which the tone is slightly lowered); then the tone is dropped.

5. The accent on certain words disappears when these words are placed next to another accented word. This accounts for the fact that words will on occasion carry an accent mark and at other times discard it.

6. Accent patterns vary more among different dialects than do grammatical patterns.

THE ALPHABET: THE SOUNDS

Many Japanese sounds are like English. Listen and repeat the following Japanese first names, and notice which sounds are similar and which are different:

Ákira	Fusao	Isoo
Áiko	Fusáko	Ítoko
Átsuko	Gantaroo	Jíroo
Chíeko	Gíichi	Jún
Émiko	Haruo	Kíyoshi
Éijiroo	Hídeko	Kúniko

Makoto	Osamu	Susumu
Máriko	Rentaroo	Tákashi
Noburu	Ryuuichi	Téruko
Nóbuko	Shinzoo	Úmeko

NOTICE:

1. that each sound is pronounced clearly and crisply; sounds are not slurred over the way they often are in English.

2. that each syllable is spoken evenly for almost an equal length of time.

3. that some names or words have an accented syllable and some don't.

4. that when a syllable is marked with an accent (´), the pitch of the voice is always lowered directly after that syllable.

Now listen to and repeat the following words which are to some extent similar in English and Japanese. Notice how the Japanese spelling and pronunciation differ from the English:

airon	iron (to press)
ákusento	accent
amáchua	amateur
Amérika	America
báree	ballet
básu	bus
báta	butter
benchi	bench
béru	bell
bóoto	rowboat
chokoréeto	chocolate
daiyamóndo	diamond
dánsu	dance
depáato	department store
dezáato	dessert

dezáin	design
dókku	dock
enameru	enamel
erebéetaa	elevator
esukaréetaa	escalator
furanneru	flannel
gáido	guide (traveler's)
gyángu	gang
garasu	glass (pane)
garéeji	garage

LESSON 2   DÁI NÍKA

THE LETTERS AND SOUNDS *(cont.)*

Here is a further group of words which have some
similarity in Japanese and English:

haihíiru	high heel
hámu	ham
handobággu	handbag
herikóputaa	helicopter
hisutérii	hysteria, hysterics
hóosu	water hose
hoomushikku	homesick
hóteru	hotel
infure	inflation
ínku	ink
interi	intelligentsia
jaanarísuto	journalist
jámu	jam, jelly
jázu	jazz
kábaa	cover
káfusu	cuffs
káppu	cup (trophy)
koppu	drinking glass
karée ráisu	curried rice

karéndaa	calendar
maagarin	margarine
máaketto	market
maikuróhon	microphone
modan	modern
náiron	nylon

PRONUNCIATION PRACTICE I

Vowels

The following groups of words will give you some additional practice in spelling and pronunciation:

1. The sound *a* as in the English word "ah" or "father," but short and crisp:

hanásu	to tell	**káta**	shoulder
akai	it's red	**wakái**	he is young

2. The sound *e,* pronounced like the "a" in the English word "many," but without the final "y":

e	picture	**te**	hand
ke	hair	**me**	eye

3. The sound *i,* pronounced like the "e" in the English word "keep" but still higher, short, and crisp:

i	stomach	**ni**	two
ki	tree	**hí**	fire

4. The sound *o* as in the English word "go," but sharply cut off:

o	tail	**otóko**	male
otó	sound	**sóto**	outside

5. The sound *u* as in the English word "put", but spoken without rounding the lips:

ushí	cow	**kutsú**	shoes
kushí	comb	**tsukue**	desk

VOWEL CLUSTERS

6. When two identical vowels such as *aa, ee, ii, oo,* or *uu* appear together, they form a sound twice as long as the single vowel.

Compare the following pairs:

to	door	**sato**	native place
tóo	ten	**satóo**	sugar
tokí	time	**kotó**	event, thing
tóoki	china	**kootoo**	high rank

Sometimes a pair of identical vowels is called a "long vowel" or a "double vowel," and it can be written as a single letter with a macron over it, e.g., *ā, ē, ō,* and *ū.* However, "long" or "double" *i* is usually written *ii*:

koohíi,	coffee	**kúuki,**	air
kōhii		*kūki*	
sóoko, *sōko*	warehouse	**tooroku,**	registration
		tōroku	

7. In a succession of two or more different vowels, each vowel is pronounced clearly and distinctly, and each vowel is articulated for the same length of time:

ué	top	**akai**	it's red
tsukue	desk	**aói**	it's blue
ookíi	it's big	**aói úmi**	blue ocean
óokíi ié	a big house	**aói kao**	a pale face

The combination *ei* forms an exception to this rule, for in everyday speech *ei* is often pronounced like *ee:*

kéiko	practice	**Beikoku**	The United
(pronounced		(pronounced	States of
kéeko)		*Beekoku*)	America
séito	pupil,	**seinen**	youth
(pronounced	student	(pronounced	
séeto)		*seenen*)	

8. The vowels *i* and *u* are "weak" vowels. They sometimes disappear altogether or are whispered in a rapid conversation. This disappearance or whispering usually occurs when these vowels are surrounded by such voiceless consonants as *ch*, *h*, *k*, *p*, *s*, *sh*, *t*, and *ts*:

kutsúshita	socks	**kitté**	stamp
kippu	ticket	**sukkári**	entirely

9. When a syllabic[1] *n* follows a vowel, it affects the sound of the vowel so that it sometimes takes on a nasal quality:

kán	tin can	**són**	less (money)
kónnan	difficulty	**món**	gate

LESSON 3 DÁI SÁNKA

PRONUNCIATION PRACTICE II

CONSONANTS

1. *B* is generally pronounced like the English "b" but less explosively:

bentoo	box lunch	**binsen**	writing pad
kaban	briefcase	**obon**	tray

2. *Ch* is pronounced like the English "ch" in "cheese":

ocha	tea	**uchi**	house
chótto	a little bit	**chúui**	caution

3. *D* is pronounced with the tip of the tongue touching the back of the upper teeth and is less explosive than the English "d":

dáre	who	**dénsha**	streetcar
dóko	where	**kádo**	corner

[1]See Lesson 4, Item 21.

4. *F* is usually pronounced by forcing the air out between the lips as though blowing out a candle:

fúne	ship	**furó**	bath
fukái	it's deep	**futatsu**	two

5. The Japanese *g* has two sounds:

   a. At the beginning of a word, it is pronounced like the English "g" in "go":

gaikoku	foreign country	**genryoo**	raw material
gín	silver	**gó**	five

   b. In the middle of a word, it usually has some nasal quality and sounds something like the "ng" in the English word "singer":

hagaki	post card	**kagí**	key
káge	shadow	**kágu**	household furniture

6. The Japanese *h* has two sounds:

   a. Before *a, e,* and *o,* it is pronounced like the English "h" in "high":

hái	yes	**hón**	book
hei	fence	**hóo**	cheek

   b. Before *i* or *y,* it is pronounced like the English "h" in "hue":

higashi	east	**hyakú**	one hundred
hirú	noon	**hyooshi**	rhythm

7. *J* is pronounced like the English "j" in "jeep":

jagaimo	potato	**shookàijoo**	letter of introduction
jibikí	dictionary	**júnsa**	policeman

8. *K* is pronounced like the English "k" in "kite":

kása	umbrella	**kón'ya**	this evening
késa	this morning	**kutsú**	shoes

9. *M* is pronounced like an English "m" but without tightening the lips as much:

máiasa	every morning	**míkan**	tangerine
mé	eye	**mushi**	bugs

10. *N* has two sounds in Japanese:
   a. *N* before *a, e, o,* and *u,* it is pronounced with the tip of the tongue touching the back of the upper teeth:

nashí	pear	**nódo**	throat
néko	cat	**numá**	marsh

   b. Before *i* or *y,* it is pronounced like the "n" in the English word "news" (with the tip of the tongue touching the back of the lower teeth and the middle part of the tongue touching the roof of the mouth):

nikú	meat	**gyuunyuu**	cow's milk
nishi	west	**nyuu-jóoryoo**	admission fee

11. *P* is pronounced like the English "p" but less explosively:

pán	bread	**pín**	pin
pén	pen	**sánpun**	three minutes

12. *R* is pronounced by first placing the tip of the tongue at the back of the upper teeth and then flapping it.[1]

[1]For more on the sound of *r,* refer to the footnote on page 2.

ráigetsu	next month	**riku**	land
rénga	brick	**rokú**	six

LESSON 4 DÁI YÓN KA

CONSONANTS *(cont.)*

13. *S* is pronounced like the English "s" in "song" but with less hiss:

saká	slope	**sóra**	sky
sékai	world	**sú**	vinegar

14. *Sh* resembles the English "sh" in "she":

shashin	photograph	**shooko**	proof
shichí	seven	**shúfu**	capital city

15. *T* is pronounced with the tip of the tongue touching the back of the upper teeth and is less explosive than the English "t":

tá	rice field	**té**	hand
takusan	a lot	**to**	door

16. *V* is pronounced like the English "v" in "vain." Note that the sound of *v* appears only in words borrowed from occidental languages. Some Japanese do not use this sound at all but replace it with a *b*, as follows:

vaiorin	violin	**baiorin**	violin
véeru	veil	**béeru**	veil
viníiru	vinyl	**biníiru**	vinyl
révyuu	revue	**rébyuu**	revue

17. *W* is pronounced somewhat like the English "w" in "want" but without rounding or protruding the lips:

| watakushi | I | kawá | river |
| wáke | meaning | uwagi | jacket |

18. *Y* is pronounced as in English:

| yamá | mountain | hayái | it's fast |
| yóru | night | fuyú | winter |

19. Z usually has two sounds in Japanese:

    a. At the beginning of a word it has a sound similar to the English "ds" in "beds":

| zashikí | guest room | zoori | sandal |
| zéi | tax | zutto | by far the |

    b. In the middle of a word it is pronounced like the English "z" in "zero":

| kaze | wind | mizu | water |
| suzume | sparrow | kázoku | family |

    Note that some Japanese mix the *dz* and *z* sounds described above without regard to the position of the letter in the word.

20. When a word contains a double *p*, *t*, *k*, or *s*, the consonant sound is also doubled in length. Note the differences in pronunciation between the following pairs of words, the first member containing a single consonant and the second containing double consonants:

haka	tomb	kasai	fire (in a house)
hakka	mint (plant)	kassai	applause
móto	formerly	mótto	more

The same kind of lengthening takes place when *t* is followed by *ch* or *ts* or when *s* is followed by *sh:*

itchi	agreement	**tassha**	being healthy
ittsuu	one letter	**késshin**	determination

21. The syllabic *n* represents another group of sounds which is independent from the *n* described above in item 10. In this manual, the syllabic *n* will be written like the ordinary *n*. Remember, however, that it differs in pronunciation from the ordinary *n* as follows:

   a. It is always held as long as one full syllable.

   b. Its own sound-value changes, depending on what follows.

      1. Before *n, t,* and *d,* it is pronounced like the English "n" in "pen":

anna	that sort of	**santóo**	third class
onna	female	**kóndo**	this time

      2. Before *m, p,* or *b,* it is pronounced like the English "m":

SPELLED	PRONOUNCED	
sánmai	**sámmai**	three sheets
shinpai	**shimpai**	worry
kanban	**kamban**	signboard

      3. Before a vowel or a semi-vowel (*y* or *w*), it is pronounced somewhat like the English *ng* in "singer," but without finishing the *g* sound and the preceding vowel is often nasalized.

gen'an	original plan
tán'i[1]	unit
hón'ya[1]	bookstore
minwa	folklores

Note that in the following pairs of words, the first has an ordinary *n* and the second has a syllabic *n*:

nana	seven	taní	valley
nán'a	South Africa	tán'i	unit
kani	crab	kuni	nation
kán'i	simplicity	kún'i	court rank

4. Before *k*, *g*, and *s*, or when it is the final letter in a word, the syllabic *n* sounds somewhat like the English "ng" in "singer" described in (3) above:

kankei	relationship	senséi	teacher
ningen	human beings	san	three
sen	one thousand	kin	gold

LESSON 5 DÁI GÓKA

THE JAPANESE SYLLABARY

The traditional writing system used in Japan is based on two different types opf symbols: "phonetic" and "ideographic." (See grammer section for a detailed explanation.) The phonetic symbols are the Japanese equivalents of our alphabet and are called *kana*. Each *kana* symbol stands for a syllable.

These are the basic syllables represented in *kana*:

[1]Notice that an apostrophe is placed after a syllabic *n* when it precedes a vowel or *y*.

a	ka	sa	ta	na	ha	ma	ya	ra	wa	n (syllabic)
a	ka	sa	ta	na	ha	ma	ya	ra	wa	
i	ki	shi	chi	ni	hi	mi		ri		
u	ku	su	tsu	nu	fu	mu	yu	ru		
e	ke	se	te	ne	he	me		re		
o	ko	so	to	no	ho	mo	yo	ro	o	

15

BUILDING A VOCABULARY

Building up a Japanese vocabulary is an easier task than you might expect. As you have already observed, a great number of English and European words have been adopted by the Japanese and are in everyday use. The following is a list of more of these words.

apáato	apartment house	**gaaru sukáuto**	girl scout
aribai	alibi	**géemu**	game
arufabétto	alphabet	*górira*	gorilla
arukooru	alcohol	*gurúupu*	group
asufáruto	asphalt	**hamonika**	harmonica
asupírin	aspirin	**hoomúran**	home run
bátto	bat (baseball)	**infuruéna**	influenza
		iyáhoon	earphone
bóonasu	bonus	**jíguzagu**	zigzag
booru	ball	**jirénma**	dilemma
booi sukáuto	boy scout	**károrii**	calorie
		katarogu	catalogue
búrashi	brush	*Katoríkku*	Catholic
chíppu	tip	*kéeki*	cake
dáasu	dozen	*konkuríito*	concrete
dámu	dam	*kóoto*	coat (woman's outer garment)
dainamáito	dynamite		
dekki	deck		
dórama	drama	*kórera*	cholera
dóru	dollar	*kóruku*	cork
emerárudo	emerald	*korusétto*	corset
episoodo	episode	*kúupon*	coupon
feruto	felt	*kúrabu*	club

kúreyon	crayon	*raion*	lion
kuríimu	cream	*rajúumu*	radium
kuríiningu	cleaning	*reenkóoto*	raincoat
makaroni	macaroni	*résutoran* ⎫	restaurant
manhóoru	manhole	*résutoranto* ⎬	(occidental
Marariya	malaria		style)
masukótto	mascot	*ríbon*	ribbon
massáaji	massage	*rokétto*	rocket
Mée dee	May Day	*rómansu*	romance
mégahon	megaphone	**sáakasu**	circus
metaru	medal	**sáiren**	siren
ményuu	menu	*sakkárin*	saccharine
mémo	memo	*sandoítchi*	sandwich
móotaa	motor	*sárarii*	salary
mottóo	motto	*sháberu*	shovel
neonsáin	neon sign	*shoouíndoo*	show
ónsu	ounce		window
ooru	oar	*sokétto*	socket
oosóritii	authority	*sooséiji*	sausage
ootóbai	motorcycle	*sunáppu*	snap (photo-
	(auto-		graph)
	bicycle)	*supái*	spy
ootomíiru	oatmeal	*supiido*	speed
Orinpíkku	Olympic	*suríppa*	slipper
	game	*súriru*	thrill
paasénto	per cent	*sutóobu*	stove
pái	pie	*suutsu*	suitcase
paináppuru	pineapple	*kéesu*	
panfurétto	pamphlet	**taipuráitaa**	typewriter
panku	flat tire	**táiru**	tile
	(puncture)	*tákushii*	taxi
panorama	panorama	*tánku*	tank (army)
párasoru	parasol	*táoru*	towel
párupu	pulp	*teeburu*	table
pianisuto	pianist	*ténto*	tent
pokétto	pocket	*tonneru*	tunnel (rail-
			road)

torákku	truck	**yótto**	yacht
uétoresu	waitress	**yúumoa**	humor
uranyúumi	uranium		

Notice that some words are used in a more restricted sense in Japanese than in English. Note too that when a word from English is added to Japanese, not only is the *sound* of the word changed to harmonize with the Japanese sound system, but the *length* of the word may be cut, as in the following examples:

infure	inflation
panku	puncture (flat tire)

Here are some more words borrowed from English but used in a restricted sense in Japanese:

JAPANESE FORM	WORD OF ORIGIN	BUT MEANS IN JAPANESE
barákku	barrack	shack; shabby-looking, flimsy wooden house
bíru **bírudingu**	building	occidental-style concrete office building
bisukétto	biscuits	tea biscuits and cookies
dóa	door	occidental-style door
dorámu	drum	drum (musical only; referring mainly to types used in jazz)
haato	heart	heart (one of a suit of playing cards)
herumétto	helmet	sun helmet of the kind usually worn in the tropics
hókku	hook	snap fastener used on garments
jám	jam	jam and jelly
jaketsu	jacket	sweater
káppu	cup	trophy
koppu	cup	drinking glass

kónpasu	compass	compass (instrument for drawing circles)
mátchi	match	match (for igniting fire)
míshin	machine	sewing machine
nóoto	note	notebook
paama-nénto	permanent	permanent wave
paipu	pipe	pipe (for smoking)
ráitaa	lighter	cigarette lighter
rekóodo	record	phonograph record
sutóroo	straw	drinking straw

LESSON 6   DÁI RÓKKA

GENERAL EQUIVALENTS

1. Japanese *aa* = English "ar," "er," "ir," "or"

| apáato | apartment | *sáakasu* | circus |
| herikó-putaa | helicopter | *móotaa* | motor |

2. Japanese *ee* = English "a"

| géemu | game | *teeburu* | table |
| kéeki | cake | *keeburu* | cable car |

3. Japanese *oo* = English "o," "oā"

| bóonasu | bonus | *hoomuran* | home run |
| bóoto | boat | *kóochi* | coach (athletic) |

4. Japanese *ui* = English "vi," "wi"

| kúizu | quiz (radio program) | *sandouitchi* | sandwich |
| shoouíndoo | show window | | |

5. Japanese *b* = English "v"

sháberu   shovel   **térebi**   television

6. Japanese *chi* = English "ti"

chíppu   tip   **chíimu**   team
                               (athletic)

7. Japanese *ji* = English "di"

rájio   radio   *jirénma*   dilemma
sutajio   studio (art,
           broad-
           casting,
           movie)

8. Japanese *k* = English "c"

kákuteru   cocktail   *kanariya*   canary
Amerika   America   *kókku*   cook
                             (occidental
                             food)

9. Japanese *kku* = English "ack," "ock"

barákku   barrack
dókku   dock

10. Japanese *kki* = English "eck," "ick"

dekki   deck
sutékki   stick (walking)

11. Japanese *ru* = English "l," "rl"

hóteru   hotel   *káaru*   curl
booru   ball

12. Japanese *suto* = English "st"

sutoráiki,   strike   *jaanarísuto*   journalist
  suto   (labor)
pianísuto   pianist

13. Japanese *tto* = English "t"

maakétto	market	*sokétto*	socket
pánfuretto	pamphlet	*yótto*	yacht

14. Japanese *tsu* = English "t"

jáketsu	jacket	*shátsu*	shirt
	(sweater)		
omuretsu	omelet		

15. Japanese *s* = English "th"

súriru	thrill	**oosóritii**	authority
	(movie)		(person)

USEFUL WORD GROUPS I

THE DAYS OF THE WEEK

Nichiyóobi	Sunday
Getsuyóobi	Monday
Kayóobi	Tuesday
Suiyóobi	Wednesday
Mokuyóobi	Thursday
Kin'yóobi	Friday
Doyóobi	Saturday

THE MONTHS

Ichigatsu	January
Nigatsu	February
Sángatsu	March
Shigatsu	April
Gógatsu	May
Rokugatsu	June
Shichigatsu	July
Hachigatsu	August
Kúgatsu	September
Juugatsu	October

| Juuichigatsu | November |
| Juunigatsu | December |

SOME NUMBERS

ichí	one
ni	two
san	three
shí	four
gó	five
rokú	six
shichí	seven
hachí	eight
kyúu, *kú*	nine
júu	ten

SOME COLORS

áo	blue
áka	red
kiiro	yellow
mídori	green
shíro	white
kúro	black
chairo	brown
nezumiiro, haiiro	gray

DIRECTIONS

| kitá | north | higashi | east |
| minami | south | nishi | west |

QUIZ 1

Try matching these two columns:

1. *Nichiyóobi*	1. Thursday
2. *Hachigatsu*	2. brown
3. *Suiyóobi*	3. ten

4. *nezumiiro*	4. Sunday
5. *Mokuyóobi*	5. red
6. *kú*	6. August
7. *chairo*	7. Monday
8. *hachí*	8. July
9. *Shichigatsu*	9. five
10. *kiiro*	10. white
11. *áka*	11. gray
12. *Getsuyóobi*	12. nine
13. *gó*	13. Wednesday
14. *shíro*	14. yellow
15. *júu*	15. eight

ANSWERS

1-4; 2-6; 3-13; 4-11; 5-1; 6-12; 7-2; 8-15; 9-8;
10-14; 11-5; 12-7; 13-9; 14-10; 15-3.

WORD STUDY

fuíito	feet
gáron	gallon
gúramu	gram
ínchi	inch
kiro meétoru	kilometer
máiru	mile
méetoru	meter
póndo	pound
ríttoru	liter
yáado	yard

LESSON 7 DÁI NANÁKA

GOOD MORNING!

Ohayoo gozaimásu.	Good morning.
-san[1]	Mr.
Yamada-san	Mr. Yamada
Yamada-san, ohayoo gozaimásu.	Good morning, Mr. Yamada.
Konnichi wa.	Good afternoon. [Good day.]
Konban wá.	Good evening.
Oyasumi nasái.	Good night (said just before going to bed).
Ogénki desu ka?	How are you? [Are you in good spirits?]
génki	well [good spirits]
Génki desu.	Very well. [Am well.]
Arígatoo gozaimásu.	Thank you.
Okagesama de.	Thank you. [Due to your kind thought, am well.]
hanáshite kudasái	Please speak
yukkúri	slowly
Yukkúri hanáshite kudasái.	Speak slowly.
dóozo	please
Dóozo yukkúri hanáshite kudasái.	Please speak slowly.
moo ichido	once more
itte kudasái	please say
Moo ichido itte kudasái.	Please repeat that. [Say it once more, please.]
Dóozo moo ichido itte kudasái.	Please repeat that. [Please once more say it.]

[1]The suffix -san is used in Japanese as a term of respect meaning "Mr.," "Mrs.," "Miss," "Sir," or "Madam."

dóomo	very much [indeed!]
Dóomo arígatoo gozaimasu.	Thank you very much.
Dóo itashimáshite.	Not at all.
Arígatoo gozaimáshita.	Thank you (for what you have done).
Kochira kóso.	It was a pleasure. [It was my side (that should have thanked).]
Déwa ashita.	Till tomorrow. See you tomorrow. [Well, then, tomorrow.]
Déwa Doyóobi ni.	Till Saturday. See you Saturday. [Well, then, on Saturday.]
Déwa Getsuyóobi ni.	Till Monday. See you Monday.
Déwa Mokuyóobi ni.	Till Thursday. See you Thursday.
Déwa kónban.	Till this evening. See you this evening.
Déwa myóoban.	Till tomorrow evening. See you tomorrow evening.
Déwa raishuu.	Till next week. See you next week.
Déwa mata.	See you later. [Well, then, again.]
Déwa sono uchi ni.	See you in a little while.
Sayonara.	Good-by.

QUIZ 2

1. *Génki désu.*	1. Speak.
2. *Konban wa.*	2. once more

3. *Hanáshite kudasái.*	3. please say
4. *Arígatoo gozaimásu.*	4. See you tomorrow.
5. *moo ichido*	5. How are you?
6. *Dóozo.*	6. I am very well.
7. *itte kudasái*	7. slowly
8. *Déwa ashita.*	8. Thank you.
9. *Ogénki désu ka?*	9. Please.
10. *yukkúri*	10. Good evening.

ANSWERS

1-6; 2-10; 3-1; 4-8; 5-2; 6-9; 7-3; 8-4; 9-5; 10-7.

LESSON 8   DÁI HACHÍKA

DO YOU HAVE...?

The particle *ka* is used at the end of an interrogative sentence and shows that what precedes it is a question; the particle *ga* is used to show that what precedes it is the grammatical subject of a verb. (See Lessons 9 and 10, for further material on particles and how to use them.)

There is usually no translation in Japanese for "some" or "any."

Arimásu ka?	Do you have...? [Is there...?]
mizu ga[1]	some water *(as the subject of the verb)*
tabako ga[1]	some (any) cigarettes
hí ga[1]	a light
mátchi ga[1]	some matches
sekkén ga, shabon ga	some soap

[1]This construction (the noun plus the particle *ga*) is used *only* when the noun is the subject of the verb.

kamí ga	some paper
Mizu ga arimásu ka?	Do you have some water?
Tabako ga arimásu ka?	Do you have any cigarettes?

WHAT WILL YOU HAVE TO EAT?

asahan	breakfast
hiruhan	lunch
yuuhan	supper
Irasshaimàse.	Good afternoon. [Welcome.]
Náni o meshiagarimasu ka?	What would you like? [What would you eat?]
Mísete kudasái.	Show me . . .
Ményuu o mísete kudasái.	Show me a menu.
. . . kudasái.	I'd like [Please give me . . .]
Pán o kudasái.[1]	I'd like some bread.
pán o	some bread
báta o	some butter
súupu o	some soup
nikú o	some meat
gyuuniku o	some beef
tamago o	some eggs
yasai o	some vegetables
jagaimo o	some potatoes
sárada o	some salad
míruku o	some milk
budóoshu o	some wine
satóo o	some sugar
shió o	some salt
koshoo o	some pepper
yakizákana o	some broiled fish

[1]This construction (the noun plus the particle *o*) is used *only* when the noun is the object of the verb.

miso shíru o	some bean soup
sashimi o	some sashimi (raw fish)
tenpura o	some tempura (fried shrimp)
. . . motte kite kudasái.	Please bring me . . .
Súupu o motte kite kudasái.	Please bring me some soup.
chasaji o	a teaspoon
fóoku o	a fork
náifu o	a knife
napukin o	a napkin
sara o	a plate
koppu o	a glass
. . . íppai kudasái.	I'd like [Please give me] a glass of . . .
. . . hitóbin kudasái.	I'd like [Please give me] a bottle of . . .
Mizu o íppai kudasái.	Please give me a glass of water.
ocha o íppai	a cup of tea
koohíi o íppai	a cup of coffee
budóoshu o hitóbin	a bottle of wine
akabudóoshu o hitóbin	a bottle of red wine
tamago o moo hitótsu	another egg
sore o sukóshi	a little of that
sore o moo sukóshi	a little more of that
pán o moo sukoshi	some more bread, a little more bread
nikú o mótto	some more meat
nikú o moo sukóshi	a little more meat
Kanjoogaki o motte kite kudasái.	The check, please.

QUIZ 3

1. *nikú o*	1. bring me
2. *akabudóoshu o*	2. matches
3. *arimásu ka?*	3. give me
4. *míruku o*	4. meat
5. *báta o*	5. some water
6. *kudasái*	6. a light
7. *mátchi o*	7. milk
8. *nikú o moo sukóshi*	8. eggs
9. *motte kite kudasái*	9. red wine
10. *mizu o*	10. the check
11. *hí o*	11. Do you have . . .
12. *shió o*	12. butter
13. *tamago o*	13. a cup of coffee
14. *koohíi o íppai*	14. some more bread
15. *kanjoogaki o*	15. salt

ANSWERS

1-4; 2-9; 3-11; 4-7; 5-12; 6-3; 7-2; 8-14; 9-1; 10-5;
11-6; 12-15; 13-8; 14-13; 15-10.

LESSON 9   DÁI KYÚUKA

COMMON VERB FORMS

This lesson and several of the following lessons are
longer than the others. They contain the grammatical
information you need to know from the start. Don't

try to memorize anything. Read each section until you understand every point and then, as you continue with the course, try to observe examples of the points mentioned. Refer back to the grammatical sections as necessary. In this way you will eventually find that you have a good grasp of the basic features of Japanese grammar without any deliberate memorizing of "rules."

There is no distinction in Japanese verbs between persons and numbers; the same forms are used for first, second, and third persons in both the singular and plural. Note, too, that in Japanese it is the verb endings that determine tenses.

1. I speak

Hanashimásu.	I speak. I will speak.
Hanashimáshita.	I spoke. I have spoken.
Hanashimashoo.	Let's speak. Let's talk.
Hanáshite imásu.	I am speaking.
Hanáshite imáshita.	I was speaking.
Hanáshite kudasái.	Please speak.

   a. Notice the endings denoting tense:

present or future	*(hanashi)masu*
past or present perfect	*(hanashi)mashita*
tentative	*(hanashi)mashoo*
present progressive	*(hanashi)te imasu*
past progressive	*(hanashi)te imashita*
polite request	*(hanashi)te kudasai*

   b. See how the same forms are used for singular and plural and for first, second, and third persons. The subject of a sentence does not have to be mentioned when it is clear who is speaking or what it is that is being spoken about.

Hanashimásu.	I speak.
Hanashimásu.	You *(sing.)* speak.
Hanashimásu.	He speaks.
Hanashimásu.	We speak.
Hanashimásu.	You *(pl.)* speak.
Hanashimásu.	They speak.

2. I don't speak (you don't speak, he doesn't speak, etc.)

Hanashimasén.	I don't speak. I will not speak.
Hanashimasén deshita.	I didn't speak.
Hanáshite imasén.	I am not speaking.
Hanáshite imasén deshita.	I wasn't speaking.

a. Notice how the negative is formed:

negative present or future	*(hanashi)masen.*
negative past	*(hanashi)masen deshita.*
negative present progressive	*(hanashi)te imasen.*
negative past progressive	*(hanashi)te imasen deshita.*
negative request	*(hanasa)naide kudasai.*

ASKING A QUESTION I

1. To ask a question, add the particle *ka* at the end of the sentence and use either a rising or falling intonation.

    Note: Again the subject of each of these sentences could be "I," "your," "he," "we," or "they." "You" is used as the subject arbitrarily in the following English translations.

Naraimásu.	You learn.
Naraimásu ka?	Do you learn?
Naraimáshita.	You learned. You have learned.
Naraimáshita ka?	Did you learn? Have you learned?
Narátte imásu.	You are learning.
Narátte imásu ka?	Are you learning?
Narátte imáshita.	You were learning.
Narátte imáshita ka?	Were you learning.

2. To ask a question with a negative, use the particle *ka* in the same way:

Naraimasén ka?	Don't you learn?
Naraimasén deshita ka?	Didn't you learn?
Narátte imasén ka?	Aren't you learning?
Narátte imasén deshita ka?	Weren't you learning?

REVIEW QUIZ 1

Choose the correct Japanese equivalent for the English word:

1. five =
   a. *rokú*
   b. *shichí*
   c. *gó*

2. eight =
   a. *hachí*
   b. *kú*
   c. *shí*

3. Tuesday =
   a. *Suiyóobi*
   b. *Kayóobi*
   c. *Kin'yóobi*

4. Sunday =
   a. *Nichiyóobi*
   b. *Doyóobi*
   c. *Getsuyóobi*

5. March =
   a. *Sángatsu*
   b. *Kúgatsu*
   c. *Shigatsu*

6. June =
   a. *Shichigatsu*
   b. *Rokugatsu*
   c. *Gógatsu*

7. red =
   a. *áo*
   b. *kiiro*
   c. *áka*

8. green =
   a. *kiiro*
   b. *midoriiro*
   c. *haiiro*

9. black =
   a. *kúro*
   b. *chairo*
   c. *shíro*

10. brown =
    a. *kúro*
    b. *áka*
    c. *chairo*

11. Good morning. =
    a. *Ohayoo gozaimásu.*
    b. *Konban wa.*
    c. *Génki desu.*

12. Very well. =
    a. *Arígatoo gozaimásu.*
    b. *Génki desu.*
    c. *Taihen.*

13. Thank you. =
    a. *Itte kudasái.*
    b. *Arígatoo gozaimásu.*
    c. *Doo itashimáshite.*

14. Please. =
    a. *Hanáshite kudasái.*
    b. *Arigatoo gozaimásu.*
    c. *Dóozo.*

15. Good-by. =
    a. *Déwa ashita.*
    b. *Sayonara.*
    c. *Konnichi wa.*

16. He learns. =
    a. *Naraimásu.*
    b. *Naraimasén.*
    c. *Narátte imásu.*

17. We are learning. =
    a. *Naratte imasu.*
    b. *Naraimáshita ka?*
    c. *Narátte kudasái.*

18. I don't learn. =
    a. *Naraimásen.*
    b. *Naraimásu.*
    c. *Naraimáshita.*

19. Do you learn? =
    a. *Naraimásu ka?*
    b. *Naraimáshita ka?*
    c. *Naraimasén ka?*

20. Please learn. =
    a. *Narátte imásu ka?*
    b. *Narátte kudasái.*
    c. *Naratte imashita.*

ANSWERS

1-c; 2-a; 3-b; 4-a; 5-a; 6-b; 7-c; 8-b; 9-a; 10-c; 11-a; 12-b; 13-b; 14-c; 15-b; 16-a; 17-a; 18-a; 19-a; 20-b.

LESSON 10   <small>DÁI JÍKKA</small>

NOUNS AND NOUN PARTICLES

In Japanese, the form of a noun remains the same no matter where it appears. Normally, every noun is followed by at least one "particle" when it is used in a sentence. (There are some exceptions to this rule, but they are very few.) The particle, which is very often not translatable, is the "tag" or "signpost" that tells what relation the word it accompanies has to another word or part of the sentence. For instance, one particle may show that the noun it follows is the *subject* of the sentence, another may show that the noun it follows is the *object* of the sentence,[1] and still another may show that the noun it follows is the *modifier of another noun*. Remember, however, that *all* particles must follow the words with which they are used.

Following is a list of important noun particles[2] with a brief description of their use:

1. *wa* shows that the noun it follows is the "topic" of the sentence. Here the word "topic" is deliberately employed as a contrast to the word

[1]See Lesson 8.
[2]See Grammar Section 10-I for more particles and their uses.

"subject" which we often use in grammar. A topic in Japanese—that is, a word or group of words which is followed by the particle *wa*—serves as advance notice of what the speaker will talk about. This practice of isolating a topic and setting it off with the particle *wa* is frequently used to start a sentence in Japanese, and can be compared to the occasional practice in English of beginning a sentence with "As for..." or "Speaking of..." For instance, in Japanese you would say:

> As for Mr. Yoshida (he), came to this country again this year.
> Talking about this morning's *New York Times,* have (you) read (it)?

Notice how a topic is first singled out and then followed by a simplified statement. Note also that a topic can be either an *implied subject* or an *implied object* of the verb, and that it may even specify a *time* or *place*.

Further examples with *wa:*

Kabukiza wa Tookyoo ni arimásu.	(The) Kabuki Theatre is in Tokyo. [As for Kabuki Theatre, (it) is in Tokyo.]
Búnraku wa mimasén deshita.	I didn't see (the) Bunraku (Puppet Play). [As for Bunraku, I didn't see (it).]
Boardman-san wa Amerika e kaerimáshita.	Speaking of Mr. Boardman, he went back to America.
Kinóo wa Tanaka-san no uchí e ikimáshita.	Speaking of yesterday, I went to Tanaka's house.

2. *ga* shows that the noun it follows is both the grammatical subject of a verb and also an "emphatic" subject. In English, you place emphasis on a subject by raising your voice. In Japanese you can create the same emphasis, usually without raising the voice, by using the particle *ga*.

   If you do *not* want to emphasize the subject, you can either introduce the subject with the topic-particle *wa* or avoid mentioning it altogether. But you omit mentioning the subject only when it is already understood by the listener. In English you always mention the subject except when using the imperative; in Japanese you may omit specifically naming the subject when you feel that the person to whom you are speaking already knows what it is.

Watakushi ga ikimáshita.	*I* (not he) *(spoken with emphasis)* went. [(It) was I who went.]
Tanaka-san ga kimáshita.	*Mr. Tanaka (spoken with emphasis)* came.
Jikan ga arimasén.	There isn't *time*.
Are ga toshókan desu.	*That* is the library (*in answer to the question:* "Which building is the library?").

3. *o* shows that the noun it follows is *the thing acted on* by the verb. It usually corresponds to the direct object of a transitive verb, but a place where movement from one point to another occurs, is also included in this notion. For example, the particle *o* marks places where actions such as "going," "coming," "passing," "walking," "running," "swimming," "flying," and "departing" take place.

Kabuki no kippu[1] *o kaimáshita.*	I bought some Kabuki (theatre) tickets.
Tegami[2] *o dashimáshita.*	I sent a letter.
Ginza Dóori o arukimáshita.	We walked on Ginza Street.
Gakkoo no máe o toorimáshita.	We passed in front of the school.

4. *no* shows that the noun it follows modifies (i.e., explains, characterizes) another noun that comes after it. It is most frequently used for the possessive (''of''):

Tookyoo no machí desu.	It is the city of Tokyo.
Yamada-san no uchí desu.	It is Mr. Yamada's house. [(It) is the house of Mr. Yamada.]
Tanaka-san no kodomo desu.	He is Mr. Tanaka's child. [He is the child of Mr. Tanaka.]

5. *ni* shows that the noun it follows modifies a verb or an adjective. *How* it modifies depends on the noun as well as the verb or adjective affected. In other words, to know how the noun with *ni* is used, one must see the noun as well as the verb or adjective with it. One thing is always sure: The noun with *ni* is to be linked to a verb or an adjective in one of the following ways:

a. The noun with *ni* may tell *where* a thing or person is (in the sense of being ''in'' or ''at'' a place):

[1]*kippu* = tickets
[2]*tegami* = a letter

| *Tanaka-san wa Tookyoo ni imásu.* | Mr. Tanaka is in Tokyo. |
| *Ginza wa Chuuóoku ni arimásu.* | Ginza is in the boro of Chuoku [. . . the boro of Chuo.] |

    b. The noun with *ni* may tell the *purpose* for which the action is performed (in the sense of "for" or "in order to"):

| *Nihón e benkyoo ni kimáshita.* | I came to Japan to study. |

    c. The noun with *ni* may tell the *person* or *thing* to which the action of the verb is directed (in the sense of "to," "from," or "of"):

| *Yamada-san ni agemáshita.* | I gave it to Mr. Yamada. |

    d. The noun with *ni* may tell the *thing into which something changes* (there is usually no translation for this usage):

| *Tookyoo Dáigaku no gakusei ni narimáshita.* | I became a student at [of] Tokyo University. |
| *Tookyoo no michi wa kírei ni narimáshita.* | The streets in Tokyo have become clean. |

    e. The noun with *ni* may tell the *manner* (how) in which the action of the verb is performed or in which a thing exists:

| *Shízuka ni hanáshite imásu.* | They are talking quietly. |

6. *de* tells that the noun which precedes it is:

    a. the *place* of action ("at," "in"):

| *Kyóoto de kaimáshita.* | I bought it in Kyoto. |

b. the *means* of action ("by," "through"):

Hikóoki de ikimáshita.	I went by [means of a] plane.

c. the *limit* to which the predicate is restricted ("in," "within"):

Nihón de ichiban takái yamá desu.	It is the highest mountain in Japan. [Restricting ourselves to Japan, (it) is the highest mountain.]

7. **kara** shows that the noun it follows is the *beginning point* of an action or state ("from," "since"):

Amerika kara kimáshita.	I came from America.
Nigatsú kara koko ni súnde imásu.	I have been living here since February.

8. **máde** shows that the noun it follows is the *ending point* of an action or event ("up to," "by," "until"):

Hiroshima máde ikimáshita.	I went as far as Hiroshima.
Juugatsú made Kyóoto ni imásu.	I shall be in Kyoto until October.

9. **e** shows that the noun it follows is the *direction toward which* a motion takes place ("to," "toward"):

Níkkoo e ikimáshita.	I went to Nikko.
Amerika e okurimáshita.	I sent it to America.

10. *to* shows that the preceding noun is one of the following:

a. a part of a complete list ("and"):

Tookyoo to Kyóoto to Oosaka e ikimáshita.	I went to Tokyo, Kyoto, and Osaka. (These are the places I went to.)
Yamada-san to Tanaka-san to Takeda-san ga kimáshita.	Mr. Yamada, Mr. Tanaka, and Mr. Takeda came. (These are the people who came.)

b. the one with whom the action of the verb is performed ("with"):

Kánai to ikimáshita.	I went with my wife.
Tanaka-san to hanashimáshita.	I spoke with Mr. Tanaka.

c. the thing into which something or somebody changes:

Ano tatemono wa Tanaka-san no monó to narimáshita.	That building became Mr. Tanaka's (property).
Daigíshi to narimáshita.	He became a member of Parliament.
Nihón no daihyoo to narimáshita.	He became the representative of Japan.

Note that in this usage *to* is often interchangeable with *ni*.

11. *ya* shows, as *to* sometimes does, that the noun it follows is part of a list, but the fact that *ya* is used implies that the list is not a complete one:

Ringo ya nashí o tabemáshita.	We ate apples, pears (and other things).
Tanaka-san ya Takáhashi-san ya Yamada-san ga kimáshita.	Mr. Tanaka, Mr. Takahashi, Mr. Yamada (and other people) came.

12. *yóri* signifies "than" and shows that the noun it follows is the thing with which a comparison is made:

Tookyoo wa Kyóoto yori ookii desu.	Tokyo is larger than Kyoto.
Hokkáidoo wa Kyúushuu yori samúi desu.	Hokkaido is colder than Kyushu.

COMMON ADJECTIVE FORMS

Adjectives in Japanese are used very much like verbs. Not only are they used to modify nouns, but they can also be used as predicate words by themselves. Adjectives have their own forms for present, past, tentative, etc., and they have "plain" and "polite" forms, as do verbs.

The following show some ways in which adjectives can be used:

1. **It is expensive.**

Takái desu.	It is expensive.
Takái deshita. ⎫ *Takákatta desu.* ⎭	It was expensive.
Takái deshoo.	It will probably be expensive.
Tákaku narimáshita.	It became expensive.
Takákute kaemasén.	It is expensive and I can't buy it.

2. It is not expensive.

Tákaku arimasén	It is not expensive.

Tákaku arimasén deshita.
Tákakunakatta desu. } It was not expensive.

Tákaku arimasén deshoo.
Tákakunái deshoo. } It will probably not be expensive.

a. Notice how the endings differ for affirmative and negative:

AFFIRMATIVE

present	*(taká)i desu.*
past	{ *(taká)i deshita.* *(táka)katta desu.*
tentative	*(taká)i deshoo.*
adverbial	*(táka)ku.*
-*te* form[1]	*(táka)kute.*

NEGATIVE

present	*(táka)ku arimasén.*
past	*(táka)ku arimasén deshita.*
tentative	*(táka)ku arimasén deshoo.*

b. Notice how the same forms are used for both singular and plural, in all persons (I, you, he, she, it, we, they):

Takái desu.	It is expensive.
Takái desu.	They are expensive.
Takái deshita.	It was expensive.

[1]For information on the -*te* form, see Lesson 12 and Grammar, Section 24.

Takái deshoo.	It is probably expensive.
Takái deshoo.	They are probably expensive.
Anáta wa kashikói desu.	You are wise.
Anó hito wa kashikói desu.	He is wise.
Uketsuke wa dóko ni arimásu ka?	Where is the reception desk?
Massúgu saki ni arimásu.	It is straight ahead.
Kyóo wa dóko e ikimásu ka?	Where are you going today?
Úmi e ikimásu.	I am going to the beach [sea].
Haizara wa dóko ni arimásu ka?	Where is the ash tray?
Teeburu no ué ni arimásu.	(It)'s on the table.
Kodomótachi wa dóko e ikimásu ka?	Where are the children going?
Doobutsúen e ikimásu.	They are going to the zoo.
Doobutsúen wa dóko ni arimásu ka?	Where is the zoo?
Hakubutsúkan no ushiro ni arimásu.	Behind the museum.
Kása wa dóko ni okimáshita ka?	Where did you put the umbrella?
To no ushiro ni okimáshita.	[I put it] behind the door.
Shinbun wa dóko ni okimáshita ka?	Where did you put the newspaper?
Anáta no hón no ué ni okimáshita.	I put it on your books.

Yamada-san wa dóko ni súnde imásu ka?	Where does Mr. Yamada live? [Where is Mr. Yamada residing?]
Kono machí ni súnde imásu.	He lives in this town.
Kono básu wa Kanda o toorimásu ka?	Does this bus pass through Kanda?
Sono hikóoki wa Tookyoo no machi no ué o tobimáshita ka?	Did that plane fly over the city of Tokyo?
Sono mannénhitsu wa dóko de kaimáshita ka?	Where did you buy that fountain pen?
Marúzen de kaimáshita.	I bought it at Maruzen's.
Sono kaban wa dóko e mótte ikimásu ka?	Where are you carrying that suitcase?
Watakushi no heyá e mótte ikimásu.	[I am carrying (it)] to my room.
Okinawa wa dóko ni arimásu ka?	Where is Okinawa located?
Nippon to Taiwán no aida ni arimásu.	It is located between Japan and Taiwan.
Kono kishá wa dóko made ikimásu ka?	How far does this train go?
Kóobe máde ikimásu.	It goes as far as Kobe.
Kono básu wa dóko kara kimásu ka?	Where does this bus come from?
Shinjuku kara kimásu.	It comes from Shinjuku.
Dónna monó o tabemáshita ka?	What sort of things did you eat?
Sukiyaki ya tenpura o tabemáshita.	We ate sukiyaki, tempura, and things like that.

Tookyoo no tenpuraya de wa dóno misé ga íi desu ka?	Of the tempura restaurants in Tokyo, which is good?
Tenkin ga íi desu.	Tenkin is good.
Sono uchí wa ookíi desu ka?	Is that house big?
Iie, anmari ookíku arimasén.	No, it isn't too big.
Sono terebi wa takái deshita ka?	Was that television (set) expensive?
Iie, tákaku arimasén deshita.	No, it wasn't expensive.

LESSON 11 DÁI JUUÍKKA

TO BE OR NOT TO BE

There is more than one way to say "is" in Japanese. A different word is used for this English verb in each of the following sentences:

Enpitsu desu.	It is a pencil.
Enpitsu ga arimasu.	There is a pencil.
Nyuu Yooku ni imasu.	He is in New York.

1. When you say that one thing is equal to another, you use *désu*.

2. When you are talking about something being located or situated in a place, use *arimásu* if the thing referred to is inanimate, and

3. You use *imásu* if the thing referred to is animate.

Note: *Désu* is called the *copula*. *Arimásu* and *imásu* are ordinary verbs and are inflected like other verbs. The negative of *désu* is not at all like *désu*: it is either *ja arimasén*, *dé wa arimasén*, or *dé arimasén*—these three expressions are interchangeable.

1. *Sore wa enpitsu desu.*

That is a pencil. (A equals B.)

2. *Soko ni enpitsu ga arimásu.*

There is a pencil there. (A—inanimate—is located at B.)

3. *Soko ni kodomo ga imásu.*

There is a child there. (A—animate—is located at B.)

1. *Sore wa tabako desu ka?*

Is that a cigarette?

2. *Tabako ga arimásu ka?*

Is there a cigarette?

3. *Yamada-san wa soko ni imásu ka?*

Is Mr. Yamada there?

1. *Shikágo wa ookíi machí desu.*

Chicago is a big city.

2. *Shikágo wa Irinoíshuu ni arimásu.*

Chicago is in the State of Illinois.

3. *Yamada-san wa Shikágo ni imásu.*

Mr. Yamada is in Chicago.

Compare the following different forms of *desu*:

A wa B desu.	A is B.
A wa B deshita.	A was B.
A wa B de C wa D desu.	A is B and C is D.
A wa B deshóo.	A is probably B.

A wa B ja arimasén.
A wa B dé wa
   arimasén. } A is not B.

A wa B ja arimasén
   deshita.
A wa B dé wa arimasén } A was not B.
   deshita.

A wa B ja arimasén
   deshoo.
A wa B de wa arimasén } A is probably not B.
   deshoo.

In the sentences which follow, notice that the word which equals the element "A" (as it is used in the illustrations above) is marked with the particle *wa, ga,* or *mo. Wa* is used when the emphasis in the sentence is not on "A." *Ga* is used when "A" is the emphasized word, and *mo* is used when something other than "A" has already been equated to "B" and you are saying that "A" also is to equal "B." The word or phrase equaling the element "B" always comes immediately before *désu* or the form derived from it. If no specific noun is used for "B," use *soo* in its place, for *desu* can never be used alone.

Dóno kata ga Tanaka-san désu ka?	Which person is Mr. Tanaka?
Watakushi ga Tanaka désu.	I (*with emphasis*) am. [Am Tanaka.]
Watakushi ga sóo desu.	I am [so].
Anata wa Beikokújin desu ka?	Are you an American?
Hai, sóo desu.	Yes, I am. [Yes, am so.]

Amerika Talshíkan wa Tookyoo ni arimásu.	(The) American Embassy is in Tokyo.
Súmisu-san wa Amerika Taishíkan ni imásu.	Mr. Smith is in the American Embassy.
Ano tatemóno wa Amerika Taishíkan desu.	That building is the American Embassy.
Kono tatemóno wa Amerika Taishíkan ja arimasén. Eikoku Taishíkan desu.	This building is not the American Embassy. It is the British Embassy.
Dóno tatemóno ga Amerika Taishíkan desu ka?	Which building is the American Embassy?
Ano tatemóno ga sóo desu.	That building is. [That building is so.]
Ano tatemóno wa Amerika Taishíkan desu ka?	Is that building the American Embassy?
Hai, sóo desu.	Yes, it is. [Yes, is so.]

ASKING YOUR WAY

1. **Where?**

Otazune itashimásu ga . . .	Excuse me. [Am asking a question, but . . .]
dóko	where
arimásu	there is
Dóko ni arimásu ka?	Where is it?
hóteru	hotel
Hóteru wa dóko ni arimásu ka?	Where is there a hotel?
Résutoran wa dóko ni arimásu ka?	Where is there a restaurant?
denwa	telephone

Denwa wa dóko ni arimásu ka?	Where is there a telephone?
. . . oshiete kudasái	can you tell me? (please teach me)
Denwa wa dóko ni arimásu ka oshiete kudasái.	Can you tell me where there is a telephone?
éki	railroad station
Éki wa dóko ni arimásu ka oshiete kudasái.	Can you tell me where the railroad station is? [. . . there is the railroad]
yuubínkyoku	post office
Yuubínkyoku wa dóko ni arimásu ka oshiete kudasái.	Can you tell me where the post office is?

2. Here and There.

koko	here, this place
soko	there, that place (nearby)
asoko	there, that place over there (outside of immediate reach)
dóko	where, which place
Dóko desu ka?	Which place is it?
kochira	this way
sochira	that way
achira	that way over there
dóchira	which way
Dóchira desu ka?	Which way is it?
Achira désu	It is over that way.
Kochira désu.	It's this way.
migi no hóo ni	to the right [in the direction of the right]

hidari no hóo ni	to the left [in the direction of the left]
Migi no hóo ni arimásu.	It's to the right. [It is in the direction . . .]
Hidari no hóo ni arimásu.	It's to the left.
Migi e omagari nasái.	Turn right (*polite command*).
Hidari e omagari nasái.	Turn left (*polite*).
Massúgu oide nasái.	Go straight ahead (*polite*)
Massúgu saki désu.	It's straight ahead.
Choodo hantaigawa desu.	It's directly opposite.
Kádo ni arimásu.	It's on the corner.
Koko ni arimasén.	It's not here.
Soko ni arimasén.	It's not there.
Asoko ni arimasú.	It's over there.
Koko ni imásu.	He is here.
Koko ni kite kudasái.	Come here, please.
Koko ni ite kudasái.	Stay here, please.
Soko de mátte ite kudasái.	Wait there, please.
Kochira o itte kudasái.	Go this way, please.
Achira o itte kudasái.	Go that way, please.
Soko ni dáre ga imásu ka?	Who's there?
Koko ni oite kudasái.	Put it here, please.
Soko ni oite kudasái.	Put it there, please.

3. Near and Far.

Chikái desu.	It's near.

Koko kara chikái desu.	It's near here. [Near from here.]
Taihen chikái desu.	It's very near. It's quite close.
Mura no chikáku desu[1]	It's near the village.
Michi no chikáku desu.	It's near the road.
Sonó hito no uchi no chikáku desu.	It's near him [his house].
Taihen chikái desu.	It's very near.
Koko kara góku chikái desu.	It's very near here.
tooi	far
Tooi desu ka?	Is it far?
Tooi desu.	It's far.
Tooku arimasén.	It's not far.
Koko kara tooi desu.	It's far from here.

QUIZ 4

1.	*Denwa wa dóko ni arimásu ka oshiete kudasái.*	1.	It's this way.
2.	*Hóteru wa dóko ni arimásu ka?*	2.	It's to the right.
3.	*Kochira desu.*	3.	Turn left.
4.	*Massúgu saki desu.*	4.	It's directly opposite.
5.	*Migi no hóo ni arimásu.*	5.	It's straight ahead.
6.	*Mura no chikáku desu.*	6.	Can you tell me where there is a telephone?

[1]*chikáku:* nearby place (*a noun*)

7. *Soko de mátte ite kudasái.*	7. Where is there a hotel?
8. *Kochira o itte kudasái.*	8. It's near the village.
9. *Hidari e omagari kudasái.*	9. It's not here.
10. *Choodo hantaigawa desu.*	10. Stay here.
11. *Tooku arimasén.*	11. Wait there.
12. *Soko ni oite kudasái.*	12. Go this way.
13. *Koko ja arimasén.*	13. Who's there?
14. *Koko ni ite kudasái.*	14. Put it there.
15. *Soko ni dáre ga imásu ka?*	15. It's not far.

ANSWERS

1-6; 2-7; 3-1; 4-5; 5-2; 6-8; 7-11; 8-12; 9-3; 10-4;
11-15; 12-14; 13-9; 14-10; 15-13.

WORD STUDY

buráusu	blouse
hankáchi	handkerchief
máfuraa	muffler
nékutai	necktie
oobaakóoto	overcoat
séetaa	sweater
shátsu	shirt
sukáafu	scarf
sukáato	skirt
suríppu	slip

LESSON 12 DÁI JUUNÍKA

PLAIN OR POLITE

For each of the forms of adjectives, verbs, and the copula[1] used at the end of a sentence, there is an additional form called a "plain form." The forms we have seen at the end of a sentence are called "polite forms." The polite forms are derived from plain forms and are characterized by ending with *-désu* or *-másu* or a form derived from one of these. The plain form is usually the one used in the *middle* of a sentence, while the polite form is usually at the *end* of a sentence. However, the plain form, too, can be used at the end of a sentence, but only when the person with whom you are talking has a special relationship to you. He or she must be a person with whom you can be very casual or familiar; for instance, a husband may use this form with his wife, or a high-school boy may use it with his classmates. But for anyone learning Japanese as a foreign language, it is best to use the polite form at the end of a sentence.

Dictionaries and glossaries usually list the plain present form of adjectives, verbs, and the copula. Here is a table showing the plain and polite present forms of some words that you have already seen:

ADJECTIVES

PLAIN PRESENT	POLITE PRESENT	MEANING
takái	*takái desu*	it is expensive
tooi	*tooi desu*	it is far

VERBS

hanásu	*hanashimásu*	I speak
kau	*kaimásu*	I buy
áru	*arimásu*	there is

[1]See Lesson 11, page 46.

| *tabéru* | *tabemásu* | I eat |
| *kúru* | *kimásu* | I come |

COPULA

| *da*[1] | *desu* | A is B |

To construct the polite present form of an adjective, add *desu* to the plain present.

Construct the polite present of a verb according to the rules set forth in the next section.

The polite present of the copula *da* is *désu*. Rarely, *dé arimásu* can also be used, but this form is considered very formal.

TO CONSTRUCT THE POLITE FORM OF A VERB

In order to construct the polite form of a verb from its plain present form, you must learn to identify the class or conjugation to which the verb belongs and for this, it is necessary to know the following basic facts:

1. All verbs belong to one of three classes: *consonant, vowel,* or *irregular.* Consonant verbs make up the largest group and irregular verbs the smallest.

2. There are only two verbs that are really irregular, and they are the most common: *suru* [does] and *kúru* [comes]. Although there are a few other verbs that are somewhat irregular, they are, basically, consonant verbs. Two examples are: *iku* [goes] and *kudasáru* [gives].

3. The vast majority of verbs that end in *-eru* or *-iru* are vowel verbs—for example, *tabéru* [eats]

[1] *na* may be used in place of *da*, but this variant form of the plain present copula *désu* is used only when certain nouns modify another noun.

and *míru* [sees]—so called because the stem[1] (which remains unchanged most of the time) ends in a vowel. However, there are a few verbs that end in *-eru* or *-iru* that are not vowel verbs; for example: *keru* [kicks], *káeru* [returns], *háiru* [enters]. Since the stem of these verbs ends in *-r* (*ker-, kaér-, hair-,* respectively) they are classified as consonant verbs.

4. All other verbs are consonant verbs, so called because the stem ends in a consonant.[2] Verbs that end in two vowels, such as *kau* [buys], or *iu,* which is sometimes spelled *yuu* [says], are also included in this class because they add *-w* at the end of the stem when appending an ending that begins with *-a;* e.g., *-anai* [not], *-areru* (*passive*), or *-aseru* (*causative*).

Once you can identify the class to which a given verb belongs, you can form the polite forms as follows:

1. Consonant Verbs

Add *-imásu* to the stem, with two exceptions:

a. When the stem ends in *s,* the letter is changed to *sh* before adding *-imásu.* For example: *hanásu* becomes *hanashimásu.*

b. When the stem ends in *ts,* the latter is changed to *ch* before adding *-imásu.* For example: *tátsu* becomes *tachimásu.*

---

[1]The stem of a vowel verb is that part remaining after the final *-ru* is dropped: i.e., *tabe(ru), mi(ru).*

[2]The stem of a consonant verb is that part remaining after the final *u* has been dropped. For example: *dás(u)* [puts out, sends out], *ár(u)* [there is], *ka(w)(u)* [buys], *kák(u)* [writes].

2. **Vowel verbs**

Add *-masu* to the stem.

3. **Irregular verbs**

Learn the polite form of each individually.

Note: In the following examples, the end of the stem has been marked with a hyphen:

CONSONANT VERBS

PLAIN PRESENT	POLITE PRESENT	MEANING
kák-u	*kakimásu*	writes
sak-u	*sakimásu*	blooms
kas-u	*kashimásu*	lends
máts-u	*machimásu*	waits
móts-u	*mochimásu*	holds
háir-u	*hairimásu*	enters

VOWEL VERBS

tabé-ru	*tabemásu*	eats
tome-ru	*tomemásu*	stops
mí-ru	*mimásu*	sees
okí-ru	*okimásu*	gets up

IRREGULAR VERBS

suru	*shimásu*	does
kúru	*kimásu*	comes

THE *-TE* AND *-TA* FORMS

When the *-te* form of a verb appears in a sentence, it signifies that one or more additional verbs will also appear in that sentence.

The *-te* form of a verb is used in such expressions as *hanáshite kudasái* (please speak) and *hanáshite imásu* (I'm speaking). Although the verb in such a construction most often ends in *-te,* it can also end in *-tte* or *-de.* The way the *-te* form ends or the way it is formed from the plain present (which is the dictionary form), depends on (a) the *class of verb* to which it belongs, and (b), if it is a consonant verb, the *pronunciation of the last syllable* of the plain present.

The *-te* form is sometimes called a "gerund," but unlike a proper gerund, is never used as a noun. (See page 61 for uses of the *-te* form.)

The *-ta* form is another way to refer to the plain past as opposed to the polite past. However, in the middle of a sentence, the *-ta* form is usually used in place of the polite form.

Remember that the polite past always ends in *-máshita,* whereas the *-ta* form can end not only in *-ta* but also in *-tta* or *-da.* The *-ta* form is derived from the plain present in exactly the same way as the *-te* form.

Be careful, when using either of these forms, not to interchange the final *-e* and *-a.* Follow these instructions:

1. **For Consonant Verbs**

   a. When the last syllable of the plain present is *-u, -tsu,* or *-ru,* drop that syllable and add *-tte* or *-tta:*

PLAIN PRESENT	*-te* FORM	*-ta* FORM	MEANING OF PLAIN PRESENT
kau	**katte**	**katta**	buys
omóu	**omótte**	**omótta**	thinks
mátsu	**mátte**	**mátta**	waits
mótsu	*mótte*	*mótta*	holds
okuru	*okutte*	*okutta*	sends
tóru	*tótte*	*tótta*	takes

Note: To learn this rule it might be helpful to memorize the following fictitious word which is made up by stringing together the three final syllables involved and the *-tta*:

u-tsu-ru-tta (utsurutta).

b. If the last syllable of the plain present is *-mu*, *-nu*, or *-bu*, drop it and replace it with *-nde* or *-nda*.

PLAIN PRESENT	*-te* FORM	*-ta* FORM	MEANING OF PLAIN PRESENT
yómu	**yónde**	**yónda**	reads
nómu	**nónde**	**nónda**	drinks
shinu	**shinde**	**shinda**	dies
yobu	*yonde*	*yonda*	calls
tobu	*tonde*	*tonda*	flies

Mnemonic device: *mu-nu-bu-nda (munu-bunda).*

c. If the last syllable of the plain present is *-ku*, drop it and replace it with *-ite* or *-ita*. If the last syllable is *-gu*, drop it and replace it with *-ide* and *-ida*.

PLAIN PRESENT	*-te* FORM	*-ta* FORM	MEANING OF PLAIN PRESENT
káku	**káite**	**káita**	writes
saku	**saite**	**saita**	blooms
oyógu	**oyóide**	**oyóida**	swims
kagu	**kaide**	**kaida**	smells

Mnemonic device: *ku-gu-ita-da (kuguitada).*

Note: *iku* [goes] is one exception. Its -*te* and -*ta* forms are *itte* and *itta* respectively.

d. When the last syllable of the plain present is -*su*, drop it and add -*shite* or -*shita*.

PLAIN PRESENT	-*te* FORM	-*ta* FORM	MEANING OF PLAIN PRESENT
hanásu	**hanáshite**	**hanáshita**	speaks
kasu	**kashite**	**kashita**	lends
hósu	**hóshite**	**hóshita**	dries
moyasu	**moyashite**	**moyashita**	burns

Mnemonic device: *su-shita (sushita)*.

2. For Vowel Verbs

Simply drop the final syllable -*ru* and add -*te* or -*ta*.

PLAIN PRESENT	-*te* FORM	-*ta* FORM	MEANING OF PLAIN PRESENT
tabéru	**tábete**	**tábeta**	eats
akeru	**akete**	**aketa**	opens
míru	**míte**	**míta**	sees
kiru	**kite**	**kita**	wears

3. For Irregular Verbs

PLAIN PRESENT	-*te* FORM	-*ta* FORM	MEANING OF PLAIN PRESENT
suru	*shite*	*shita*	does
kúru	*kite*	*kita*	comes

VARIOUS USAGES OF THE -*TE* FORM

The basic function of a -*te* form is to name an action or condition. It serves to show that the sentence is not complete. That is why, as a rule, it does not appear at the end of a sentence.

The -*te* form verb is used in many ways. Some of the more important follow:

1. When a sentence contains several verbs, each different, the -*te* form is usually used for all but the last.

Nippon e itte kaimáshita.	I bought it in Japan. [(I) went to Japan and bought it (there).]
Éiga o míte ginza de góhan o tábete uchi e kaerimáshita.	I saw a movie, ate [my meal] on Ginza, and returned home.

Notice that the feeling of time, mood, and level of politeness are expressed in *the terminal verb only* and not in the -*te* form verbs. In translation, however, the same feeling of time, mood, and level of politeness are expressed for the -*te* form verbs as well.

2. Sometimes the function of a -*te* form verb is merely to explain *how* the action of the following verb is performed:

Hashítte[1] kimáshita.	He went running.
Isóide[2] kimáshita.	He came hurriedly.

3. The phrase -*te imasu* is used to express an action going on or a state or condition resulting from

[1]*hashiru* = runs
[2]*isogu* = hurries

an action which occurred in the past. (The latter usage is limited to intransitive verbs):

Áme ga futte imásu.	It is raining. [The rain is falling.]
Íma góhan o tábete imásu.	We are eating [the meal] now.
Okyaku sáma ga kite imásu.	We have a visitor. [(A) visitor came and is with us.]

4. The phrase *-te arimásu* is used to express a state or condition which is the result of the past action of a transitive verb. In English it is often translated by the passive voice.

Sore wa harátte arimasu.	That has been paid for. That is paid. [That is in the state of my having paid for it.]
Sono tegami wa moo káite arimásu.	That letter (you are speaking of) is already written. [The letter is already in the state of my having written it.]

5. The phrase *-te kudasai* is used to express a request and corresponds most closely to the imperative in English.

Koko ni onamae[1] o káite kudasái.	Please write your name here. Write your name here.
Doyóobi ni kité kudasái.	Come on Saturday.

[1] *namae* = name; *onamae* = your *or* his name

MY, YOUR, HIS

There are no separate words for "my," "your," and "his." To express the idea of these words, add the particle *no* to the words for "I," "you," "he."

Watakushi no hón wa dóko ni arimásu ka?	Where is my book?
Anáta no hón wa dóko ni arimásu ka?	Where is your book?
Sonó hito no hón wa dóko ni arimásu ka?	Where is his book?
Sonó hitotachi no hón wa dóko ni arimásu ka?	Where are their books?
Anáta no tegami wa dóko ni arimásu ka?	Where is your letter?
Sono hito no tegami wa dóko ni arimásu ka?	Where is his (her) letter?
Sono hitotáchi no tegami wa dóko ni arimásu ka?	Where are their letters?

Sometimes the idea of "your" may be suggested by prefixing the noun referred to with *o-* or *go-*. In such cases, *anata no* [your] is usually not used. Notice that the nouns to which *o-* or *go-* can be added are limited in number.

Otaku[1] wa dóchira desu ka?	Where is your house?
Gokázoku[2] wa dóchira desu ka?	Where is your family [staying]?

[1] *taku* = house; *otaku* = your house
[2] *kázoku* = family

Okuni[1] was dóchira desu ka?   Where are you from?

Onamae wa nán desu ka?   What is your name?

QUIZ 5

1. *Nihón e itte kaimáshita.*
2. *Isóide kimáshita.*
3. *Áme ga futte imásu.*
4. *Doyóobi ni kite kudasái.*
5. *Hashítte ikimáshita.*
6. *Sono tegami wa moo kaite arimásu.*
7. *Anáta no hón wa dóko ni arimásu ka?*
8. *Koko ni onamae o káite kudasái.*
9. *Watakushi no hón wa dóko ni arimásu ka?*
10. *Sonó hito no tegami wa dóko ni arimásu ka?*

1. He came hurriedly.
2. I went to Japan and bought it there.
3. That letter is already written.
4. Where is your book?
5. Where is my book?
6. Please write your name here.
7. Come on Saturday.
8. We have a visitor.
9. He went running.
10. It is raining.

[1]kuni = home, country

11. *Okyaku sáma ga kite imásu.*

11. That is paid.

12. *Sore wa harátte arimásu.*

12. Where is her letter?

13. *Íma góhan o tábete imásu.*

13. Where are their books?

14. *Éiga o mite Ginza de góhan o tábete uchi e kaerimáshita.*

14. We are eating now.

15. *Sono hitótachi no hón wa dóko ni arimásu ka?*

15. I saw a movie, ate on Ginza, and returned home.

ANSWERS

1-2; 2-1; 3-10; 4-7; 5-9; 6-3; 7-4; 8-6; 9-5; 10-12; 11-8; 12-11; 13-14; 14-15; 15-13.

WORD STUDY

aisukuríimu	ice cream
bifuteki	beefsteak
chíizu	cheese
kecháppu	catsup
mayonéezu	mayonnaise
omuretsu	omelet
sárada	salad
sóosu	sauce (Worcestershire)
súupu	soup
tóosuto	toast

LESSON 13 DÁI JUUSÁNKA

IT IS

Íi desu. Yói desu.	It is good.
Yóku arimasen.	It's not good.
Anmari yóku arimasen.	It's not very good.
Taihen yói desu.	It's very good.
Warúi desu.	It's bad.
Wáruku arimasen.	It's not bad.
Anmari wáruku arimasen.	It's not very bad.
Oishíi desu.	It's delicious.
Oishóikatta desu.	It was delicious.
Óishiku arimasén.	It doesn't taste very good.
Óishiku arimasén deshita.	It was not very tasty.
Oishíi deshoo.	It probably tastes very good.
Oishikunái deshoo.	It probably doesn't taste very good.
Sono hóo ga oishíi deshoo.	That would probably be more delicious.
Sono hóo ga kore yóri oishíi deshoo.	That would probably taste better than this.
Sore wa kore hodo oishikunái deshoo.	It would probably not taste as good as this one.
Sore wa kore hodo oishiku arimasén.	It is not as good-tasting as this one.
Hayái desu.	It is fast.
Sono kishá wa hayái desu.	That train is fast.
Sono kishá wa háyaku arimasén.	That train is not fast.

Sono kishá wa hayakunái desu.	That train is not fast.
Sono kishá wa kono kishá hodo[1] háyaku arimasén.	That train is not as fast as this train.
Sono kishá wa kono kisha gúrai hayái desu.	That train is as fast as this train.
Sono kishá wa kono kisha no yóo ni hayái desu.	That train is as fast as this train.
Atarashíi desu.	It's new.
Sono jidóosha wa atarashíi desu.	That car is new.
Sono jidóosha wa ataráshiku arimasén.	That car is not new.
Sono jidóosha wa kono jidóosha hodo ataráshiku arimasén.	That car is not as new as this one [car].
Sono jidóosha wa kono jidoosha gúari atarashíi desu.	That car is as new as this one [car].
Sono jidóosha wa kono jidóosha no yóo ni atarashíi desu.	That car is as new as this one [car is].
Kono jidóosha no hóo ga ano jidóosha yori atarashíi desu.	This car is newer than that one [car].
Kono jidóosha ga ichiban atarashíi desu.	This car is the newest.

ASKING A QUESTION II

There are several ways to ask a question:

1. Add the particle *ka* at the end of a declarative

[1]hodo = not as . . . as

sentence, and either raise the pitch of your voice
at the end (i.e., use the "question-intonation"),
or not, as you like.

2. Phrase the sentence like a declarative statement
   and use the question-intonation but do not use
   the particle *ka* at the end. This is a very informal
   usage.

3. When you ask a question which demands an
   answer, and the answer can be one of several
   alternatives, add *ka* to each of the alternatives
   you offer.

Kore desu ka?	Is it this?
Kore desu.	It's this.
Sore desu ka?	Is it that?
Kore desu ka sore desu ka?	Is it this or is it that?
Koko ni imásu ka?	Is he here?
Asoko ni imásu ka?	Is he over there?
Koko ni imásu ka asoko ni imásu ka?	Is he here or is he over there?
Dóko ni imásu ka?	Where is he?
Dóko desu ka?	Where is it? [Which place is (it)?]
Dáre desu ka?	Who is it?
Dónata desu ka?	Who is it (*extra polite*)?
Nán desu ka?	What is it?
Ítsu desu ka?	When is it?
Íkura desu ka?	How much is it?
Íkutsu desu ka?	How many? How old is he?
Náze desu ka?	Why is it?
Dóoshite desu ka?	How is it?
Dóo desu ka?	Which way is it? also
Dóchira desu ka?	Which of the two is it?

Dóre desu ka?	Which is it (*used for more than two*)?
Dóno tatémono desu ka?	Which building is it?
Dóno hito desu ka?	Which person is it?
Ikimáshita ka?	Did you go?
Dáre ga ikimáshita ka?	Who went?
Náze ikimáshita ka?	Why did you go?
Ítsu ikimáshita ka?	When did you go?
Nán de ikimáshita ka?	How did you go? [By what means (of transportation) did (you) go?]
Dáre to ikimáshita ka?	With whom did you go?
Ítsu dáre to ikimáshita ka?	When and with whom did you go?
Dóoshite Tanaka-san to ikimáshita ka?	Why did you go with Mr. Tanaka?
Kabuki wa dóo deshita ka?	How was the Kabuki play?
Búnraku wa dóoshite mimasén deshita ka?	Why didn't you see the Bunraku (puppet play)?
Kabuki é wa dáre to ikimáshita ka?	With whom did you go to the Kabuki?

LESSON 14   DÁI JUUYÓNKA

TO HAVE AND HAVE NOT

1. **I (you, he, she . . .) have.**

Mótte imásu.	I have [Am holding.]

2. I (you, he, she ...) don't have.

Mótte imasén.	I don't have.
Kore o mótte imásu.	I have this. I've got this.
Nani mo mótte imasén.	I have nothing. I don't have anything.
Okane o mótte imásu.	I have money.
Okane o juubun mótte imásu.	I have enough money.
Okane o sukoshi mo mótte imasén.	I haven't any money. [I haven't even a little bit of money.]

3. Do I (you, he, she ...) have?

Mótte imásu ka?	Do I have (it)?

4. Don't I (you, he, she ...) have?

Mótte imasén ka?	Don't I have (it)?
Okane o mótte imásu ka?	Does he have (any) money?
Okane o juubun mótte imásu ka?	Does he have enough money?
Enpitsu o mótte imásu ka?	Do you have a pencil?
Pén o mótte imásu ka?	Do you have a pen?
Kitte o mótte imásu ka?	Do you have a stamp?
Kamí o mótte imásu ka?	Do you have any paper?
Okane o juubun mótte imasén ka?	Don't you have enough money?
Enpitsu o mótte imasén ka?	Don't you have a pencil?
Pén o mótte imasén ka?	Don't you have a pen?

| **Kitte o mótte imasén ka?** | Don't you have a stamp? |
| **Kamí o mótte imasén ka?** | Don't you have any paper? |

5. I (you, he, she . . .) have to have.

| *Mótte inákereba narimasén.* | I have to have (it). [If (I) don't have (it), it won't do.] |

6. Do I (you, he, she . . .) have to have?

| *Mótte inákereba narimasén ka?* | Do I have to have (it)? |

7. I (you, he, she . . .) don't have to have.

| *Mótte inákute mo íi desu.* | I don't have to have (it). [Even if (I) don't have (it), I will be all right.] |

8. Don't I (you, he, she . . .) have to have?

Mótte inákute mo íi desu ka?	Don't I have to have it?
Pasupooto o mótte inákereba narimasén.	You have to have a passport.
Kippu o mótte inákereba narimasén.	You have to have a ticket.
Shookáijoo o mótte inákereba narimasén.	You have to have a letter of introduction.
Pasupooto o mótte inákereba narimasén ka?	Do you have to have a passport?

Kippu o mótte inákereba narimasén ka?	Do you have to have a ticket?
Shookáijoo o mótte inákereba narimasén ka?	Do you have to have a letter of introduction?
Pasupooto o mótte inákute mo íi desu.	You don't have to have a passport.
Kippu o mótte inákute mo íi desu.	You don't have to have a ticket.
Shookáijoo o mótte inákute mo íi desu.	You don't have to have a letter of introduction.
Pasupooto o mótte inákute mo íi desu ka?	Don't I have to have a passport? [Is it all right (to go) even if I don't have a passport?]
Kippu o mótte inákute mo íi desu ka?	Don't I have to have a ticket?
Shookáijoo o mótte inákute mo íi desu ka?	Don't I have to have a letter of introduction?

9. I (you, he, she . . .) may have it.

Mótte iru ká mo shiremasén.	I may have (it). [I cannot tell if I have (it).]

10. I (you, he, she . . .) may not have it.

Mótte inái ka mo shiremasén.	I may not have (it).
Okane o mótte iru ká mo shiremasén.	He may have (some) money.

Pasupooto o mótte iru ká mo shiremasén.	He may have the passport.
Kippu o mótte iru ká mo shiremasén.	He may have the ticket.
Okane o mótte inái ká mo shiremasén.	He may not have any money.
Pasupooto o mótte inái ká mo shiremasén.	He may not have the passport.
Kippu o mótte inái ká mo shiremasén.	He may not have the ticket.

LESSON 15   DÁI JUUGÓKA

SOME WORDS AND IDIOMS

1. **I have been to...**

Hakone e itta kotó[1] ga arimásu.	I have been to Hakone. [(I) have the experience of having gone to Hakone.]
Taiwan e itta kotó ga arimásu.	I have been to Taiwan.
Nihon ryóori o tábeta kotó ga arimásu.	I have eaten Japanese cooking. [(I) have had the experience of eating Japanese cooking.]
Kabuki o míta kotó ga arimásu.	I have seen (the) Kabuki.
Yamada-san ni átta kotó ga arimásu.	I have met Mr. Yamada.

[1]*Kotó* = act, event, experience

2. Sometimes I go.

Hakone e iku kotó ga arimásu.	Sometimes I go to Hakone. [The act of my going to Hakone exists.]
Taiwan e iku kotó ga arimásu.	Sometimes I go to Taiwan.
Nihon ryóori o tabéru kotó ga arimásu.	Sometimes I eat Japanese cooking.
Kabuki o míru kotó ga arimásu.	Sometimes I see Kabuki plays.
Yamada-san ni áu kotó ga arimásu.	Sometimes I see [meet with] Mr. Yamada.

3. I can, I am able to . . .

Ashita wa Hakone e iku koto ga dekimásu.	Tomorrow I can go to Hakone. [The act of my going to Hakone tomorrow is possible.]
Rainen wa Taiwán e iku kóto ga dekimásu.	Next year I can go to Taiwan.
Nihon ryóori o tabéru kotó ga dekimásu.	I can eat Japanese cooking.
Nyuu Yóoku de Kabuki o míru kotó ga dekimáshita.	I could see the Kabuki in New York.
Yamada-san ni áu kotó ga dekimáshita.	I was able to see Mr. Yamada.

4. I've decided to . . .

Ashita wa Hakone e iku kóto ni shimáshita.	I've decided to go to Hakone tomorrow.

Rainen wa Taiwán e iku kóto ni shimáshita.	I've decided to go to Taiwan next year.
Nihon ryóori o tabéru kotó ni shimáshita.	I've decided to have [eat] Japanese cooking.
Kabuki o míru kotó ni shimáshita.	We've decided to see the Kabuki plays.
Yamada-san ni áu kotó ni shimáshita.	I've decided to see Mr. Yamada.

5. Ago

máe	ago
ichijikan máe	an hour ago
nijíkan máe	two hours ago
sanjikan máe	three hours ago
ichinichi máe	a day ago
futsuka máe	two days ago
sanshuukan máe	three weeks ago
gokágetsu máe	five months ago
gonen máe	five years ago
júunen máe	ten years ago
zutto máe	a long time ago
kánari máe	a rather long time ago, quite a long time ago
sukóshi máe	a short time ago

6. Also

mo	also, too
watakushi mo	I also, I too
anáta mo	you also
anó hito mo	he also
ano onna no hitó mo	she also
watakushitachi mo	we also
anátatachi mo	you also
ano hitótachi mo	they also
Ano hito mo kimásu.	He's coming too.

Ano hitótachi mo kimásu.	They are coming too.
Ano hitó mo shimáshita.	He did it too.
Watakushi mo kimásu.	I'm coming too.

7. As (so) . . . as . . .

Ano hitótachi mo hoka no hitótachi hodo séi ga takái desu.	They're as tall as the others.
Ano hitótachi wa hoka no hitótachi hodo séi ga tákaku arimasén.	They are not as tall as the others.
Sore wa moo hitótsu no monó hodo yóku arimasén.	That's not as good as the other one.
Sore wa moo hitótsu no mono hodo óokiku arimasén.	That's not as large as the other one.

8. As . . . as possible

Dekiru dake háyaku kite kudasái.	Come as quickly as you can.
Dekiru dake háyaku shite kudasái.	Do it as soon as possible.
Dekiru dake yóku shite kudasái.	Do it as well as you can.

QUIZ 6

1. Oishíi desu.	1. He may have a ticket.
2. Atarashíi desu.	2. That train is not as fast as this train.
3. Sore desu ka?	3. I haven't any money.

4. *Dóko ni imásu ka?*

5. *Oishíi deshoo.*

6. *Ítsu desu ka?*

7. *Nán desu ka?*

8. *Dóno tatemóno desu ka?*

9. *Dáre to ikimáshita ka?*

10. *Oishiku arimasén deshita.*

11. *Kabuki wa dóo deshita ka?*

12. *Ítsu ikimáshita ka?*

13. *Okane o juubun mótte imásu.*

14. *Enpitsu o mótte imasu ka?*

15. *Sono hoo ga oishíi deshoo.*

16. *Pasupooto o mótte inákereba narimasén.*

17. *Okane o sukoshi mo mótte imasén.*

18. *Kippu o mótte inákute mo íi desu.*

4. You don't have to have a ticket.

5. Come as quickly as you can.

6. I have seen (the) Kabuki.

7. Why didn't you see the Bunraku?

8. You have to have a passport.

9. It isn't as delicious.

10. I was able to see Mr. Yamada.

11. I have enough money.

12. It's delicious.

13. When is it?

14. Which building is it?

15. It probably tastes very good.

16. It's new.

17. Where is he?

18. Have you a pencil?

19. *Kippu o mótte iru ka mo shiremasén.*

19. Is it that?

20. *Sore wa kore hodo oishiku arimasén.*

20. What is it?

21. *Kabuki o míta koto ga arimásu.*

21. It wasn't very tasty.

22. *Yamada-san ni áu koto ga dekimáshita.*

22. When did you go?

23. *Dekiru dake háyaku kite kudasái.*

23. That would probably taste better.

24. *Búnraku wa dóo shite mimasén deshita ka?*

24. With whom did you go?

25. *Sono kishá wa kono kishá hodo háyaku arimasén.*

25. How was the Kabuki play?

ANSWERS

1-12; 2-16; 3-19; 4-17; 5-15; 6-13; 7-20; 8-14; 9-24; 10-21; 11-25; 12-22; 13-11; 14-18; 15-23; 16-8; 17-3; 18-4; 19-1; 20-9; 21-6; 22-10; 23-5; 24-7; 25-2.

LESSON 16 DÁI JUURÓKKA

DO YOU SPEAK JAPANESE?

Nihongo ga dekimásu ka?

Do you speak Japanese? [Is Japanese possible?]

lie, dekimasén.	No, I don't speak Japanese.
hetá désu.	speak poorly [be poor (in skill)]
taihen hetá désu	speak very poorly [be very poor]
Taihen hetá désu.	I (speak) very poorly.
sukóshi	a little
Hái, sukóshi dekimásu.	Yes, I speak a little.
hon no sukóshi	very little
Hon no sukóshi dekimásu.	I speak very little.
amari . . . dekimasén	not much *(used with a negative verb)*
wázuka daké	just a little
Wakarimásu ka?	Do you understand (it)?
lie, wakarimasén.	No, I don't understand (it).
Amari yóku wakarimasén.	I don't understand (it) very well.
Nihongo wa amari yóku wakarimasén.	I don't understand Japanese very well.
Hai, wakarimásu.	Yes, I understand.
Hai, sukóshi wakarimásu.	Yes, I understand a little.
Yomemásu ga[1] hanasemasén.	I read but I can't speak. (I can read but . . .)
Wakarimásu ka?	Do you understand?
Sukóshi mo wakarimasén.	Not at all.
Yóku wakarimasén.	I don't understand very well.
Káite kudasái.	Write it, please.

[1] *ga* = but

| Dóo kakimásu ka? | How do you write it? |
| Sono kotoba wa shirimasén. | I don't know that word. |

PLEASE SPEAK A LITTLE SLOWER

| Yukkúri hanáshite kudasáreba . . . | if you speak slowly (for me) |
| Yukkúri hanáshite kudasáreba wakarimásu. | If you speak slowly, I'll be able to understand you. |

LESSON 17 DÁI JUUNANÁKA

PLEASE SPEAK A LITTLE SLOWER (cont.)

Nán to osshaimáshita ka?	What did you say?
Sore wa Nihongo de dóo iimásu ka?	How do you say that in Japanese?
"Thank you" wa Nihongo de dóo iimásu ka?	How do you say, "Thank you," in Japanese?
Dóo yuu ími désu ka?	What do you mean?
. . . kudasaimasén ka?	would you not . . . ?
hanásu	speak
mótto yukkúri	slower
Mótto yukkúri hanáshite kudasaimasén ka?	Would you speak slower? [Would you not speak. . . .]
dóozo	please
Dóozo mótto yukkúri hanáshite kudasaimasén ka?	Would you mind speaking a little slower, please?
Moo ichido itte kudasaimasén ka?	Would you please say (that) again?

THANKS

Yukkúri hanáshite kudasái.	Please speak slowly.
Arígatoo.	Thanks.
Dóomo arígatoo gozaimásu.	Thank you very much.
Dóo itashimáshite.	Don't mention it.
Arígatoo gozaimásu.	Thanks. [(I) thank (you).]
Dóo itashimáshite.	Not at all.
Gomennasái.	Excuse me.
Dóozo.	Certainly. [Please (go ahead.)]
Dóozo osaki ni.	Go ahead!
Shitsúrei. Nán to osshaimáshita ka?	Pardon? What did you say?
Nán to osshaimáshita ka?	What did you say?
Déwa mata.	See you soon.
Déwa nochihodo.	See you later.
Déwa kónban.	See you this evening.

QUIZ 7

1. Káite kudasái.	1. I don't speak Japanese.
2. Nihongo wa dekimasén.	2. A few words.
3. Nihongo wa yóku wakarimasén.	3. Do you understand?
4. Wakarimásu ka?	4. I don't understand Japanese very well.
5. Hon no sukóshi.	5. Write it down.

6. *Moo ichido itte kudasaimasén ka?*

6. How do you write it?

7. *"Thank you" wa Nihongo de dóo iimasu ka?*

7. I don't know that word.

8. *Dóo yuu ími désu ka?*

8. How do you say, "Thank you," in Japanese?

9. *Dóo kakimásu ka?*

9. What do you mean?

10. *Sono kotoba wa shirimasén.*

10. Would you please say that again?

ANSWERS

1-5; 2-1; 3-4; 4-3; 5-2; 6-10; 7-8; 8-9; 9-6; 10-7.

WORD STUDY

bánana	banana
karifuráwaa	cauliflower
kyábetsu	cabbage
méron	melon
orénji	orange
páseri	parsley
remon	lemon
rétasu	lettuce
sérori	celery
tómato	tomato

THIS AND THAT

1. *Kono* This

kono hón   this book

konó hito	this man
kono hóteru	this hotel
kono tegami	this letter
kono hanashi	this story

2. *Sono* That

Sono refers to some thing or place which is near by.

sono hón	that book
sono hí	that day
sonó kotoba	that word
sonó hito	that man
sono hóteru	that hotel
sonó tegami	that letter

3. *Kore* This

Kore wa doo yuu ími désu ka?	What does this mean?
Kore wa watakushi nó désu.	This is mine.

4. *Sore* That

Sore refers to things within immediate reach, both physical and abstract:

Sore désu.	That's it. It's that.
Sore wa kangaénaide kudasái.	Don't think about that.
Sore wa mochíron désu.	That goes without saying.
Kore wa watakushi nó désu; are wa anáta no désu.	This one is mine; that one is yours.

5. *Are* That

Are refers to things ouside of immediate reach:

Are désu.	It's that (over there).
Are ja arimasén.	It isn't that. That's not it.
Are o kudasái.	Give me that over there.

QUIZ 8

1.	*Are wa anáta no désu ka?*	1.	What does this mean?
2.	*Kore wa dóo yuu ími désu ka?*	2.	It isn't that.
3.	*Are o kudasái.*	3.	That goes without saying.
4.	*Sore wa kangaénaide kudasái.*	4.	This one is mine; that one is yours.
5.	*Sore désu.*	5.	This is mine.
6.	*Kore wa watakushi no désu.*	6.	Give me that.
7.	*Are désu.*	7.	That's it.
8.	*Sore wa mochíron désu.*	8.	Don't think about that.
9.	*Kore wa watakushi no désu; are wa anáta no désu.*	9.	It's that.
10.	*Are ja arimasén.*	10.	Is that yours?

ANSWERS

1-10; 2-1; 3-6; 4-8; 5-7; 6-5; 7-9; 8-3; 9-4; 10-2.

WORD STUDY

baree bóoru	volleyball
basukétto bóoru	basketball
bókushingu	boxing
górufu	golf
háikingu	hiking
pínpon	Ping-pong (table tennis)
résuringu	wrestling
sukéeto	skating
sukíi	ski, skiing
ténisu	tennis

LESSON 18   DÁI JUUHACHÍKA

USEFUL WORD GROUPS II
NOT

Yóku arimasén.	It's not good.
Wáruku arimasén.	It's not bad.
Soré ja arimasén.	It's not that.
Koko ni arimasén.	It's not here.
Amari takusan de náku.	Not too much.
Amari háyaku náku.	Not too fast.
Máda désu.	Not yet. [It's yet (to come).]
Sukóshi mo . . . masén.	Not at all *(with a negative predicate).*
Sukóshi mo jínkam ga arimasén.	I haven't any time.
Dóo suru ka shirimasén.	I don't know how to do it.
Ítsu ka shirimasén.	I don't know when.

Dóko ka shirimasén.	I don't know where.
Nani mo shirimasén.	I don't know anything.
Nani mo iimasén déshita.	He didn't say anything.
Náni mo arimasén.	Nothing. [There is nothing.]
Náni mo mótte imasén.	I haven't anything.
Kesshite.	Never *(with a negative predicate)*.
Kesshite kimasén.	He (she) never comes.
Dáre ga kimáshita ka?	Who came?
. . . Dare mo kimasén déshita.	. . . Nobody came.
Dáre mo miemasén.	I don't see anyone. [No one is in sight.]
Moo soko e ikimasén.	I don't go there any more.
Moo kimasén.	He doesn't come any more.
Hyakuen shika arimasén.	I have only a hundred yen. [(I) don't have but a hundred yen.]
Ichijíkan shika arimasén.	You have only one hour.
Tóo shika mótte imasén.	He has only ten of them.

ISN'T IT

Hontoo désu ne?	It's true, isn't it?
Kimásu ne?	You are coming, aren't you?
Juubun mótte imásu ne?	You have enough of it, haven't you?
Sukóshi mo mótte imasén ne?	You haven't any of it, have you?
Sansei désu ne?	You agree, don't you?

QUIZ 9

1. *Sore ja arimasén.*	1. I don't see anyone.
2. *Ítsu ka shirimasén.*	2. I have only a hundred yen.
3. *Sukóshi mo jikan ga arimasén.*	3. You have only one hour.
4. *Nani mo arimasén.*	4. You are coming, aren't you?
5. *Kimásu ne?*	5. You haven't any of it, have you?
6. *Ichijíkan shika arimasén.*	6. It's not that.
7. *Dare mo miemasén.*	7. I haven't any time.
8. *Hyakuen shika arimasén.*	8. I don't know when.
9. *Sukoshi mo mótte imasén ne?*	9. He didn't say anything.
10. *Nani mo iimasén déshita.*	10. Nothing.

ANSWERS

1-6; 2-8; 3-7; 4-10; 5-4; 6-3; 7-1; 8-2; 9-5; 10-9.

I, YOU, HE

1. **It's me (I)**

Watakushi désu.	It's me.
Anáta desu.	It's you.
Anó hito désu.	It's him (her).
Watakushitachi désu.	It's us.

2. It's mine.

Notice that when a noun appears together with *no* but the combination is not followed by another noun, it often means, literally, "a thing pertaining to (that noun)." For example:

watakushi no	a thing pertaining to me; my thing, mine

Notice also that when the sequence *no desu*, or *n desu* follows immediately after a predicate, it means, "That's what it is," or, "It's a fact that," and the predicate itself is usually in the plain form.

Watakushi nó désu.	It's mine.
Anáta no désu.	It's yours.
Anó hito nó désu.	It's his (hers).
Watakushítachi no désu.	It's ours.
Anatagata nó désu.	It's yours *(polite)*.
Anó hitotachi nó désu.	It's theirs.

3. About me

Anáta no koto o hanáshite iru no désu.	I'm talking about you. [(I'm) talking of things pertaining to you.]
Watakushi no kotó o hanáshite irú no desu ne?	You are talking about me, aren't you? [. . . that's what it is, isn't it?]

4. To me

Watakushi ni kudasái.	Give it to me, please.
Watakushítachi ni kudasái.	Give it to us, please.

Watakushi ni kudasaimáshita.	He gave it to me.
Watakushítachi ni kudasaimáshita.	He gave it to us.

THE MODIFIERS

In Japanese, a modifer *always* precedes the word modified, whether the modifier is a single word, a phrase, or a clause. An adjective that modifies a noun is always placed before the noun, and an adverb that modifies a verb is always placed before the verb. Even a long clause, which in English would follow the noun, precedes it in Japanese. In fact, the very act of placing a clause before a noun makes it a modifier of that noun.

Here are some examples:

ie	a house
akai	it is red *(plain)*
akai ie	a red house
yáne	a roof
Yáne ga akai.	The roof is red.
Yáne ga akai ie. ⎫ **Yáne no akai ie.** ⎭	The house whose roof is red. [The-roof-is-red house.]
Yáne no akai ie ni súnde imásu.	He lives in a house with a red roof.
hito	a person
súnde imásu	he lives [is residing]
súnde iru	he lives *(plain)*
súnde iru hito	the person who lives (there)
sono ie ni súnde iru hito	the person who lives in that house

yáne no akai ie ni súnde iru hito	the person who lives in the house with a red roof
Ano yáne no akai ie ni súnde iru híto ga kyónen Amerika kara kitá hito desu.	The person who lives in that house with a red roof is the man who came from America last year.

THE NOUN-MAKER *NO*

In addition to the particle *no* that follows a noun and links it to another noun, there is a "noun-maker" *no* which appears only *after* a clause. (As you have already seen, a clause *can* be a single adjective or a verb or a series of words ending in an adjective or verb.) This *no* makes a noun out of the clause and is usually translated "one who," "one which," "the act of doing," "the time when," or "the place where."

Akai no o kudasái.	Give me one which is red. Give me a red one.
Akakunái no o kudasái.	Give me one which is not red.
Yáne ga akái no ga watakushi no ie desu.	The one (house) with a red roof is my house. [The-roof-is-red one (house) is my house.]
Tabemáshita.	I ate.
Tábeta.	I ate *(plain)*.
sakana	fish
Tábeta no wa sakana déshita.	The food [thing] that I ate was fish.
Sakana o tábeta.	I ate fish *(plain)*.
Sakana o tábeta no wa kinóo deshita.	It was yesterday that I ate fish. [The day that (I) ate fish was yesterday.]

WORD STUDY

baketsu	bucket
booru	bowl
fóoku	fork
furaipan	frying pan
gásu	gas
míkisaa	mixer
nafukin	napkin
náifu	knife
supúun	spoon
tóosutaa	toaster

QUIZ 10

1. *Watakushi nó desu.*
2. *Tábeta no wa sakana déshita.*
3. *Anáta no kotó o hanáshite irú no desu.*
4. *Anatagáta no desu.*
5. *Watakushítachi ni kudasái.*
6. *Watakushi ni kudasaimáshita.*
7. *Y'ane no akai uchi ni súnde imásu.*
8. *Akakunái no o kudasái.*
9. *Akái no o kudasái.*
10. *Sakana o tábeta no wa kinóo deshita.*

1. It was yesterday that I ate fish.
2. Give me one which is not red.
3. Give it to us, please.
4. Give me one which is red.
5. He lives in a house with a red roof.
6. It's yours.
7. He gave it to me.
8. The food that I ate was fish.
9. It's mine.
10. I'm talking about you.

LESSON 19   DÁI JUUKYÚUKA

HELLO!

Konnichi wa.	Hello. Good afternoon.
Ohayoo gozaimásu.	Good morning.
Ogénki desu ka?	How are you?
Okagesama de génki desu.	Very well, thanks. [Thanks to your thinking of me . . .]
Betsu ni kawari arimasén.	So so. [No special change.]
Anáta wa?	And how are you? [And you?]
Dóo ni ka yatte orimásu.	Not bad.
Okagesama de dóo ni ka yatte orimásu.	Not bad, thanks.
Okawari arimasén ka?	How are you? How are things?
Okagesama de tasshá désu.	All right. Fine. [Thanks to your thinking of me, I am in good health.]

I'D LIKE YOU TO MEET . . .

Sákata-san no ókusan o goshookai itashimásu.	Allow me to present Mrs. Sakata. [May (I) introduce Mrs. Sakata.]
Sákata-san o goshookai itashimásu.	Allow me to present Mr. Sakata.

Hajímete ome ni kakarimásu.	Glad to meet you. [It is a pleasure to meet you.]
Dóozo yoroshiku.	Glad to meet you. [Am at your service.]
Kochira wa Sakata désu.	This is (Mr.) Sakata.
Dóozo yoroshiku.	Glad to meet you.

HOW ARE THINGS?

Konnichi wa.	Hello.
Gokigen ikága desu ka?	How are you?
Okage sama de.	Fine, thanks.
Kawatta kotó wa arimasén ka?	What's new?
Betsu ni arimasén.	Nothing much. [There isn't anything especially.]
Nisánnichi shitára denwa o kákete kudasái.	Phone me one of these days.
Wasurenáide kudasái.	Don't forget.
Shoochi shimáshita.	I'll certainly do so.
Daijóobu desu ne?	Are you sure? You're sure?
Daijóobu desu.	Sure!
Déwa mata.	See you soon. [Well then, again.]
Getsuyóobi ni ome ni kakarimásu.	See you on Monday.
Isshúukan shitára ome ni kakarimásu.	I'll see you in a week.
Nishúukan shitára ome ni kakarimásu.	I'll see you in two weeks.
Kin'yóobi no yóru ome ni kakarimásu.	I'll see you Friday evening.

Kono Mokuyóobi ni ome ni kakarimásu.	I'll see you this coming Thursday.
Kono Mokuyóobi no yóru hachíji ni ome ni kakarimásu.	I'll see you this coming Thursday at eight o'clock in the evening. [This coming Thursday evening at eight o'clock (I'll) see you.]
Kón'ya ome ni kakarimásu.	I'll see you this evening.

QUIZ 11

1.	*Gokigen ikága desu ka?*	1.	So so.
2.	*Ashita ome ni kakarimásu.*	2.	Very well, thanks.
3.	*Dóozo yoroshiku.*	3.	Not too bad.
4.	*Kawatta kotó wa arimasén ka?*	4.	How are you?
5.	*Mokuyóobi ni ome ni kakarimásu.*	5.	I'll see you tomorrow.
6.	*Okagesama de.*	6.	I'm happy to know you.
7.	*Betsu ni arimasén.*	7.	What's new?
8.	*Konnichi wa.*	8.	I'll see you on Thursday.
9.	*Doo ni ka yatte orimásu.*	9.	Good afternoon. Hello.

10. *Betsu ni kawari arimasén.*	10. Nothing much.
11. *Sono uchi ni ome ni kakarimásu.*	11. Allow me. . . . ("I would like to introduce")
12. *Nísannichi shitara denwa o kákete kudasái.*	12. Phone me one of these days.
13. *Jiki ome ni kakarimásu.*	13. See you Monday.
14. *Goshookai itashimásu.*	14. See you soon.
15. *Getsuyóobi ni ome ni kakarimásu.*	15. See you in a little while.

ANSWERS

1-4; 2-5; 3-6; 4-7; 5-8; 6-2; 7-10; 8-9; 9-3; 10-1;
11-15; 12-12; 13-14; 14-11; 15-13.

LESSON 20 DÁI NÍJIKKA

HAVE YOU TWO MET?

Kono katá o gozónji de irasshaimásu ka?	Do you know my friend [this person]?
Iie, kyoo hajímete ome ni kakarimásu.	No, I don't think so. [Am meeting him for the first time today.]
Iie, kore máde ome ni kakátta kotó wa arimasén.	No, I haven't had the pleasure.

Máe kara gozónji de irasshaimásu ne?	I believe you already know one another.
Hái, máe kara zonjiágete orimásu.	Yes, we've already met. [Have known him from before.]
Iie, zonjiágete orimasén.	No, I don't believe we've met before. [No, (I) don't know (the gentleman]

GLAD TO HAVE MET YOU

Ome ni kakáru koto ga dékite saiwai déshita.	Glad to have met you. [Has been good fortune (for me) to have been able to see you.]
Mata zéhi oai shitái to omoimásu.	Hope to see you soon.
Dóozo yoroshiku.	Same here.
Moo ichido sono uchi ni hi o kimete oide itadakimashoo.	Let's get together again one of these days.
Arígatoo gozaimasu.	Fine. [Thank you.]
Watakushi no júusho to denwa bángoo wa omochi deshóo ka?	Do you have my address and telephone number?
Iie, mótte orimasén. Itadaite okimashóo.	No, let me have it.
Banchi wa Bunkyóoku Oiwakéchoo[1] juugo bánchi desu.	My address is 15 Oiwake Street, Bunkyoku.

[1]The word for "street" *(choo)* is sometimes added to the name proper, as in *Oiwakechoo*. When *-me* is added to *choo* to make *choome*, it signifies that the street is an ordinal (i.e., *Ginza yon choome* = Ginza Fourth Street).

Denwa bángoo wa Koishikawa no go yon go ni ban desu.	My telephone number is Koishikawa 5452.
Jimúsho no banchi mo itadaite okimashóo.	Give me your office address, too,
Okaki itashimashóo. Ginza yon choome no ni bánchi desu.	I'll write it for you. It's 2 Ginza Fourth Street.
Ása wa kuji máe deshitara uchi ni orimásu.	You can get me at home before nine in the morning. [If it is before nine (I'll) be at home.]
Sono áto wa jimúsho no hóo ni orimásu.	Otherwise [afterwards] at the office.
Aa sóo desu ka. Déwa, táshika ni gorenraku itashimásu.	Good. I'll be sure to get in touch with you.
Déwa shitsúrei itashimásu. Odénwa o omachi shite orimásu.	Good-by. [And] (I) shall be waiting for your phone call.
Déwa mata.	See you soon.

QUIZ 12

1. Iie, kyoo hajímete ome ni kakarimásu.	1. Yes, we've already met.
2. Hái, máe kara zonjiágete orimásu.	2. No, I haven't had the pleasure.

3. *Iie, mótte orimasén. Itadaite okimashóo.*

3. No, not yet.

4. *Jimúsho no banchi mo itadaite okimashóo.*

4. Glad to have met you.

5. *Déwa mata.*

5. I hope to see you soon.

6. *Aa sóo desu ka. Déwa táshika ni gorenraku itashimásu.*

6. Give me your office address, too.

7. *Watakushi no júusho to denwa bángoo wa omochi deshóo ka?*

7. No, let me have it.

8. *Iie, kore máde ome ni kakátta koto wa arimasén.*

8. Do you have my address and telephone number?

9. *Mata zéhi oai shitái to omoimásu.*

9. Good. I will be sure to get in touch with you.

10. *Ome ni kakáru koto ga dékite saiwai déshita.*

10. See you soon.

ANSWERS
1-3; 2-1; 3-7; 4-6; 5-10; 6-9; 7-8; 8-2; 9-5; 10-4.

WORD STUDY
baiorin	violin
furúuto	flute
gítaa	guitar

háapu	harp
kurarinétto	clarinet
mandorin	mandolin
paipu órugan	pipe organ
piano	piano
sakisóhon	saxophone
séro	cello

REVIEW QUIZ 2

1. *Dóozo moo sukóshi yukkúri_____(speak)
   kudasaimásen ka?*
   a. *káite*
   b. *hanáshite*
   c. *kákete*

2. *Dóozo_____ (slowly) hanáshite kudasái.*
   a. *hakkíri*
   b. *yóku*
   c. *yukkúri*

3. *Kodomo_____(direction-particle) hón o
   yarimáshita.*
   a. *ga*
   b. *ni*
   c. *no*

4. *Ókusan ni tegami_____(object-particle)
   yarimáshita.*
   a. *o*
   b. *ga*
   c. *no*

5. *Sonna ni_____(far) arimasén.*
   a. *tooku*
   b. *chikaku*
   c. *takaku*

6. *Anó hito*_____(topic-particle) *kodǫmo ni okane*
   o yarimáshita.
   a. *o*
   b. *wa*
   c. *to*

7. *Watakushi wa heya no náka ni*_____(am).
   a. *desu*
   b. *imásu*
   c. *arimásu*

8. _____(Late) *kimáshita.*
   a. *Háyaku*
   b. *Tooku*
   c. *Osoku*

9. *Sono hón wa dóko ni*_____(is)?
   a. *imásu*
   b. *arimásu*
   c. *désu*

10. *Koppu o*_____(bring) *kudasái.*
    a. *katte*
    b. *tótte*
    c. *mótte kite*

11. *Sore wa*_____(easy) *desu.*
    a. *yasashíi*
    b. *muzukashíi*
    c. *ookíi*

12. *Kodomo no*_____(house) *desu.*
    a. *monó*
    b. *uchi*
    c. *tokoro*

13. *Okane ga*_____(there isn't).
    a. *arimasén*
    b. *imasén*
    c. *kimasén*

14. *Tabako o*_____(have) *imásu ka?*
    a. *míte*
    b. *káite*
    c. *mótte*

15. *Nihongo wa yóku*_____(don't understand).
    a. *wakarimasén*
    b. *kakemasén*
    c. *shimasén*

16. *Dóo mo*_____(thank) *gozaimásu.*
    a. *osamuu*
    b. *arígatoo*
    c. *otakoo*

17. _____(Here) *ni imásu ka?*
    a. *Dóko*
    b. *Soko*
    b. *Koko*

18. _____(Letter) *wa dekimáshita ka?*
    a. *Tegami*
    b. *Shitaku*
    c. *Benkyoo*

19. *Sore wa*_____(yesterday) *deshita ka?*
    a. *kón'ya*
    b. *hontoo*
    c. *kinóo*

20. _____(A little) *wakarimásu.*
    a. *Yóku*
    b. *Takusan*
    b. *Sukóshi*

ANSWERS

1-b; 2-c; 3-b; 4-a; 5-a; 6-b; 7-b; 8-c; 9-b; 10-c; 11-a;
12-b; 13-a; 14-c; 15-a; 16-b; 17-c; 18-a; 19-c; 20-c.

LESSON 21 DÁI NÍJUU ÍKKA

NUMBERS

1. One, Two, Three

For one to ten only, there are two sets of numbers.

ichí	one
ní	two
san	three
shí	four
gó	five
rokú	six
shichí	seven
hachí	eight
kú, kyúu	nine
júu	ten
juuichí	eleven
juuní	twelve
júusan	thirteen
juushí	fourteen
hitótsu	one
futatsu	two
mittsú	three
yottsú	four
itsútsu	five
muttsú	six
nanátsu	seven
yattsú	eight
kokónotsu	nine
tóo	ten
júugo	fifteen
juurokú	sixteen
juunána	seventeen
juuhachí	eighteen
júuku	nineteen
níjuu	twenty

níjuu ichí	twenty-one
níjuu ní	twenty-two
níjuu san	twenty-three
sánjuu	thirty
sánjuu ichí	thirty-one
sánjuu ní	thirty-two
sánjuu san	thirty-three
yónjuu, *shijuú*	forty
yónjuu ichí	forty-one
yónjuu ní	forty-two
yónjuu san	forty-three
gojúu	fifty
gojuu ichí	fifty-one
gojuu ní	fifty-two
gojuu san	fifty-three
rokujúu	sixty
rokujuu ichí	sixty-one
rokujuu ní	sixty-two
rokujuu san	sixty-three
nanájuu	seventy
nanájuu ichí	seventy-one
nanájuu ní	seventy-two
nanájuu san	seventy-three
hachijúu	eighty
hachijuu ichí	eighty-one
hachijuu ní	eighty-two
hachijuu san	eighty-three
kujúu, kyúujuu	ninety
kyúujuu ichí	ninety-one
kyúujuu ní	ninety-two
kyúujuu san	ninety-three
hyakú	one hundred
hyaku ichí	one hundred and one
hyaku ní	one hundred and two
hyaku san	one hundred and three
sén	one thousand
sén ichí	one thousand and one

| sén ní | one thousand and two |
| sén san | one thousand and three |

LESSON 22 DÁI NÍJUU NÍKA

NUMBERS (cont.)

2. More Numbers

hyaku níjuu	one hundred and twenty
hyaku níjuu ichí	one hundred and twenty-one
hyaku sánjuu	one hundred and thirty
hyaku yónjuu, *hyaku shijúu*	one hundred and forty
hyaku gojúu	one hundred and fifty
hyaku rokujúu	one hundred and sixty
hyaku nanájúu	one hundred and seventy
hyaku nanájuu ichí	one hundred and seventy-one
hyaku nanájuu hachí	one hundred and seventy-eight
hyaku hachijúu	one hundred and eighty
hyaku kujúu	one hundred and ninety
hyaku kujuu hachí	one hundred and ninety-eight
hyaku kujuu kú	one hundred and ninety-nine
nihyaku	two hundred
sánbyaku[1] *níjuu shí*	three hundred and twenty-four

[1](Notice the *b* in *sánbyaku*) See Grammar, Section 10, for letter changes with use of a "counter."

happyaku[1] schichijuu gó   eight hundred and seventy-five

sanzén sánbyaku sánjuu san   three thousand three hundred and thirty-three

The pronunciation of numbers often differs before "counters" beginning with certain consonants. "Counters" are words like "sheet" in "ten sheets of paper" or "cup" in "ten cups of water." Most things have to be counted with a counter in Japanese. Before a counter beginning with *h, k, s,* or *t,* the pronunciation of the *ichi* (one), *bachi* (eight), and *juu* (ten) usually changes. When a counter begins with *h,* the *h* changes to *p.* Before a counter beginning with *h* or *k,* the numbers *roku* (six) and *hyaku* (one hundred) also change form. Following are some examples of these changes in form:

ichí, íppun	one, one minute
rokú, róppun	six, six minutes
hachí, háppun, hachifun	eight, eight minutes
júu, júppun, jíppun	ten, ten minutes
hyaku, hyáppun	one hundred, one hundred minutes
ichí, íkken	one, one house
rokú, rókken	six, six houses
hachí, hachiken	eight, eight houses
júu, júkken, jíkken	ten, ten houses
hyakú, hyákken	one hundred, one hundred houses
ichí, issatsu	one, one volume
hachí, hassatsu	eight, eight volumes
júu, jussatsu, jissatsu	ten, ten volumes
ichí, ittén	one, one point

[1] (Notice the *p* in *happyaku*) See Grammar, Section 10.

hachí, hattén	eight, eight points
júu, juttén, jittén	ten, ten points

3. First, Second, Third

dái ichí[1]	first
dái ní	second
dái san	third
dái yon	fourth
dái gó	fifth
dái rokú	sixth
dái nána	seventh
dái hachí	eighth
dái kyúu	ninth
dái júu	tenth
dái ichí no gyoo ⎫ **hajime no gyoo** ⎭	the first line
dái ní maku	the second act
san too ⎫ *shi'kai* ⎭	the third class
yón kai	the fourth floor
dái gó ka	the fifth lesson
dái rokkái	the sixth time
dái naná shuu	the seventh week
dái hachikágetsu	the eighth month
dái kyuu nen	the ninth year
dái júu	the tenth
dái juuichi ninmé no hito	the eleventh person
dái juuní shoo	the twelfth chapter
dái juusán nichi	the thirteenth day
juushi séiki ⎫ *juuyon séiki* ⎭	the fourteenth century
dái juugo kenmé no uchi	the fifteenth door, the fifteenth building

---

[1]When *dái* precedes a numeral, it shows that the number which follows is an ordinal. Occasionally, an ordinal is used without *dái*.

juuroku banmé no fúne	the sixteenth boat
juushichi choome ⎫ *juunana choome* ⎬	the seventeenth street
dái juuháppan	the eighteenth edition
juuku banme no jidóosha	the nineteenth car
nijikkenmé no ié.	the twentieth house

QUIZ 13

1. *rókkiro*	1. the third class
2. *yon kai*	2. the eighth month
3. *jíppun*	3. the ninth year
4. *sántoo*	4. six kilometers
5. *juuyon séiki*	5. the fourth floor
6. *juuichi ninmé no hito*	6. ten minutes
7. *dái gó ka*	7. the eleventh person
8. *dái hakkágetsu*	8. the thirteenth day
9. *dái juusán nichi*	9. the fifth lesson
10. *dái kyúunen*	10. the fourteenth century

ANSWERS

1-4; 2-5; 3-6; 4-1; 5-10; 6-7; 7-9; 8-2; 9-8; 10-3.

4. Two and Two

Ichi to ní de san ni narimasu.	Two and one are [become] three.
Ni tasu ichi wa san desu.	Two and [plus] one are three.

Ní to ní wa yon desu.	Two and two are four.
Ní tasu ní wa yón desu.	Two and [plus] two are four.
Yon to san wa shichi desu.	Four and three are seven.
Yón tasu san wa shichí desu.	Four and [plus] three are seven.
Gó to ní de shichí ni narimásu.	Five and two are seven.
Gó tasu ní wa shichí desu.	Five and [plus] two are seven.
Shichí to ichí de hachí ni narimásu.	Seven and one are eight.
Shichí tasu ichí wa hachí desu.	Seven and [plus] one are eight.

LESSON 23   DÁI NÍJUU SÁNKA

IT COSTS...

Kore wa . . . shimásu.	This costs . . .
Kore wa góen shimásu.	This costs five yen.
Kono hón wa hyaku gojúu en shimasu.	This book costs one hundred fifty yen.
Kono booshi wa nisen en shimáshita.	This hat cost me two thousand yen.
Kono kimono ni hassen en haraimáshita.	I paid eight thousand yen for this dress.
Kono jidóosha o gojúuman en de kaimáshita.	I bought this car for five hundred thousand yen.
Ichi ríttoru nisén en desu.	It's two thousand yen a liter.
Ichi meetoru nihyaku gojúu en desu.	That costs two hundred fifty yen a meter.

Sén nihyakú en
shimásu.

The price is twelve
hundred yen. It costs
twelve hundred yen.

Hitótsu gojúu en desu.

They cost fifty yen
apiece.

THE TELEPHONE NUMBER IS . . .

Watakushi no denwa
bángoo wa Aóyama
no san roku yon ní
ban desu.

My telephone number is
Aoyama 3642.

Kanda no go ni sán
rokú ban ni kákete
míte kudasai.

Try number Kanda
5236.

Denwa bángoo ga
kawarimáshita. Íma
no wa Azabu no ni
ni ní yón ban desu.

My telephone number
has been changed; it's
now Azabu 2224.

Denwa wa Nakano no
san sán rei nana ban
desu.

Their phone number is
Nakano 3307.

THE NUMBER IS . . .

Oiwakechoo juu nana
bánchi ni súnde
imásu.

I live at 17 Oiwake
Street.

Shoowa dóori yon
bánchi ni súnde
imásu.

He lives at 4 Showa
Boulevard.

Yamanechoo juuni
bánchi desu.

Our address is 12
Yamane Street.

Yanakachoo nihyaku
rokujuusan bánchi
ni súnde imásu.

We live at 263 Yanaka
Street.

Heya no bangoo wa
yónjuu ní desu.

My room number is 42.

SOME DATES

Amerika wa sén yónhyaku kyúujuu ní nen ni hakken saremáshita.	America was discovered in 1492.
Sén happyaku kyúujuu ichí nen ni okorimáshita.	It happened in 1891.
Sén kyúuhyaku juuní nen ni umaremáshita.	I was born in 1912.
Kore wa mina sén kyúuhyaku níjuu yó nen ni okorimáshita.	All this happened in 1924.
Nyuu Yóoku no Sekai hakuránkai wa sén kyúuhyaku sánjuu kyúu nen ni arimáshita.	The New York World's Fair took place in 1939.
Watakushi wa sen kyúuhyaku rokujuu nen ni wa Tookyoo ni imáshita.	I was in Tokyo in 1960.

QUIZ 14

1. *Kore wa gosen en shimásu.*

2. *Denwa bángoo wa Nakano no san sán rei nana ban desu.*

3. *Kono jidóosha o gojuumán en de kaimáshita.*

1. This costs five thousand yen.

2. I bought this car for five hundred thousand yen.

3. Their phone number is Nakano 3307.

4. *Watakushi wa sén kyúuhyaku rokujuu nen ni Tookyoo ni imáshita.*

4. They cost fifty yen apiece.

5. *Sore wa hitótsu gojúu en desu.*

5. I was in Tokyo in 1960.

ANSWERS

1-1; 2-3; 3-2; 4-5; 5-4.

LESSON 24 DÁI NÍJUU YÓNKA

WHAT TIME IS IT?

Nánji desu ka?	What time is it?
Nánji ka oshiete kudasaimasén ka?	Do you have the time, please?
Ichíji desu.	It's one o'clock.
Níji desu.	It's two o'clock.
Sánji desu.	It's three o'clock.
Yóji desu.	It's four o'clock.
Góji desu.	It's five o'clock.
Rokúji desu.	It's six o'clock.
Shichíji desu.	It's seven o'clock.
Hachíji desu.	It's eight o'clock.
Kúji desu.	It's nine o'clock.
Júuji desu.	It's ten o'clock.
Juuichíji desu.	It's eleven o'clock.
Juuníji desu.	It's noon. It's twelve o'clock.
Gógo ichíji desu.	It's 1:00 P.M.
Gógo níji desu.	It's 2:00 P.M.
Gógo sánji desu.	It's 3:00 P.M.
Gógo yóji desu.	It's 4:00 P.M.
Gógo góji desu.	It's 5:00 P.M.

Gógo rokúji desu.	It's 6:00 P.M.
Gógo shichíji desu.	It's 7:00 P.M.
Gógo hachíji desu.	It's 8:00 P.M.
Gógo kúji desu.	It's 9:00 P.M.
Gógo júuji desu.	It's 10:00 P.M.
Gógo juuichíji desu.	It's 11:00 P.M.
Gógo juuníji desu.	It's 12:00 P.M.
Yóru no juuníji desu.	It's midnight.

THE TIME IS NOW...

byóo	second
fún, pún	minute
ji	hour
Níji juugófun desu.	It's two fifteen.
Níji juugofún sugí desu.	It's a quarter after two.
Yóji juugofún máe desu.	It's a quarter to four.
Sánji yonjuugófun desu.	It's three forty-five.
Niji-hán desu.	It's half-past two.
Níji sánjippun desu.	It's two thirty.
Góji nijippun máe desu.	It's twenty to five.
Kúji sanjuugófun desu.	It's nine thirty-five.
Shóogo desu.	It's noon.
Juuníji gofun máe desu.	It's five to twelve.
Juuníji gofun sugí desu.	It's five past twelve.
Gózen ichíji desu.	It's one o'clock in the morning.
Goji góro desu.	It's about five.

Shichiji góro desu.	It's about seven.
Juuichíji sukóshi máe desu.	It's almost eleven.
Máda rokuji-hán desu.	It's only half-past six.
Goji sugí desu.	It's after five.

A MATTER OF TIME

Ítsu oide ni narimásu ka?	When will you come *(polite)?* What time will you come?
Sánji ni soko e ikimásu.	I'll be there at three o'clock.
Sánji nijuppun máe ni kimáshita.	He came at twenty to three.
Gógo níji ni kimásu.	He'll come at 2:00 P.M.
Kúji nijuugofun góro ni soko e ikimásu.	We'll be there about nine twenty-five.
Kónban no juuji-hán ni káette kimásu.	He'll be back at ten thirty tonight.
Hachíji juugofun góro ni soko de ome ni kakarimashóo.	I'll see you there about eight fifteen.
Rokúji ni aimásu.	We'll meet at six.
Yóji ni dekakemásu.	I'm going out at four o'clock.
Shichíji to hachíji no aida ni kité kudasái.	Come between seven and eight.
Yóru no rokúji ni kimásu.	He'll come at six in the evening.
Kónban júuji ni kité kudasái.	Come at ten o'clock tonight.
Kishá wa shichíji níjuu sánpun ni tsukimásu.	The train arrives at seven twenty-three.
Kishá wa kúji yónjippun ni demásu.	The train leaves at nine forty.

WORD STUDY

anpaia	umpire
baaténdaa	bartender
dezáinaa	designer
doresuméekaa	dressmaker
enjiniya	engineer
manéejaa	manager
sararíiman	salaried man
seerusúman	salesman
supónsaa	sponsor
taipísuto	typist

QUIZ 15

1. Niji-hán desu.

2. Níji júugofun desu.

3. Kúji sánjuu gófun desu.

4. Shichíji to hachíji no aida ni kité kudasái.

5. Soko de hachíji juugofun góro ni ome ni kakarimásu.

6. Kishá wa shichíji níjuu sánpun ni tsukimásu.

7. Kónban júuji ni kité kudasái.

1. I'll see you there about eight fifteen.

2. The train arrives at seven twenty-three.

3. Come between seven and eight.

4. Come at ten o'clock tonight.

5. It's one o'clock in the morning.

6. He'll come at 2:00 P.M.

7. We'll be there about nine twenty-five.

8. *Yóru no ichíji desu.*

8. It's two fifteen. It's a quarter after two.

9. *Kúji níjuugofun góro ni soko e ikimásu.*

9. It's half-past two. It's two thirty.

10. *Níji ni kimásu.*

10. It's nine thirty-five.

ANSWERS

1-9; 2-8; 3-10; 4-3; 5-1; 6-2; 7-4; 8-5; 9-7; 10-6.

LESSON 25   DÁI NÍJUU GÓKA

IT'S TIME

Jikan desu.	It's time.
Sore o suru jikan desu.	It's time to do it. [(It) is to-do-it time.]
Déru jikan desu.	It's time to leave.
Uchi e káeru jikan desu.	It's time to go home.
Jikan ga arimásu.	I have time.
Juubun jikan ga arimásu.	I have enough time.
Jikan ga arimasén.	I haven't the time.
Dono kurai nágaku soko ni iru tsumori desu ka?	How long do you intend to stay here?
Dono kurai nágaku koko ni imáshita ka?	How long have you been here?
Jikan no muda o shite imásu.	He's wasting his time.

Suru jikan o agete kudasái.	Give him time to do it.
Kimono o kikaéru aida dake mátte kudasái.	Just give me enough time to get dressed. [Please wait just for the duration that I am dressing.]
Tokidoki kimásu.	He comes from time to time.

MORNING, NOON AND NIGHT

ása	morning
hirú ⎱	
shóogo ⎰	noon
gógo	afternoon
ban	evening
yóru	night
hi	the day
shúu	the week
isshúukan	a week
nishúukan	two weeks
tsukí	month
nén	year
kinóo	yesterday
kyóo	today
ashita	tomorrow
ototói	the day before yesterday
tsugí no hi	the next day
asátte	the day after tomorrow
chótto máe	a moment ago
íma	now
súgu	in a moment, soon
zutto máe	a long time ago
sukóshi máe	a little while ago
késa	this morning
kinoo no ása	yesterday morning

ashita no ása	tomorrow morning
kyoo no gógo	this afternoon [today's afternoon]
kinoo no gógo	yesterday afternoon
ashita no gógo	tomorrow afternoon
kónban	this evening
kinoo no ban ⎫ **sakúban** ⎭	yesterday evening
ashita no ban ⎫ **myóoban** ⎭	tomorrow evening
kónban	tonight
kinoo no yóru ⎫ **sakúban** ⎬ **yuube** ⎭	last night
ashita no yóru ⎫ **myóoban** ⎭	tomorrow night

LESSON 26   DÁI NÍJUU RÓKKA

EXPRESSIONS OF TIME

konshuu	this week
senshuu	last week
raishuu	next week
saraishuu	in two weeks, the week after next
senshuu	last week
kongetsu	this month
séngetsu	last month
ráigetsu	next month
rairáigetsu ⎫ **saraigetsu** ⎭	in two months, the month after next
senséngetsu	two months ago, the month before last
kotoshi	this year

kyónen \} sakunen	last year
rainen	next year
sarainen	in two years, the year after next
nínen máe \} issakúnen \} otótoshi	two years ago, the year before last
ása	in the morning
ban	in the evening
hiru góro	towards noon
yuushokugo	after dinner (the evening meal)
shuumatsu	at the end of the week
getsumatsu	at the end of the month
konshuu no owari góro ni	towards the end of the week
ichijíkan mae	an hour ago
juugohun inai ni	in a quarter of an hour
sono uchi ni	one of these days
Sono uchi ni ome ni kakarimasu.	See you one of these days.
máinichi	everyday
ichinichi juu	all day (long)
hitoban juu	all night (long)
Asa kara ban made hatarakimasu.	He works from morning to night.
Kyóo wa nannichi desu ka?	What's the date?

PAST, PRESENT, FUTURE

PAST	PRESENT	FUTURE
imashígata	**íma**	**súgu ato de**
a moment ago	now	in a moment

kinoo no asa	**késa**	**ashita no ása**
yesterday morning	this morning	tomorrow morning

kinoo no gógo	**kyóo no gógo**	**ashita no gógo**
yesterday afternoon	this afternoon	tomorrow afternoon

sakúban	**kónban**	**myóoban**
yesterday evening, last night	this evening, tonight	tomorrow evening, tomorrow night

senshuu	**konshuu**	**raishuu**
last week	this week	next week

séngetsu	**kongetsu**	**ráigetsu**
last month	this month	next month

sakunen	**kotoshi**	**rainen**
last year	this year	next year

LESSON 27 DÁI NÍJUU NANÁKA

WHAT DAY IS THIS?

Nichiyóobi	Sunday
Getsuyóobi	Monday
Kayóobi	Tuesday
Suiyóobi	Wednesday
Mokuyóobi	Thursday
Kin'yóobi	Friday
Doyóobi	Saturday

WHAT'S THE DATE TODAY?

1. The Days of the Month

In Japanese, each day of the month has a name, and these, except for the word for the first day, are also used to count the *number* of days.[1] To count "one day," you say *ichinichi*.

tsuitachi	First day (of the month)
futsuka	Second day
mikka	Third day
yokka	Fourth day
itsuka	Fifth day
muika	Sixth day
nanoka or nanuka	Seventh day
yooka	Eighth day
kokonoka	Ninth day
tooka	Tenth day
juuichinichi	Eleventh day
juuninichi	Twelfth day
juusánnichi	Thirteenth day
júuyokka	Fourteenth day
juugónichi	Fifteenth day
juurokunichi	Sixteenth day
juushichinichi	Seventeenth day
juuhachinichi	Eighteenth day
juukúnichi	Nineteenth day
hatsuka	Twentieth day
níjuu ichinichi	Twenty-first day
níjuu ninichi	Twenty-second day
níjuu sánnichi	Twenty-third day
níjuu yokka	Twenty-fourth day
níjuu gónichi	Twenty-fifth day
níjuu rokunichi	Twenty-sixth day
níjuu shichinichi	Twenty-seventh day

[1]For ordinal numbers, see Grammar, Section 11.

níjuu hachinichi	Twenty-eighth day
níjuu kúnichi	Twenty-ninth day
sanjúunichi	Thirtieth day
sánjuu ichinichi	Thirty-first day

2. What's the date today?

Kyóo wa nánnichi desu ka?	What's the date today?
Doyóobi wa nánnichi desu ka?	What will be the date Saturday? [As for Saturday, what is the date?]
Kyóo wa tooka desu.	Today's the tenth.
Kyóo wa hatsuka desu.	Today's the twentieth.
Kyóo wa Kayóobi desu ka Suiyóobi desu ka?	Is today Tuesday or Wednesday?
Kyóo wa Suiyóobi desu.	Today's Wednesday.
Kyóo wa Getsuyóobi desu.	Today's Monday.
Raishuu no Doyóobi ni kite kudasái.	Come next Saturday.
Raishuu no Kayóobi ni tachimásu.	He's leaving next Tuesday.
Senshuu no Getsuyóobi ni tsukimáshita.	He arrived last Monday. [He arrived last week's Monday.]
Raishuu no Getsuyóobi ni tsukimásu.	He's arriving next Monday.
Soko ni mikka imáshita.	I was there three days.
Soko ni ichinichi shika imasén deshita.	I was there only one day. [(I) wasn't there any more than one day.]

QUIZ 16

1.	*ototói*	1.	afternoon
2.	*kyóo*	2.	day before yesterday
3.	*gógo*	3.	today
4.	*imashígata*	4.	day after tomorrow
5.	*ashita no gógo*	5.	a moment ago
6.	*kyóo no gógo*	6.	tomorrow afternoon
7.	*asátte*	7.	all night long
8.	*Jikan o muda ni shite imásu.*	8.	He's wasting his time.
9.	*hitoban juu*	9.	this afternoon
10.	*Dono kurai nágaku koko ni imáshita ka?*	10.	How long have you been here?
11.	*raishuu*	11.	the month after next
12.	*senshuu*	12.	the week before last
13.	*sensenshuu*	13.	next week
14.	*saraigetsu*	14.	the year before last
15.	*otótoshi*	15.	last week
16.	*Jikan desu.*	16.	It's time to go home.
17.	*Jikan ga arimásu.*	17.	tomorrow night

18.	*Uchi e káeru jikan desu.*	18.	tonight
19.	*myóoban*	19.	It's time.
20.	*kónban*	20.	I have time.

ANSWERS

1-2; 2-3; 3-1; 4-5; 5-6; 6-9; 7-4; 8-8; 9-7; 10-10; 11-13; 12-15; 13-12; 14-11; 15-14; 16-19; 17-20; 18-16; 19-17; 20-18.

THE MONTHS

Ichigatsu	January
Nigatsu	February
Sángatsu	March
Shigatsu	April
Gógatsu	May
Rokugatsu	June
Shichigatsu	July
Hachigatsu	August
Kúgatsu	September
Juugatsu	October
Juuichigatsu	November
Juuinigatsu	December

Kyoo wa Rokugatsu tsuitachí desu.	Today is the first of June.
Watakushi wa Shigatsu juuninichí ni umaremáshita.	I was born on April twelfth.
Imooto wa Gógatsu itsuka ni umaremáshita.	My sister was born on May fifth.
Watakushi no tanjóobi wa Nigatsu futsuka desu.	My birthday is February second.

Shichigatsu júuyokka ni kimásu.	I'll come on the fourteenth of July.
Gakkoo wa Kúgatsu hatsuka ni hajimarimásu.	School begins on the twentieth of September.
Sángatsu níjuu ninichí ni kaerimásu.	I'll be back on March twenty-second.
Juuichigatsu juuichinichí wa yasumí desu.	November eleventh is a holiday.
Shichigatsu mikka ni tachimásu.	He's leaving on July third.
Tegami wa Rokugatsu muika zuke désu.	The letter is dated June sixth.
Gógatsu juuichinichí ni otazune shimásu.	We'll come to see you on May eleventh.
Kyóo wa sén kyúuhyaku rokujúunen Gógatsu itsuka desu.	Today is May fifth, 1985.

THE SEASONS

háru	spring
natsú	summer
áki	autumn
fuyú	winter
fuyú ni	in winter
natsú ni	in summer
áki ni	in autumn, in the fall
háru ni	in spring

QUIZ 17

1. Kyóo wa nan'yóobi desu ka?	1. Sunday

2. *Sono uchi ni ome ni kakarimásu.*

2. in a quarter of an hour

3. *ichinichi juu*

3. See you one of these days.

4. *natsú ni*

4. all day

5. *júugo fun de*

5. What's today?

6. *Raishuu no Getsuyóobi ni tsukimásu.*

6. in the summer

7. *Kyóo wa Getsuyóobi desu.*

7. winter

8. *Raishuu no Doyóobi ni kite kudasái.*

8. What's the date Saturday?

9. *fuyú*

9. Today's the twentieth.

10. *Nichiyóobi*

10. Today's Monday

11. *Kyoo wa hatsuka desu.*

11. Come next Saturday.

12. *Doyóobi wa nánnichi desu ka?*

12. He'll arrive next Monday.

13. *Shichigatsu no júuyokka ni kimásu.*

13. The letter is dated June sixth.

14. *Kyóo wa Rokugatsu no tsuitachí desu.*

14. I'll come on the fourteenth of July.

15. *Tegami wa Rokugatsu muika zuke ni nátte imásu.*

15. Today is the first of June.

ANSWERS

1-5; 2-3; 3-4; 4-6; 5-2; 6-12; 7-10; 8-11; 9-7; 10-1;
11-9; 12-8; 13-14; 14-15; 15-13.

WORD STUDY

bíiru	beer
júusu	juice
kákuteru	cocktail
kokoa	cocoa
koohíi	coffee
míruku	milk
shanpén	champagne
sóoda	soda
uísukii	whiskey
yoogúruto	yogurt

SHINBUN ÚRIBA DE

(AT THE NEWSSTAND)

(SEE THE NOTES BELOW FOR AN EXPLANATION OF
IDIOMS.)

Kyaku: Japan Taimuzu o kudasái. Komakai okane
o mótte inái n desu ga, sen en de tótte
moraemásu ka?[1]
Uriko: Ashitá de kékkoo desu.[2]
Kyaku: Démo kóna'ya jidóosha ka nan ka ni
hikarete shinde shimattára[3] dóo shimásu?
Uriko: Kamaisén. Táishita kotó ja arimasén kara.[4]

[1] totte moraemasu ka = can I have you take it (from)?
[2] *Ashitá de kékkoo desu.* = Tomorrow will do.
[3] *hikarete shinde shimattára: hikareru* is a passive form of *hiku* [run
over]; *shinde shimau* = (and) die [end up in death]—*tára* = if,
suppose
[4] *kara* = and so, and therefore (when used after a sentence-ending
form of a verb or an adjective)

Customer: Give me the *Japan Times,* please.
  However, I don't have any small change. Can
  you give me change for one thousand yen?
Dealer: Pay me tomorrow.
Customer: But suppose I get run over by a car or
  something tonight?
Dealer: So what! It wouldn't be a great loss.

LESSON 28 DÁI NÍJUU HACHÍKA

TO GO

IKU To go *(irregular verb)*

PLAIN	POLITE	
iku	**ikimásu**	I, you, we, they go; he, she goes[1]
itta	**ikimáshita**	I went
itte	**itte**	I go and . . .
ikanai	**ikimasén**	I don't go
ikitái	**ikitái desu**	I wish to go
ikéba } **ittára**		if I go
ikanákereba } **ikanákattara**		If I don't go
ittári[2]		sometimes I go
ikóo	**ikimashóo**	I think I'll go. Let's go.
iké		Go! (Sharp command)

[1] See Lesson 9b for rule governing use of the verb with persons and number.
[2] See footnote 1, page 130.

Some Japanese words have three forms: "humble," "honorific," and "plain." The speaker uses the humble form only when referring to himself. The speaker may use an equivalent honorific form for the second or third person. The plain form may be used for any person. The three forms have exactly the same meaning in English.

1. Some Common Expressions With *iku*

Itte kudasái!	Please go!
Ikanáide kudasái.	Please don't go.
Yukkúri itte kudasái.	Go slowly.
Itte sagashite kudasái.	Go look for it. [Go and look for (it), please.]
Soko e ikanákereba narimasén.	We have to go there. [If (I) don't go, (it) won't do.]
Itté wa ikemasén.	You must not go.
Ikanákute mo íi desu.	We don't have to go. [Even if (we) don't go (it) will be all right.]
Itté mo ikanákute no íi desu.	It doesn't matter whether we go or not. [Even if (we) go, even if we don't go, (it) will be all right.]
Itté mo íi desu.	You may go. You have my permission to go. [Even if (you) go (it) will be all right.]
Ikitái desu ga iku kotó ga dekimasén.	I want to go but I can't [go].
Itta kotó ga arimásu.	I have been there.
Itta kotó wa arimasén.	I have never been there.
Iku kotó ga arimásu.	I sometimes go.

2. Verb particles with *iku*

Soko e iku to[1] kau kotó ga dekimásu.	If you go there, you can buy.
Ashita ikú to[2] iimáshita.	He said he would go tomorrow.
Ittá keredomo[3] áu kotó ga dekimasén deshita.	I went but couldn't meet him.
Kinóo wa ikimáshita ga[4] kyóo wa ikimasén.	I went yesterday but I am not going today.
Tákushii de ittá kara[5] ma ni aimáshita.	I went by taxi and so I was able to make it.
Tookyoo e itté kara[6] Kyooto e ikimáshita.	I went to Tokyo and then [after that] I went to Kyoto. After I went to Tokyo, I went to Kyoto.
Áme ga futtá node[7] ikimasén deshita.	It rained and so [because of that fact] I didn't go
Hiroshima e ikimáshita shi[8] Nagásaki é mo ikimashita.	I went to Hiroshima and, in addition [not only that], I even went to Nagasaki.
Hanashinágara[9] ikimashóo.	Let's talk [discuss that] as we go.

[1] *to* = if, when
[2] *to* marks the end of a quote.
[3] *keredomo* = but
[4] *ga* (particle) = but
[5] *kara* (when it follows a sentence-ending form) = and so, and therefore, because of that
[6] *kara* (when it follows a *-te* form) = and after that, and subsequently
[7] *node* = and because of that fact, the situation being what it is
[8] *shi* = and not only that, and in addition to that
[9] *-nagara* = as, while (denotes simultaneous actions by the same subject)

| Nichiyóobi ni wa Enoshima e ittári Hakone e ittári[1] shimásu. | On Sundays I sometimes go to Enoshima and sometimes [go] to Hakone. |

A FEW SHORT EXPRESSIONS

Abunai!	Watch out! [(It) is dangerous!]
Ki o tsukéte kudasái!	Be careful! Pay attention!
Háyaku itte kudasái.	Please go fast.
Mótto háyaku itte kudasái.	Please go faster.
Sonna ni háyaku ikanáide kudasái.	Do not go so fast.
Anmari háyaku ikanáide kudasái.	Don't go too fast.
Mótto yukkúri itte kudasái.	Go slower.
Mótto háyaku kité kudasái.	Please come sooner.
Mótto osoku kité kudasái.	Please come later.
Déwa mata.	See you later. [Well then, again]
Isóide kudasái.	Please hurry up.
Isogánaide kudasái.	Don't hurry.
Isóide imásu.	I'm in a hurry.
Isóide imasén.	I'm not in a hurry.
Dóozo goyukkúri.	Take your time.
Chótto mátte kudasái.	Just a minute!
Súgu.	Soon, in a minute. Right away.

[1]-tári . . . -tári when followed by suru = sometimes do A, sometimes do B; do such things as A and B

Mairimásu.[1] I'm coming.

LESSON 29 DÁI NÍJUU KYÚUKA

ONE, THEY, PEOPLE: (USEFUL WORD GROUPS III)

▭▭ ▭▭

1. **They say that . . .**

sóo desu	They say that . . . It's said that . . . People say that . . . I understand that . . . I hear . . .
Soko wa taihen kírei da sóo desu.[2]	They say that that place is very pretty.
Sore wa hontoo da sóo desu.	They say that it is true.
Yamada-san no piano wa taihen yókatta sóo desu.	People say that Mr. Yamada played the piano very well. [Talking about Mr. Yamada's piano (-playing), it was very good, so I hear.]
Tanaka-san wa kinoo Yokohama ni tsúita soo desu.	I understand that Mr. Tanaka arrived in Yokohama yesterday.
Tanaka-san wa kinoo kónakatta soo desu.	I understand that Mr. Tanaka did not come yesterday.
Tanaka-san wa íma Tookyoo ni inai sóo desu.	I hear that Mr. Tanaka is not in Tokyo now.

[1]*mairu* (humble verb) = come, go
[2]Notice that the predicate appearing before *soo desu* is in the plain form.

Takeda-san wa rainen	I hear that Mr. Takeda
Amerika e iku sóo	will be going to
desu.	America next year.

2. *Nákereba narimasén* Have to, must

Góhan o tabénakereba	I must eat [my meal].
narimasén.	
Kisóku o yóku	You have to remember
oboénakereba	the regulations [well].
narimasén.	
Isogánakereba	I have to hurry.
narimasén.	
Yukkúri	You must walk slowly.
arukánakereba	
narimasén.	
Nihongo de	You have to speak in
hanasánakereba	Japanese.
narimasén.	

Nihón de kawanákereba	I have to buy it in
narimasén.	Japan.
Yamada-san ni	I have to see Mr.
awánakereba	Yamada.
narimasén.	
Yamada-san ni denwa o	I have to telephone Mr.
kakénakereba	Yamada.
narimasén.	
Júnsa ni kikanákereba	I had to ask a
narimasén.	policeman.
Tookyoo e jidóosha de	I had to go to Tokyo by
ikanákereba	car.
narimasén deshita.	
Éki de Yamada-san ni	I had to see Mr.
awánakereba	Yamada at the
narimasén deshita.	station.

Éki kara Yamada-san ni denwa o kakénakereba narimasén deshita.	I had to phone Mr. Yamada from the station.
Béru o narashite hito ga déte kuru no o matánakereba narimasén deshita.	I had to ring the bell and wait for someone to answer.
To ga shimátte itá node soko ni tátte mátte inákereba narimasén deshita.	The door was closed so I had to stand there and wait.
Okane o mótte inákatta node karinákereba narimasén deshita.	I had no money (and) so I had to borrow (some).

QUIZ 18

1. *Tookyoo e jidóosha de ikanákereba narimasén deshita.*

2. *Kisóku o yóku oboénakereba narimasén.*

3. *Isogánakereba narimasén.*

4. *Yukkúri arukánakereba narimasén.*

5. *To ga shimátte itá node soko ni tátte mátte inákereba narimasén deshita.*

6. *Yamada-san e denwa o kakénakereba narimasén.*

7. *Okane ga nákatta node karinákereba narimasén deshita.*

8. *Góhan o tabénakereba narimasén.*

9. *Júnsa ni kikanákereba narimasén deshita.*

10. *Éki de Yamade-san ni awánakereba narimasén deshita.*

1. I have to hurry.

2. You have to walk slowly.

3. I had to go to Tokyo by car.

4. You have to learn the regulations.

5. I have to phone Mr. Yamada.

6. The door was closed so I had to stand there and wait.

7. I must eat.

8. I had no money so I had to borrow some.

9. I had to see Mr. Yamada at the station.

10. I had to ask a policeman.

ANSWERS
1-3; 2-4; 3-1; 4-2; 5-6; 6-5; 7-8; 8-7; 9-10; 10-9.

WORD STUDY

faindaa	finder
fírutaa	filter
fuirumu	film
furasshu ranpu	flash lamp
kámera	camera
néga	negative
póji	positive
rénzu	lens
serufu taimaa	self-timer
sháttaa	shutter

A LITTLE AND A LOT

Sukóshi. — A little.

Sukóshi desu ka takusán desu ka? — A lot or a little. [Is (it) a little or is (it) a lot?]

Hon no sukóshi.	Very little.
Sukoshi zútsu.	Little by little.
Moo sukóshi kudasái.	A little bit more. [Give (me) a little bit more.]
Sukóshi shika hanashimasén.	He doesn't talk much. [(He) doesn't talk except a little.]
Sukoshi hoshíi desu ka takusan hoshíi desu ka?	Do you want a little or a lot of it?
Sukóshi koko de yasúnde ikimashóo.	Let's rest here a little and (then) go.
Sukóshi kudasái.	Give me a little of it.
Sukóshi mizu o kudasái.	Give me a little water.
Hon no sukóshi daké desu.	It's only a very little bit.
Nihongo wa sukóshi shika dekimasén.	I speak very little Japanese. [(I) can't speak Japanese except a little.]
takusan	a lot, much
Okane wa takusan arimasén.	I haven't much money.
Jikan wa takusan arimasén.	I haven't much time.

TOO MUCH

amari	too
amari takusan	too much
Amari takusan desu. } **Amari oosugimasu.** }	It's too much.
Amari takusan ja arimasén.	It's not too much.
amari sukóshi	too little

Amari atsúi desu.
Amari atsusugi másu. } It's too hot.

Amari samúi desu.
Amari samusugimásu. } It's too cold.

Amari mizu ga
oosugimásu. There is too much water.

MORE OR LESS

tashoo more or less
óokute mo at the most
sukunákute mo at the least
mótto mótto more and more
mótto mótto sukunáku less and less
moo rokubai six times more
mótto háyaku earlier *(adv.)*
mótto osoku
mótto áto de } later *(adv.)*

mótto átsuku hotter
Mótto átsuku shite Please make it hotter.
kudasái.
mótto tákaku more expensive
Mótto tákaku It became more
narimáshita. expensive.
Moo arimasén. There is no more of it. There is no more of it left.

Sore íjoo desu. It's more than that.
Sore íka desu. It's less than that.
Ichiban omoshirói hón This is the most
desu. interesting book.
Ano hito wa níisan yori He is taller than his
sé ga takái desu. older brother.
Watakushi hodo sé ga She isn't as tall as I.
tákaku arimasén.
Watakushi yóri hikúi She is shorter than I.
desu.

ENOUGH, SOME MORE

juubun	enough
Juubun desu ka?	Is it enough?
Juubun desu.	It's enough.
Juubun ja arimasén.	It's not enough.
Juubun ookíi desu.	It's large enough.
Okane wa juubun mótte imasu ka?	Do you have enough money?
mótto	some more
Mótto desu ka?	(Do you want) some more?
moo sukóshi	a little more
Mizu o moo íppai kudasái.	Give me another glass of water.
Pán o moo sukóshi kudasái.	Please give me some more bread.
Nikú o moo sukóshi kudasái.	Please give me some more meat.
mótto mótto	much more, lots more
Moo ichido kité kudasái.	Come again [visit us once more], please.
Moo ichido itte kudasái.	Say it again [once more], please.
Moo ichido kurikáeshite kudasái.	Please repeat it [Repeat it once more . . .]

GOOD

Kékkoo desu.	It's good.
Taihen kékkoo desu.	It's very good.
Amari kékkoo ja arimasén.	It's not very good.
Kono budóoshu wa kékkoo desu.	This wine is good.
Kono nikú wa kekkoo desu.	This meat is good.

Kékkoo na oténki desu ne.	The weather is fine, isn't it?
Mótto ikága desu ka?	How about some more?
Moo kékkoo desu.	No, thanks. I am fully satisfied.

I WANT TO HAVE...

Mizu ga hoshíi desu.	I want some water. [Water is wanted.]
Mizu ga hoshíi desu ka?	Do you want some water? [Is water wanted?]
Mizu wa hóshiku arimasén.	I don't want any water.
Ocha wa ikága desu ka?	How about some tea?
Koohíi wa ikága desu ka?	How about some coffee?
Kuríimu wa ikága desu ka?	How about some cream?
Osatoo wa ikága desu ka?	How about some sugar?
Kuríimu wa dono kurai iremashóo ka?	How much cream shall I put in?
Osatoo wa dono kurai iremashóo ka?	How much sugar shall I put in?
Ocha wa dono kurai kaimashóo ka?	How much tea shall I buy?
Koohíi wa dono kurai kaimashóo ka?	How much coffee shall I buy?
Dónna ocha o kaimashóo ka?	What sort of tea shall we buy?
Dónna koohíi o kaimashóo ka?	What sort of coffee shall we buy?

Dóno koohíi o kaimashóo ka?	Which coffee shall we buy?
Dóno koohíi ga hoshíi desu ka?	Which coffee do you want?
Dónna koohíi ga sukí desu ka?	What sort of coffee do you like?
Dóno koohíi ga ichiban sukí desu ka?	Which coffee do you like best?
Dóno koohíi ga ichiban hoshíi desu ka?	Which coffee do you want most?

QUIZ 19

1. *Sukóshi hoshíi desu ka takusan hoshii desu ka?*	1. I speak very little English.
2. *Nihongo wa sukóshi shika hanasemasén.*	2. It became more expensive.
3. *Anmari atsusugimásu.*	3. She is not as tall as I.
4. *Anmari mizu ga oosugimásu.*	4. Which coffee do you like best?
5. *Mótto tákaku narimáshita.*	5. How about some tea?
6. *Watakushi hodo sé ga tákaku arimasén.*	6. There is too much water.
7. *Okane wa juubun mótte imásu ka?*	7. Do you want a little or do you want a lot?
8. *Moo ichido itte kudasái.*	8. It's too hot.

9. *Ocha wa ikága*
   desu ka?

9. Do you have
   enough money?

10. *Dóno koohíi ga*
    ichiban sukí desu
    ka?

10. Say it again.

ANSWERS

1-7; 2-1; 3-8; 4-6; 5-2; 6-3; 7-9; 8-10; 9-5; 10-4.

WORD STUDY

buromáido	bromide
kuraimákkusu	climax
rabu shíin	love scene
rokéishon	location
shíin	scene
shinario	scenario
sukuríin	screen
sutáa	star
sutajio	studio
táitoru	title

I WANT TO...

When you want to *have* something you say *ga hoshii desu:* when you want to *do* something you use *ga* plus *infinitive* plus *tai desu*.

The combination of an infinitive plus *tai* acts exactly like an adjective. The action you want to perform is normally marked by *ga* or *wa* but the use of *o* is becoming acceptable.

Nomitái desu.	I want to drink it.
Tabetái desu.	I want to eat it.
Kaitái desu.	I want to buy it.
Mitái desu.	I want to see it.
Nomitáku arimasén.	I'm not thirsty [(I) don't want to drink (it).]

Tabetáku arimasén.	I'm not hungry. [(I) don't want to eat (it).]
Kaitáku arimasén.	I don't want to buy it.
Mitáku arimasén.	I don't want to see it.
Koohíi ga nomitái desu.	I'd like some coffee. [(I) want to drink coffee.]
Kudámono ga tabetái desu.	I'd like some fruit. [(I) want to eat fruit.]
Kutsú ga kaitái desu.	I want to buy (a pair of) shoes.
Éiga ga mitái desu.	I want to see a movie.
Koohíi ga nomitáku narimáshita.	I want to drink coffee now (though I didn't before). [(I) became desirous of drinking coffee.]
Kudámono ga tabetáku narimáshita.	I want to eat fruit now.
Kutsú ga kaitáku narimáshita.	I want to buy shoes now.
Éiga ga mitáku narimáshita.	I want to see a movie now.

I INTEND TO . . .

Iku tsumori desu.	I intend to go.
Ryokoo suru tsumori desu.	I intend to travel.
Benkyoo suru tsumori desu.	I intend to study.
Kekkon suru tsumori desu.	I intend to marry.
Iku tsumori désu ka?	Do you intend to go?
Iku tsumori déshita ka?	Did you intend to go?
Iku tsumori ja arimasén ka?	Don't you intend to go?

Iku tsumori ja arimasén deshita ka?	Didn't you intend to go?
Ryokoo suru tsumori deshita ga shimasén deshita.	I (had) intended to travel but didn't.
Ryokoo suru tsumori deshita ga dekimasén deshita.	I (had) intended to travel but couldn't.
Ryokoo suru tsumori deshita ga akiramemáshita.	I (had) intended to travel but I gave it up [the idea].
Ryokoo suru tsumori deshita ga dekíru ka doo ka wakarimasén.	I (had) intended to travel but I can't tell (now) if I can or not.

IT IS SUPPOSED...

Kúru hazu desu.	It is supposed to come.
Tegami ga kúru hazu desu.	A letter is supposed to come.
Tomodachi ga kúru hazu desu.	A friend of mine is supposed to come.
Denwa ga áru hazu desu.	There is supposed to be a telephone. He is supposed to have a telephone.
Shiranai hazu desu.	He is supposed not to know it.
Kitá hazu desu.	It is supposed to have come.
Tegami o uketotta hazu desu.	He is supposed to have received a letter.
Tomodachi ga shiraseta hazu desu.	My friend is supposed to have notified (him about it).

Tomodachi kara denwa ga átta hazu desu.	There is supposed to have been a phone call from a friend of mine.
Minna yónda hazu desu.	He is supposed to have read all of it.
Minna dékite iru hazu desu.	Everything is supposed to have been done.

SOMETHING, EVERYTHING, NOTHING

náni = what

náni ka = something

nán demo (used with affirmative) = everything, anything at all

nani mo (used with negative) = nothing, not anything

Náni ka kaimáshita ka?	Did you buy something?
Dáre ka[1] *kimáshita ka?*	Did someone come?
Ítsu ka ikimashóo.	Let's go sometime.
Dóko ka de kikimáshita.	I heard it somewhere.
Nán de mo kaimáshita.	I bought everything.
Dáre de mo hairemásu.	Anybody at all can enter.
Ítsu de mo ikimásu.	I can go any time.
Dóko de mo kaemásu.	You can but it at any place.
Nani mo kaimasén deshita.	I didn't buy anything.

[1]See Grammar, Section 15, for uses of question words with particles.

Dare mo kimasén deshita.	Nobody came.
Ítsu mo imasén deshita.	He wasn't there at any time. He was always absent.
Doko mo mimasén deshita.	I didn't see any place.
Náni ka tsumetai monó o nomimashóo.	Let's drink something cool.
Dáre ka Nihongo no yóku dekíru hito ni kikimashóo.	Let's ask someone who can speak Japanese well.
Ítsu ka anmari isogashikunái toki ni ikimashóo.	Let's go there when we are not too busy.
Dóko ka mótto shízuka na tokoró e ikimashóo.	Let's go somewhere quieter.
Náni o míte mo kaitaku narimásu.[1]	Whatever I see, I [get to] want to buy.
Dáre ga kité mo kyóo wa au kotó ga dekimasén.	No matter who comes [Whoever may come], I can't meet him today.
Ítsu itté mo anó hito wa jimúsho ni imasén deshita.	No matter when I went to his office, he wasn't there. [Whenever (I) went, he wasn't at his office.]
Dóko e itté mo Eigo no dekíru hito ga imáshita.	Wherever I went, there was someone who would speak English.

[1]Note the construction: The interrogative plus the *to* form plus *mo* = "-ever" plus the verb.

QUIZ 20

1. *Kaitái desu.*
2. *Iku tsumori désu.*
3. *Kúru hazu desu.*
4. *Náni ka kaimáshita ka?*
5. *Kaitaku arimasén.*
6. *Ryokoo suru tsumori désu.*
7. *Dóko ka de kikimáshita.*
8. *Kitá hazu desu.*
9. *Dáre dé mo hairemásu.*
10. *Dáre ka Nihongo no yóku dekíru hito nikikimashóo.*
11. *Ryokoo suru tsumori ja arimasén deshita.*
12. *Nani mo kaimasén deshita.*

1. Everything is supposed to have been done.
2. I didn't buy anything.
3. Let's drink something cool.
4. Nobody came.
5. I didn't intend to travel.
6. Anybody at all can enter.
7. Let's ask someone who can speak Japanese well.
8. Did you buy something?
9. It is supposed to come.
10. I intend to travel.
11. I don't want to buy it.
12. I intend to go.

13. *Minna dékite iru hazu desu.*	13. I want to buy it.
14. *Dare mo kimasén deshita.*	14. I heard it somewhere.
15. *Náni ka tsumetai monó o nomimashóo.*	15. It is supposed to have come.

ANSWERS

1-13; 2-12; 3-9; 4-8; 5-11; 6-10; 7-14; 8-15; 9-6; 10-7; 11-5; 12-2; 13-1; 14-4; 15-3.

LESSON 30 DÁI SANJUKKA

SMALL TALK

Mochíron desu.	Of course, Certainly.
Shoochi itashimáshita.	Fine! [(I) have understood.]
Sóo desu ka?	Indeed? Is that so?
Soo omoimásu.	I think so.
Soo omoimasén.	I don't think so.
Tanaka-san désu ka?	Are you Mr. Tanaka?
Hái, sóo desu.	Yes, I am. [("Am so.")]
tábun	perhaps, probably
Tábun sóo deshoo.	I suppose so. Probably it is so.
Tábun sóo ja nái deshoo.	I suppose not. Probably it is not so.
Sóo da to íi to omoimásu.	I hope so. [If (it) is so it would be good, that way (I) think.]

Sóo ja nái to íi to omoimásu.	I hope not. [If (it) is not so it would be good, that way (I) think.]
Táshika ni sóo desu.	Certainly. [Certainly (it) is so.]
Táshika ni sóo ja arimasén.	Certainly not. [Certainly (it) is not so.]
Oki no dóku desu.	It's a pity! It's a shame! You have my sympathy.
Sore wa baai ni yorimásu.	That depends [on the occasion.]
Kamaimasén.	That's nothing. That's not important. That doesn't matter. [(I) don't mind.]
Zenzen kamaimasén.	That doesn't matter at all.
Gotsugoo ga yoróshikereba.	If you have no objections. If it doesn't inconvenience you. [If (it) is convenient.]
Dóchira de mo kékkoo desu.	I don't care. It's all the same to me. [Either will do.]

QUIZ 21

1. *Soo omoimásu.*	1. It's a pity.
2. *Mochíron desu.*	2. I suppose not.
3. *Tábun sóo deshoo.*	3. I hope so.
4. *Shoochi itashimáshita.*	4. That's nothing.

5. *Sóo da to íi to omoimásu.*	5. I don't care.
6. *Tábun sóo ja nái to omoimásu.*	6. Certainly it is so.
7. *Táshika ni sóo desu.*	7. I think so.
8. *Oki no dóku desu.*	8. Agreed!
9. *Kamaimasén.*	9. Of course.
10. *Dóchira de mo kékkoo desu.*	10. I suppose so.

ANSWERS

1-7; 2-9; 3-10; 4-8; 5-3; 6-2; 7-6; 8-1; 9-4; 10-5.

THE SAME

onaji	same
Onaji monó desu.	It's the same thing *(a tangible article).*
Onaji kotó desu.	It's the same thing *(abstract).*
Kore wa onaji ja arimasén.	This isn't the same. These aren't the same.
dóoji ni **onaji tokí ni** }	at the same time
onaji shunkan ni	at the same moment
onaji machí ni	in the same town

ALREADY

móo	already

móo mukoo ni itte imásu.	He is already there. [(He) is already in the state of having gone there.]
Móo shite shimaimáshita.	He has already done that. [(He) has already done that and (it) is all finished.]
Móo dáshite shimaimáshita ka?	Has he sent it already?
Móo sumásete shimaimáshita ka?	Have you finished already?

WORD STUDY

abunóomaru	abnormal
cháamingu	charming
derikéeto	delicate
éreganto	elegant
kuráshikku	classic
modan	modern
nóomaru	normal
ríberaru	liberal
senchiméntaru	sentimental
yuníiku	unique

LESSON 31   DÁI SÁNJUU ÍKKA

LIKING AND DISLIKING

1. **I like it.**

| Sukí desu. | I like it. ["That's (my) favorite."] |
| Nihon ryóori ga sukí desu. | I like Japanese cooking. |

Kodomo ga sukí desu.	I like children.
Hón o yómu koto ga sukí desu.	I like reading books.
Oyógu koto ga sukí desu.	I like swimming.
Kékkoo desu.	Good! It's good.
Taihen kékkoo desu.	It's very good.
Subarashíi desu.	It's wonderful.
Mígoto desu.	It's admirable.
Kanzen désu.	It's perfect.
Taihen ki ni irimáshita.	I'm very pleased with it. I like it very much.
Taihen íi hito desu.	He's very nice. [(He) is a very good person.]
Taihen kanji no íi hito desu.	He's very pleasant.
Goshínsetsu sama.	You're very kind. That's very kind of you.

2. I don't like it.

Sukí ja arimasén.	I don't like it. It's not good. [That's not (my) favorite.]
Sakana wa sukí ja arimasén.	I don't like fish. [Fish is not (my) favorite.]
Kirai desu.	I dislike it.
Sakana wa kirai desu.	I dislike fish.
Yamada-san wa kirai desu.[1]	I dislike Mr. Yamada.
Yókunai desu.	It's not good.
Warúi desu.	It's bad.
Mazúi desu.	It tastes bad.
Kanshin dekimasén.	It's not good.

[1]Note that this same sentence can also mean "Mr. Yamada dislikes it."

Hón o yómu koto wa sukí ja arimasén.	I don't like reading books.
Hón o yómu koto wa kirai desu.	I dislike reading books.

QUIZ 22

1.	*Taihen kékkoo desu.*	1.	He's very nice.
2.	*Kanshin dekimasén.*	2.	It's perfect.
3.	*Subarashíi desu.*	3.	I'm very pleased with it.
4.	*Kanzen désu.*	4.	I dislike fish.
5.	*Taihen ki ni irimáshita.*	5.	He's very pleasant.
6.	*Sakana wa kirai désu.*	6.	It tastes bad.
7.	*Goshinsetsu sama.*	7.	You're very kind.
8.	*Mazúi desu.*	8.	It's wonderful.
9.	*Taihen kanji no íi hito desu.*	9.	It's very good.
10.	*Taihen íi hito desu.*	10.	It's not good.

ANSWERS

1-9; 2-10; 3-8; 4-2; 5-3; 6-4; 7-7; 8-6; 9-5; 10-1.

REVIEW QUIZ 3

1. *Uchi no_____(in) ni imasu.*
   a. *náka*
   b. *sóto*
   c. *máe*

2. *Kí no*_____(under) *ni imásu.*
   a. *ué*
   b. *shita*
   c. *sóba*

3. *Sono tatemóno no*_____(outside) *ni imásu.*
   a. *sóto*
   b. *chikáku*
   c. *urá*

4. *Shinbun no*_____(under) *ni okimáshita.*
   a. *ué*
   b. *shita*
   c. *sóba*

5. *Sore wa*_____(true) *desu.*
   a. *hontoo*
   b. *táshika*
   c. *hantai*

6. *Ginkoo e*_____(am going).
   a. *haraimásu*
   b. *kashimásu*
   c. *ikimásu*

7. *Jimúsho e*_____(come) *kudasái.*
   a. *kite*
   b. *harátte*
   c. *itte*

8. *Okane o*_____(a little) *kashite kudasái.*
   a. *sukóshi*
   b. *takusan*
   c. *nisen en*

9. *Okane o*_____(much) *mótte imasu.*
   a. *sukóshi*
   b. *takusan*
   c. *sukoshi mo*

10. _____(More) *arimásu.*
   a. *Sukóshi*
   b. *Mótto*
   c. *Moo sukóshi*

11. _____(Enough) *arimasén.*
   a. *Nani mo*
   b. *Takusan*
   c. *Juubun*

12. _____(Expensive) *desu.*
   a. *Yasúi*
   b. *Takái*
   c. *Hikúi*

13. *Sore wa kore*_____(as) *oishiku arimasen.*
   a. *wa*
   b. *hodo*
   c. *mo*

14. _____(All) *yonde shimaimashita.*
   a. *Hanbun*
   b. *Sukóshi*
   c. *Minna*

15. _____(Anybody) *hairemasu.*
   a. *Dáre demo*
   b. *Dáre ga*
   c. *Dáre ka*

16. *Soo*_____(don't think)
   a. *hurimasén*
   b. *omoimasén*
   c. *kaimasén*

17. *Iku*_____(intend to) *desu.*
   a. *hazu*
   b. *tsumori*
   c. *yóo*

18. _____(Nothing) *kaimasén deshita.*
    a. *Dáre mo*
    b. *Náni mo*
    c. *Dóre mo*

19. *Dóre mo*_____(same).
    a. *onaji desu.*
    b. *chigaimásu.*
    c. *hoshíi desu.*

20. _____(Already) *sumasete shimaimashita ka?*
    a. *Mótto mótto*
    b. *Mótto*
    c. *Móo*

ANSWERS

1-a; 2-b; 3-a; 4-b; 5-a; 6-c; 7-a; 8-a; 9-b; 10-b; 11-c; 12-b; 13-b; 14-c; 15-a; 16-b; 17-b; 18-b; 19-a; 20-c.

WORD STUDY

bakkumíraa	rear-view mirror (of a car)
bánpaa	bumper
buréeki	brake
énjin	engine
gasorin	gasoline
gíya	gear
handoru	handle (of a tool), steering wheel
heddoráito	headlight
kurátchi	clutch
taiya	tire

WARAIBANASHI

A Witticism

Tanaka-san to Yamada-san ga resutoran e itte bifuteki o chuumon shimáshita. Shibáraku tátte bifuteki ga kimáshita. Hitókire wa ookíkute hitótsu wa chiisakatta no desu. Tanaka-san wa súgu ookíi hoo o torimáshita. Sore o míte Yamada-san wa okorimáshita. Soshite "Nán to reigi no nái hitó daroo. Hito yóri saki ni tóru tokí wa chiisái hoo o tóru mon da" to iimáshita.

Kore o kiite Tanaka-san wa: "Anáta ga watashi dáttara dóo shimásu ka?" to tazunemáshita.

"Mochíron chiisái hoo o torimásu yo!" to Yamada-san wa kotaemásshita.

Tanaka-san wa "Sóre gorannasai, mónku wa nái hazu ja arimásen ka? Chiisái hoo o anata ga, moratta n da kara," to iimashita.

Tanaka and Yamada went to a restaurant and ordered steak. A few minutes later the steaks arrived. One piece was large and one piece was small. Tanaka took the large piece. Yamada was furious and said to him: "What bad manners you have! Don't you know that since you were the first to help yourself you should have taken the smaller piece?"

Tanaka answered: "If you were in my place, which piece would you have taken?"

"The smaller one, of course," said Yamada.

"Well, then," Tanaka answered, "what are you complaining about? You've got it, haven't you?"

Notes

waraibanashi: "a story to laugh"
chuumon shimashita: ordered

shibáraku tátte: after a short while

okórimáshita: got furious

soshite: and

Nán to . . . daroo: What a . . . !

reigi: manners

shiranai: (negative of *shiru*): don't know

. . . *monó da:* that's what one should do; that's an accepted way to do.

dáttara: if (you) were

torimásu yo: *yo* is an emphatic particle corresponding to an exclamation mark.

mónku: complaint

nái hazu desu: there is supposed to be not; there isn't supposed to be.

WHO? WHAT? WHEN?

dóno	which, . . . ?
Dóno hon desu ka?	Which book is it?
Dóno tegami desu ka?	Which letter (is it)?
dóre	which one?
ítsu	when?
dáre	who?
náni, nán	what?
náze, dóoshite	why?
dóko	where?
íkura	how much?
dóo, dóoshite	how?

1. *Náni, Nán* **What?**

Use *nán* when the word which follows it begins with *d, n, s, t,* or *z,* use *náni* everywhere else.

Nán desu ka?	What is it?
Nán to iimáshita ka?	What did you say?

Nán to osshaimáshita ka?

What did you say *(extra polite)*?

Sore ni tsúite wa nán to osshaimashita ka?

What did he say about it?

Náni o shite imásu ka?

What are you doing?

Náni ga hoshíi desu ka?

What do you want? What would you like?

Kore kara náni o shitái desu ka?

What do you want to do now?

Náni o sagashite imásu ka?

What are you looking for?

Sore wa náni o ími shimásu ka?

What does it mean? What is the significance of it?

Dóo shita n desu ka?

What's happening? What's going on?

Onamae wa nán desu ka?

What's your name?

Kono machi no namae wa nán desu ka?

What's the name of this town?

Kono toori no namae wa nán desu ka?

What's the name of this street?

Kyóo wa nánnichi desu ka?

What's today?

Nángatsu desu ka?

What month is it?

Nánji desu ka?

What time? [What hour is it?]

Nán to iu chigai deshoo!

What a difference!

Sono futatsú no chigai wa nán desu ka?

What is the difference between the two things?

Sono futatsú wa dóo chigaimásu ka?

What is the difference between the two? [As for the two, how do they differ?]

| *Náni o kangaete imásu ka?* | What are you thinking about? |
| *Náni ga irimásu ka?* | What do you need? |

2. *Dore* Which one?

dóre	which one?
Dóre desu ka?	Which one is it?
Dóre ga sonó hito desu ka?	Which is he?
Watakushi nó wa dóre desu ka?	Which is mine?
Dóre ga íi hoo desu ka?	Which is the better one?
Dóre ga hoshíi desu ka?	Which one do you want?
Dóre ga tadashíi desu ka?	Which one is right?

3. *Ítsu* When?

ítsu	when?
Ítsu desu ka?	When is it?
Ítsu made desu ka?	Until when is (it)?
Ítsu kimásu ka?	When are you coming?
Ítsu oide ni narimásu ka?	When are you coming *(extra polite)*?
Ítsu tachimásu ka?	When are you leaving?
Ítsu otachi ni narimásu ka?	When are you leaving *(extra polite)*?

4. *Dare* Who?

dáre	who?
Dáre desu ka?	Who is it?
Dáre desu ka?	Who are you?
Dónata desu ka?	Who are you *(extra polite)*?

Dáre ga sore o shitte imásu ka?	Who knows that?
Dáre ga watakushítachi to ikimásu ka?	Who is coming with us?
Dáre no desu ka?	Whose is it?
Dáre no tamé desu ka?	Who(m) is it for? [Whose sake is it?]
Dáre ni hanáshite imásu ka?	Who(m) are you talking to?
Dáre no kotó o hanáshite imásu ka?	Who(m) are you speaking about? [Whose matters are you speaking?]
Dáre to kimásu ka?	Who(m) are you coming with?
Dáre ni aitái desu ka?	Who(m) do you want to see?
Dónata ni oai ni naritái desu ka?	Who(m) do you want to see *(extra polite)*?
Dáre o sagashite imásu ka?	Who(m) are you looking for?
Dónata o sagashite irasshaimásu ka?	Who(m) are you looking for *(extra polite)*?

5. *Náze, Dóoshite* Why?

náze, dóoshite	why?
Náze desu ka?	Why is it?
Dóoshite desu ka?	Why is it?
Dóoshite damé desu ka?	Why not? [Why is it no good?]
Náze sonna kóto o iú n desu ka?	Why do you say that [such a thing]?
Dóoshite sonna kóto o shitá n desu ka?	Why did he do such a thing?

6. *Dóo, Dóoshite* How?

dóo	how?
Dóo desu ka?	How is it?
Dóo shimásu ka?	How do you do it?
Dóo iu ími desu ka?	What do you mean?
Onamae wa dóo osshaimásu ka?	What's your name? [How do you call (yourself) *(extra polite)*?]
Nihongo de kono kotobá wa dóo kakimásu ka?	How do you write this word in Japanese?
Sore wa Eigo de dóo iimásu ka?	How do you say that in English?
"Thanks" wa Nihongo de dóo iimásu ka?	How do you say "thanks" in Japanese?
Nihongo de "Thanks" wa dóo iimásu ka?	What's the Japanese word for "thanks?"
Dóo shita n desu ka?	How did it happen?
Dóo shitara íi n desu ka?	How does one go about it?
Dóo sureba íi n desu ka?	How does one go about it?
Sore wa dóo shite tsukurimásu ka?	How's it made? [Acting how do you make (it)?]
Sore wa dóoshite tsukurimáshita ka?	How did you make it?
Soko é wa dóo ikimásu ka?	How do you go there?
Dóo shimashoo ka?	What's to be done? What can one do? [How shall we do?]

QUIZ 23

1. *Dóno hon desu ka?*

2. *Nán to iimáshita ka?*

3. *Náni o sagashite imásu ka?*

4. *Dóno tegami desu ka?*

5. *Onamae wa nán desu ka?*

6. *Náni o shite imásu ka?*

7. *Kyóo wa nánnichi desu ka?*

8. *Náni ga hoshíi desu ka?*

9. *Nángatsu desu ka?*

10. *Kono toori no namae wa nán desu ka?*

11. *Kore kara náni o shitái desu ka?*

12. *Nánji desu ka?*

13. *Sono futatsú wa dóo chigaimásu ka?*

1. How is it?

2. What is the difference between the two?

3. Why did he do such a thing?

4. Who are you looking for?

5. What are you thinking about?

6. How do you go there?

7. Until when?

8. Which one do you want?

9. What is the name of the street?

10. What do you want to do now?

11. What time?

12. What do you want to do now?

13. What month is it?

14. *Náni o kangaete imásu ka?*　　14. Which letter?

15. *Dóre ga hoshíi desu ka?*　　15. What is your name?

16. *Ítsu made desu ka?*　　16. What are you looking for?

17. *Dónata o sagashite irasshaimásu ka?*　　17. What's today?

18. *Dóoshite sonna kóto o shitá n desu ka?*　　18. What are you doing?

19. *Dóo desu ka?*　　19. Which book is it?

20. *Soko é wa dóo ikimásu ka?*　　20. What did you say?

ANSWERS

1-19; 2-20; 3-16; 4-14; 5-15; 6-18; 7-17; 8-12; 9-13; 10-9; 11-10; 12-11; 13-2; 14-5; 15-8; 16-7; 17-4; 18-3; 19-1; 20-6.

WORD STUDY

akademíkku	academic
dándii	dandy
ekizochíkku	exotic
gurotésuku	grotesque
nóoburu	noble
nyúansu	nuance
pedanchíkku	pedantic
romanchíkku	romantic
senséeshonaru	sensational
sumúusu	smooth

HOW MUCH?

Nedan wa?	The price? How much is this?
Nedan wa íkura desu ka?	What's the price?
Íkura?	How much?
Íkura desu ka?	How much is it? How much do you want for it?
Zénbu de íkura desu ka?	How much for everything? How much does it all cost?
Hitótsu íkura desu ka?	How much each?

HOW MANY?

Íkutsu?	How many?
Íkutsu nokótte imásu ka?	How many are left?
Íkutsu mótte imásu ka?	How many of them do you have?
Nánnin desu ka? } **Íkunin desu ka?** }	How many persons?
Nanjíkan? } **Ikujíkan?** }	How many hours?
Nándo? Íkudo?	How many times?
Dono kurai désu ka?	How much time?
Dono kurai nagái desu ka?	How long?
Soko e ikú ni wa dono kurai jíkan ga kakarimásu[1] ka?	How long [how much time] does it take to get there?

[1]*kakaru:* to require, take

QUIZ 24

1.	*Íkutsu arimasu ka?*	1.	How many persons?
2.	*Íkura desu ka?*	2.	How much for everything?
3.	*Íkutsu nokótte imasu ka?*	3.	How long does it take to get there?
4.	*Nedan wa íkura desu ka?*	4.	How much each?
5.	*Dono kurai nágaku desu ka?*	5.	What's the price?
6.	*Zénbu de íkura desu ka?*	6.	How much is it?
7.	*Íkunin desu ka?*	7.	How many are left?
8.	*Íkutsu mótte imásu ka?*	8.	How much time?
9.	*Hitótsu íkura desu ka?*	9.	How many of them do you have?
10.	*Soko e ikú ni wa dono kurai jikan ga karimásu ka?*	10.	How many are there?

ANSWERS

1-10; 2-6; 3-7; 4-5; 5-8; 6-2; 7-1; 8-9; 9-4; 10-3.

LESSON 32   DÁI SÁNJUU NÍ KA

USEFUL WORD GROUPS IV

1. Some, Someone, Something

íkura ka no	some *(an undetermined amount of)*
íkutsu ka no	some *(an indeterminate number of)*
íkura ka no okane	some money
íkura ka no híyoo	some expense
íkura ka no jikan	some time
íkura ka no jikan ga kakarimásu.	It takes some time.
íkura ka no okane ga irimásu.	We need some money.
Íkutsu ka no kotobá o shitte imásu.	I know some words. I know a number of words.
íkunin ká no	some *(an indeterminate number of persons)*
Íkunin ká no hitó ni kikimáshita.	I have asked a number of persons.
Íkunin ka kité imásu.	Several people are here.
náni ka	something, anything *(not a specific thing).*
náni ka atarashíi monó	something new, anything new
náni ka kaitai monó	something you want to buy, anything you want to buy

Náni ka kaitai monó ga arimásu ka?	Have you anything you want to buy?
Náni ka kikitái koto ga arimásu ka?	Have you anything you want to ask?
Náni ka kudasai.	Give me something, please.
Náni ka káku mono o kudasái.	Give me something to write with.
Náni ka ochimáshita.	Something fell down.
Náni ka kaimáshita.	He bought something.
Náni ka shirimasén. ⎫ *Nán desu ka shirimasén.* ⎭	I don't know what it is.
dáre ka	someone
Dáre ka sore no dekíru hito ga imásu ka?	Is there anyone who can do it?
Dáre ka Eigo no yóku dekíru hito ga imásu ka?	Is there anyone who can speak English well?
áru hito	someone
Áru hito ga hoshíi to itte imásu.	Someone (a certain person who shall be nameless) says that he wants to have it.
áru tokoro	some place
Áru tokoro e ikimáshita.	He went some place.
ítsu ka	sometime
Ítsu ka kité kudasai.	Please come sometime.
Ítsu ka ikimashóo.	Let's go there sometime.
tokidoki	sometimes, occasionally
Sonó hito ni tokidoki aimásu.	I see him sometimes.
Soko de tokidoki góhan o tabemásu.	I eat [my meal] there sometimes.

2. Once, Twice

-do, -kai	a time
ichido, ikkái,	once, one time
nido, nikái	twice, two times
maido, maikai	every time, each time
kóndo	this time, this coming time
dái ikkái	the first time
Dái ikkái wa sen kyúuhyaku gojuu gonen déshita.	The first time was (in) 1955.
hajímete	for the first time
Hajímete ikimáshita.	I went there for the first time.
tsugí	the next time, the next item, the next number, etc.
kono máe	the last time
betsu no toki	another time, another occasion
mata	again
moo ichido	once more

3. Up to

máde	up to
ima máde	up to now
soko máde	up to there
owari máde	(up) to the end
éki made	up to the station
kónban made	up to this evening
ashitá made	up till tomorrow
Getsuyóobi made	up to Monday

4. I need it

Irimásu.	I need it.
Kore wa irimasén.	He doesn't need this one.
Náni ka irimásu ka?	Do you need anything?
Nani mo irimasén.	I don't need anything.
Zenzen irimasén.	I don't need it at all.

5. It's necessary, One has to

Zéhi oai shinákereba narimasén.	It's absolutely necessary that I see you.
Anó hito ni hanasánakereba narimasén.	You have to tell him.
Háyaku uchi e káette kónakereba narimasén.	You must come home early.
Hontoo da to iu kotó o mitomenákereba narimasén.	One must recognize the truth.

6. I feel like

Hoshíi[1] desu.	I'd like to have it. I feel like having it. I want to have it.
Ikitaku[2] arimasén.	I don't feel like going there. I don't want to go.
Aisukuríimu ga hoshíi desu.	I feel like having some ice cream.

[1] Used when referring to a tangible thing.
[2] Used when referring to a state of mind or emotion.

Aisukuríimu ga tabetaí desu.	I feel like eating some ice cream.
Kono éiga wa mitái desu ka?	Would you like to see this movie?

7. **At the home of**

    · The choice of the particle *de* or *ni* depends on the verb which follows it. (See Grammar.)

... **otaku de** ⎫ ... **otaku ni** ⎭	at the home of (someone else)
taku de ⎫ **taku ni** ⎭	at my home
Senséi no otaku ni imáshita.[1]	We were at the home of our teacher.
Yamada-san no otaku de[2] **oai shimashóo**	I'll see you at the Yamada's.
Taku e oide kudasái.	Come over to our place.
Yamada-san wa otaku désu ka?	Is Mr. Yamada at home?
Dóozo oraku ni.	Make yourself at home.
Isha no tɔkoró[3] **e ikanákereba narimasén.**	I have to go to the doctor's [place].

QUIZ 25

1. Íkura ka no okane.	1. To the end.
2. Ichido.	2. I need that.
3. Owari máde.	3. Please come sometime.

[1]Notice that *ni* is used here because it appears in conjunction with a form of the verb *imasu*.
[2]Notice that *de* is used here because it appears in conjunction with a form of the verb *au*.
[3]*tokoro* = place

4. *Irimásu.*

4. Some money.

5. *Ítsu ka kite kudasái.*

5. Once.

ANSWERS

1-4; 2-5; 3-1; 4-2; 5-3.

REVIEW QUIZ 4

1. *Kono machí no namae wa* _____ (what) *desu ka?*
   a. *dáre*
   b. *nán*
   c. *dóko*

2. *Anáta wa* _____ (who) *desu ka?*
   a. *dónata*
   b. *dónna*
   c. *dótchi*

3. _____ (When) *kimásu ka?*
   a. *Íkutsu*
   b. *Ítsu*
   c. *Íkura*

4. _____ (Why) *sonna koto o iú n desu ka?*
   a. *Dónna*
   b. *Dóo*
   c. *Dóoshite*

5. *Dái* _____ (twelfth) *kai.*
   a. *juuní*
   b. *níjuu*
   c. *nijuuní*

6. *Kono booshi wa* _____ (two thousand) *en shimáshita.*
   a. *niman*
   b. *nihyaku*
   c. *nisen*

7. *Oiwakéchoo* _____ (seventeen) *bánchi ni súnde imásu.*
   a. *shichijuu*
   b. *juushichi*
   c. *juuhachi*

8. _____ (Noon) *desu.*
   a. *Hirú*
   b. *Yóru*
   c. *Ása*

9. _____ (Six) *ji ni oai shimashóo.*
   a. *San*
   b. *Kú*
   c. *Rokú*

10. *Sore o suru* _____ (time) *desu.*
    a. *hito*
    b. *jikan*
    c. *tokoro*

11. *Kyóo wa* _____ (Wednesday) *desu.*
    a. *Kayóobi*
    b. *Suiyóobi*
    c. *Getsuyóobi*

12. *Raishuu no* _____ (Tuesday) *ni demásu.*
    a. *Kayóobi*
    b. *Mokuyóobi*
    c. *Nichiyóobi*

13. *Kyóo wa* _____ (June) *no tsuitachi desu.*
    a. *Rokugatsu*
    b. *Shichigatsu*
    c. *Hachigatsu*

14. *Kore wa* _____ (doesn't need).
    a. *ikimasén*
    b. *irimasén*
    c. *arimasén*

15. *Kono kotobá wa Nihongo de* _____ (how)
    kakimásu ka?
    a. *dóre*
    b. *dóo*
    c. *dáre*

16. *Watakushi wa Shigatsu* _____ (twelfth) *ni*
    umaremáshita.
    a. *júuyokka*
    b. *níjuuninichi*
    c. *juuninichi*

17. _____ (How many) *nokótte imásu ka?*
    a. *Íkutsu*
    b. *Kokónotsu*
    c. *Mittsú*

18. _____ (Intend to go) *desu.*
    a. *Iku hazu*
    b. *Iku tsumori*
    c. *Iku koto ga dekínai*

19. *Ashita* _____ (I must go).
    a. *ikanákereba narimasén.*
    b. *ikanákute mo íi desu.*
    c. *itté mo íi desu.*

20. *Yamada-san wa sono koto o* _____ (is
    supposed to know).
    a. *shitte imásen deshita.*
    b. *shitte iru hazu desu.*
    c. *shiritái deshoo.*

ANSWERS

1-b; 2-a; 3-b; 4-c; 5-a; 6-c; 7-b; 8-a; 9-c; 10-b; 11-b;
12-a; 13-a; 14-b; 15-b; 16-c; 17-a; 18-b; 19-a; 20-b.

WORD STUDY

anaúnsaa	announcer
antena	antenna
daiyaru	dial
nyúusu	news
purojúusaa	producer
puroguramu	program
rájio	radio
sáikuru	cycle
suítchi	switch
terebíjon	television

LESSON 33   DÁI SÁNJUU SÁN KA

GETTING AROUND

Chótto otazune itashimásu ga, kono machi no namae wa nán to iimásu ka?	Excuse me, but what is the name of this town?
Tookyoo made dono kurai arimásu ka?	How far are we from Tokyo?
Koko kara Tookyoo máde nán kiro arimásu ka?	How many kilometers from here to Tokyo?
Koko kara júkkiro desu.	It's ten kilometers from here.
Koko kara níjukkiro desu.	That's twenty kilometers from here.
Koko kara Tookyoo made dóo ikimásu ka?	How do I get to Tokyo from here?
Kono michi o oide nasái.	Follow this road.

Kono banchi e dóo iku no ka oshiete kudasái.	Can you tell me how I can get to this address?
Koko e dóo iku no ka oshiete kudasái.	Can you tell me how I can get to this place?
Kono toori no namae wa nán to iimásu ka?	What is the name of this street?
Ginza Doori wa dóko desu ka?	Where is Ginza Doori?
Koko kara tooi désu ka?	Is it far from here?
Koko kara chikái desu ka?	Is it near here?
Migi e sánchoo desu.	It's the third block to the right.
Kono michi o oide nasái.	Go this way.
Massúgu oide nasái.	Go straight ahead.
Kádo made itte hidari e omagari nasái.	Go to the corner and turn left.
Migi ni omagari nasái.	Turn right.
Garéeji wa dóko ni arimásu ka?	Where is the garage?
Keisatsusho wa dóko desu ka?	Where is the police station?
Shiyákusho wa dóko desu ka?	Where is City Hall?
Básu no teiryuujoo wa dóko desu ka?	Where is the bus stop?
Dóno eki de orimásu ka?	What station do I get off at?
Dóko de orimásu ka?	Where do I get off?
Kisha no éki wa dóko ni arimásu ka?	Where is the railroad station?

Tookyoo yuki no kishá ni wa dóko kara norimásu ka?	Where do I get the train for Tokyo?
Niban sen désu.	On track two.
Kishá wa íma demáshita.	The train just left.

LESSON 34 DÁI SÁNJUU YÓN KA

WRITING, PHONING, TELEGRAPHING

Tsugí no kishá wa nánji ni demásu ka?	What time does the next train leave?
Kyooto yuki no oofukugíppu o kudasái.	May I have a round-trip ticket for Kyoto?
Íkura desu ka?	How much is that?
Sen gohyaku gojúu en desu.	One thousand five hundred and fifty yen.
Jikan wa dono kurai kakari másu ka?	How long does it take to get there?
Kujíkan to chótto desu.	A little over nine hours.
Tegami o kakitái n desu ga . . .	[I'd like to write a letter, but (would you mind if I did?)]
Enpitsu o mótte imásu ka?	Have you a pencil?
Pén o mótte imásu ka?	Do you have a pen?
Suitorígami o mótte imásu ka?	Do you have a blotter?
Fuutoo o mótte imásu ka?	Do you have an envelope?
Kitté o mótte imásu ka?	Do you have a stamp?

Kitté wa dóko de kaemásu ka?	Where can I buy a stamp?
Kookuubin no kitté o mótte imásu ka?	Do you have an airmail stamp?
Yuubínkyoku wa dóko desu ka?	Where is the post office?
Kono tegami o dashitái n desu ga . . .	I'd like to mail this letter.
Kitte wa nánmai irimásu ka?	How many stamps do I need on this letter?
Pósuto wa dóko ni arimásu ka?	Where is the mailbox?
Kádo ni arimásu.	At the corner.
Denpoo o uchitái n desu ga . . . dóko de utemásu ka?	I'd like to send a telegram. Where can I send a telegram?
Denpoo Denwa Kyoku wa dóko ni arimásu ka?	Where is the telegraph-telephone office?
Yuubínkyoku ni arimásu.	It's in the post office.
Tookyoo ate no denpoo wa íkura desu ka?	How much is a telegram to Tokyo?
Soko e tsukú no ni dono kurai kakarimásu ka?	How long will it take to get there?
Koko ni denwa ga arimásu ka?	Is there a phone here?
Dóko de denwa ga kakeraremásu[1] ka?	Where can I phone?
Denwa wa dóko ni arimásu ka?	Where is the telephone?
Denwa no bókkusu wa dóko ni arimásu ka?	Where is the phone booth?

[1]*kakerareru* = can phone

Tabakoya ni arimásu.	In the cigar store [tobacco shop].

LESSON 35 DÁI SÁNJUU GÓ KA

WRITING, PHONING, TELEGRAPHING
(cont.)

Denwa o kashite kudasái?	May I use your phone?
Dóozo otsukai kudasái.	Go ahead! [Please use (it).]
Chookyori dénwa o onegai shimásu.	May I have long distance, please?
Tookyoo é no tsuuwa[1] wa íkura desu ka?	How much is a call to Tokyo?
Kyoobashi no ichi ichi ichi ni ban o onegai shimásu.	Kyobashi 1112, please.
Chótto omachi kudasái.	One moment, please.
Ohanashichuu desu.	The line's busy.
Móshi moshi, chigau bangóo ni kakarimáshita.	[Hello, hello,] Operator, you gave me the wrong number.
Ohenji ga gozaimasén.	There is no answer *(extra polite)*.
Yamada-san o onegai shimásu.	May I speak to Mr. Yamada, please?
Watakushi désu.	Speaking.
Kochira wa Táitasu desu.	This is Titus speaking. [This side (it) is Titus.]

[1]*tsuuwa* = telephone toll charge

FAMILY AFFAIRS

Onamae wa nán to osshaimásu ka?	What is your name?
Yamada Yoshio to mooshimásu.[1]	My name is Yoshio Yamada.
Anó hito no namae wa nán to iimasu ka?	What is his name?
Anó hito no namae wa Tanaka Makoto desu.	His name is Makoto Tanaka.
Anó hito no namae wa nán to iimásu ka?	What is her name?
Anó hito wa Sátoo Míchiko to iimásu.	Her name is Michiko Sato.
Anó hitótachi no namae wa nán to iimásu ka?	What are their names?
Ano otoko no hito no namae wa Shimada Yukio de, ano onna no hito no namae wa Takáhashi Nóriko desu.	His name is Yukio Shimada and hers is Noriko Takahashi.
Anó hito no namae wa nán to iimasu ka?	What's his first name?
Anó hito no namae wa Nobuo desu.	His first name is Nobuo.
Anó hito no myóoji wa nán to iimasu ka?	What is his last name?
Anó hito no myóoji wa Yasuda to iimasu.	His last name is Yasuda.
Okuni wa dóchira desu ka?	Where are you from?

[1]*moosu* = call, say *(humble verb)*

Tookyoo desu.	I'm from Tokyo.
Anáta wa dóko de umaremáshita ka?	Where were you born?
Nágoya de umaremáshita.	I was born in Nagoya.

LESSON 36 DÁI SÁNJUU RÓKKA

FAMILY AFFAIRS *(cont.)*

Anáta wa íkutsu desu ka?	How old are you?
Hátachi¹ desu.	I'm twenty.
Kúgatsu de níjuu ichí ni narimásu.	I'll be twenty-one in September.
Watakushi wa sén kyúuhyaku sánjuu kyúu nen no Hachigatsu juukú nichi ni umaremáshita.	I was born August 19, 1939.
Kyóodai wa nánnin arimásu ka?	How many brothers do you have?
Kyóodai wa futarí desu.	I have two brothers.
Áni wa níjuu gó sai desu.	My older brother is twenty-five.
Sono áni wa daigaku ni itte imásu.	He attends the university.
Otootó wa juushichí desu.	My younger brother is seventeen.
Otootó wa kootoogákkoo no sannénsei desu.	He's in the last year of senior high school.

¹*hátachi* = twenty years old

Onéesan ya imooto san wa nánnin desu ka?	How many sisters do you have?
Imootó ga hitóri áru daké desu.	I have just one younger sister.
Imootó wa juugó desu.	She's fifteen.
Imootó wa chuugákkoo no sannénsei desu.	She is in the third year of junior high school.
Otóosan no oshígoto wa nán desu ka?	What does your father do?
Chichí wa bengóshi desu.	He's [Father is] a lawyer.
Chichí wa kenchikuka desu.	He's an architect.
Kyóoshi desu.	He's a teacher.
Daigaku kyóoju desu.	He's a university professor.
Isha desu.	He's a doctor.
Kaisháin desu.	He's in business.
Orimonogáisha o yatte imásu.	He's in the textile business.
Hyakushóo desu.	He's a farmer.
Yakunin desu.	He's a government employee.
Roodóosha desu.	He's a worker.
Jidoosha kóojoo de hataraite imásu.	He works in an automobile factory.
Anáta no otanjóobi wa ítsu desu ka?	When is your birthday?
Watakushi no tanjóobi wa nishúukan saki no Ichigatsu níjuu sánnichi desu.	My birthday is in two weeks—January twenty-third.
Koko ni goshinseki ga oari desu ka?	Do you have any relatives here?

Gokázoku wa minna koko ni súnde irasshaimásu ka?	Does your whole family live here?
Sofúbo no hoka wa kázoku wa minna koko ni súnde imásu.	All my family except my grandparents.
Sofúbo wa Nágoya ni súnde imásu.	They live in Nagoya.
Anáta wa Taketomisan no goshinseki desu ka?	Are you related to Mr. Taketomi?
Watakushi no oji desu.	He's my uncle.
Anó hito wa watakushi no itóko desu.	He's my cousin.
Anáta wa Sákata-san no ókusan no goshinseki desu ka?	Are you related to Mrs. Sakata?
Watakushi no oba désu.	She's my aunt.
Watakushi no itóko desu.	She's my cousin.

REVIEW QUIZ 5

1. _____ (This) *machi no namae wa nán to iimásu ka?*
   a. *Koko*
   b. *Kore*
   c. *Kono*

2. *Koko kara Tookyoo máde* _____ (how) *ikimásu ka?*
   a. *dóko*
   b. *dóo*
   c. *dóre*

3. *Kono toori no namae wa* _____ (what) *to iimásu ka?*
   a. *dóre*
   b. *náze*
   c. *nán*

4. *Ginza Doori wa* _____ (where) *desu ka?*
   a. *dóko*
   b. *nán*
   c. *dóre*

5. *Kono michi o* _____ (go).
   a. *oide nasái*
   b. *okake nasái*
   c. *oake nasái*

6. *Kádo made itte* _____ (left) *e omagari nasái.*
   a. *hidari*
   b. *migi*
   c. *migi no hóo*

7. _____ (How much) *desu ka?*
   a. *íkutsu*
   b. *íkura*
   c. *ítsu*

8. *Tagami o* _____ (would like to write) *n desu ga.*
   a. *dashitái*
   b. *kakitái*
   c. *mitái*

9. _____ (Stamp) *wa dóko de kaemásu ka?*
   a. *kitte*
   b. *zasshi*
   c. *shinbun*

10. _____ (Corner) *ni arimásu.*
    a. *Kádo*
    b. *Tonari*
    c. *Asoko*

11. _____ (Here) *ni denwa ga arimásu ka?*
    a. *Koko*
    b. *Soko*
    c. *Asoko*

12. _____ (Wrong) *bangóo ni kakarimáshita.*
    a. *Chigau*
    b. *Hoshíi*
    c. *Byooin no*

13. *Anó hito no* _____ (first name) *wa nán to iimásu ka?*
    a. *namae*
    b. *myóoji*
    c. *jimúsho*

14. *Anáta wa dóko de* _____ (was born) *ka?*
    a. *kaimáshita*
    b. *umaremáshita*
    c. *aimáshita*

15. *Otootó wa* _____ (seventeen) *desu.*
    a. *juushichí*
    b. *juuichí*
    c. *juuhachí*

16. *Chichí wa* _____ (lawyer) *desu.*
    a. *kusuriya*
    b. *bengóshi*
    c. *isha*

17. _____ (Worker) *desu.*
    a. *Roodóosha*
    b. *Kyóoshi*
    c. *Kaisháin*

18. *Anáta wa Taketomi-san no* _____ (relative) *desu ka?*
    a. *goshinseki*
    b. *tomodachi*
    c. *bengóshi*

19. _____ (Birthday) *wa ítsu desu ka?*
    a. *Goryokoo*
    b. *Tanjóobi*
    c. *Gokekkon*

20. *Koko kara* _____ (far) *desu ka?*
    a. *tooi*
    b. *chikái*
    c. *nán kiro*

21. *Niban* _____ (track) *desu.*
    a. *sen*
    b. *me*
    c. *réssha*

22. _____ (Next) *kishá wa nánji ni demásu ka?*
    a. *Tsugí no*
    b. *Ása no*
    c. *Gógo no*

23. *Kyooto yuki no* _____ (round-trip ticket) *o kudasai.*
    a. *oofuku gippu*
    b. *katamichi*
    c. *kyuukooken*

24. _____ (Line's busy) *desu.*
    a. *Ohanashichuu*
    b. *Chigau bangóo*
    c. *Táshika*

25. *Sofúbo* _____ (except) *kázoku wa minna koko ni súnde imásu.*
    a. *no boka wa*
    b. *to issho ni*
    c. *to*

ANSWERS

1-c; 2-b; 3-c; 4-a; 5-a; 6-a; 7-b; 8-b; 9-a; 10-a; 11-a; 12-a; 13-a; 14-b; 15-a; 16-b; 17-a; 18-a; 19-b; 20-a; 21-a; 22-a; 23-a; 24-a; 25-a;

LESSON 37 DÁI SÁNJUU NANÁ KA

EVERYDAY JAPANESE CONVERSATION

🔲 🔲

KAIMONO
(SHOPPING)

Study the notes at the end of this section for greater comprehension.

1. **Íkura desu ka?**
   How much is it?

2. **Sén en désu.**
   One thousand yen.

3. **Chótto takasugimásu ga hoka ni arimasén ka?**
   It's [a little] too expensive. Haven't you anything else?

4. **Onaji shúrui no desu ka?**
   Of the same kind?

5. **Onaji shúrui no ka nitá no ga hoshíi n desu ga.**
   Yes, the same kind or something similar.

6. **Koo yuu no ga gozaimásu.**
   We have this (sort).

7. **Móo hoka ní wa arimasén ka?**
   Don't you have anything else (to show me)?

8. **Mótto oyasúi no de gozaimásu ka?**
   Less expensive [one]? [Cheaper one?]

9. **Móshi áttara.**
   If possible. [If there is.]

10. **Kore wa ikága de gozaimásu kam?**
    Would you like this? [How about this one?]

11. **Sore wa nedan ni yorimásu ne.**
That depends on the price. [(I think it is all right) depending on the price.]

12. **Kore wa hassen en de gozaimásu.**
This is eight thousand yen.

13. **Kore wa dóo desu ka? Máe no yori yasúi n desu ka takái n desu ka?**
How about this? Is it cheaper or more expensive [than the former one]?

14. **Mótto otakóo gozaimásu.**
More expensive.

15. **Hoka ni arimasén ka née?**
Haven't you anything else?

16. **Tadáima wa gozaimasén ga atarashíi kata nó ga kinkin kúru hazu de gozaimásu ga . . .**
Not at the moment, but I'm expecting some new styles soon. [. . . new style ones are supposed to come soon.]

17. **Itsu goro désu ka?**
When? [About when?]

18. **Moo jikí da to zonjimásu ga. Konshuu matsu goro otachiyori kudasái máse.**
Any day now. Drop in toward the end of the week. [I think it'll be very soon . . .]

19. **Ja soo shimashóo. Tokoró de kore wa íkura desu ka?**
I'll do that. By the way, how much is this?

20. **Issoku sanbyakú en de gozaimásu.**
Three hundred yen a pair.

21. **Ichi dáasu kudasai.**
Let me have a dozen. [Give me a dozen.]

22. **Omochi ni narimásu ka?**
    Will you take (them with you)?

23. **Iie, haitatsu shite kudasái.**
    No. Please deliver them.

24. **Gojúusho wa onaji désu ne?**
    At the same address? [The address is the same, isn't it?]

25. **Onaji desu.**
    It's still the same.

26. **Maido arígatoo gozaimásu.**
    Thank you very much. [Thank you (for your patronage) each time (you come).]

27. **Sayonara.**
    Good-by.

28. **Sayonara.**
    Good-by.

NOTES

Title: *Kaimono* = Shopping

4. *Shúrui no:* same as *shúrui no mono* = one(s) of the same kind. See also #13 for similar construction.

5. *Nita no ga* = one (that) resembles (it).

6. *Gozaimásu:* an extra-polite form of *arimásu* which would be used by the shopkeeper to the customer.

8. *Oyasúi:* an extra-polite form of *yasúi* of *yasúi desu* containing the "honorific" prefix o-. Nearly all adjectives can take this prefix "honoring" the person to whom or about whom you are speaking. However, an adjective that itself

begins with *o* cannot add the honorific prefix *o*. For instance, *omoshiroi* [It is interesting] cannot become *oomoshiroi*.

10. *Ikága* is extra-polite for *dóo*.

11. *Ni yorimásu* = depending on.

13. *Máe no:* same as *máe no mono* = one(s) of the previous time.

14. Extra polite.

16. *Tadáima* = just now.
    Kinkin = very recently.
    Kúru hazu désu ga: When the particle *ga* is used to terminate a clause, it signifies "but" or "and," but does not have quite the same force. It serves to make the sentence less sharp or less pointed, and is commonly used in extra-polite speech.

18. *Zonjimásu* (extra polite): same as *omoimasu* = think, believe. (*Zonjite imasu:* same as *shitte imasu* = know.)
    Otachiyori kudasái (extra polite): same as *tachiyotte kudasai*.

    Note the construction: *o* plus the radical (or infinitive) plus *kudasái*. A radical consists (in the case of a consonant verb) of the stem plus *i* or (in the case of a vowel verb) of the stem itself.

    For example: *okaki kudasái* = *káite kudasái; otabe kudasái* = *tábete kudasái.*

19. *Ja:* same as *de wa* = well, then.
    Tokoró de = by the way.

20. *Soku* = a counter for socks, stockings, shoes.

22. *Omochi ni narimásu ka* (extra polite): same as *mochimasu ka* or *motte ikimasu ka*. Notice the construction: *o* plus the radical plus *ni narimasu*. This method for the construction of the extra-polite form of a verb can be used for almost any plain verb (i.e., a verb which is not already extra polite). Further examples: *okaki ni narimásu = kakimásu; otabe ni narimásu = tabemásu; okai ni narimáshita = kaimáshita.*

24. *Gojúusho* (extra-polite): same as *júusho. Gojúusho* and all other extra-polite words of expressions introduced here cannot be used for things or actions pertaining to the speaker or persons identified with the speaker.

26. *Maido arígatoo gozaimásu:* The usual expression used by shopkeepers.

QUIZ 26

1. _____ (How much) *desu ka?*
   a. *Íkura*
   b. *Ikága*
   c. *Íkutsu*

2. *Onaji* _____ (kind) *no desu ka?*
   a. *shúrui*
   b. *nedan*
   c. *tokoro*

3. *Onaji shurui no* _____ (or) *nita no ga hoshíi n desu ga . . .*
   a. *ga*
   b. *ka*
   c. *to*

4. _____ (This type) *no ga gozaimásu ga . . .*
   a. *Dóo yuu no*
   b. *Soo yuu no*
   c. *Koo yuu no*

5. _____ (Less) *oyasúi no de gozaimásu ka?*
   a. *Sukóshi*
   b. *Mótto*
   c. *Taihen*

6. _____ (That) *wa nedan ni yorimásu ne.*
   a. *Sore*
   b. *Kore*
   c. *Dóre*

7. *Tadaima wa gozaimasen* _____ (but) *atarashíi kata nó ga kinkin kuru hazu désu ga . . .*
   a. *kara*
   b. *ga*
   c. *noni*

8. _____ (Around when) *desu ka?*
   a. *Ítsu*
   b. *Nanji gurai*
   c. *Itsu goro*

9. _____ (One dozen) *kudasái.*
   a. *Ichí mai*
   b. *Ichi dáasu*
   c. *Issátsu*

10. _____ (Deliver) *shite kudasái.*
    a. *Haitatsu*
    b. *Benkyoo*
    c. *Kekkon*

ANSWERS

1-a; 2-a; 3-b; 4-c; 5-b; 6-a; 7-b; 8-c; 9-b; 10-a.

ORDERING BREAKFAST

Study the notes at the end of this section for greater comprehension.

1. **Y:[1] Onaka ga suitaroo.**
   Y: You must be hungry.

2. **Mrs. Y: Ée, náni ka itadakitái wa.**
   Mrs. Y: Yes, I'm starved. [(I) would like to have something.]

3. **Y: Kono hóteru ni wa íi resutoran ga áru to yuú kara sokó e itte miyóo.**
   Y: They say there is a good restaurant in this hotel. Let's have breakfast there.

4. **Mrs. Y: Sore ga íi wa. Soo shimashoo.**
   Mrs. Y: That's a good idea.

5. **Y: Booi-san!**
   Y: Waiter!

6. **W: Oyobi de gozaimásu ka?**
   W: Yes: [(You) called, (sir)?]

7. **Y: Asahan o tabetái n da ga . . .**
   Y: We'd like some breakfast.

8. **Mrs. Y: Náni ga itadakemásu no?**
   Mrs. Y: What can we have?

9. **W: Onomímono wa koohíi koocha hotto chokoréeto. Nán ni itasimashóo ka?**
   W: Coffee, tea, or hot chocolate. What would you like to have? [What shall I make it to be?]

10. **Mrs. Y: Hoka no móno wa?**
    Mrs. Y: What else?

[1]Y stands for "Mr. Yamada," *Mrs. Y* for "Mrs. Yamada," *W* for "Waiter."

11. **W: Roorú pan ni tóosuto, sore kara hotto kéeki mo dekimásu.**
W: Rolls, toast, and hot cakes, too.

12. **Mrs. Y: Báta wa tsukánai n desu ka?**
Mrs. Y: No butter?

13. **W: Mochíron tsukimásu. Hoka ni jámu mo otsuke itashimasu.**
W: Of course, butter and jelly. [Of course, (we) will serve (it). (We) will serve jelly also.]

14. **Mrs. Y: Déwa watakushi wa koohíi to tóosuto daké ni shimashoo.**
Mrs. Y: I'd like to have some coffee and toast.

15. **Y: Kochira mo sore to onaji ni shite sonó hoka ni hanjuku támago o tsukéte kudasái.**
Y: The same for me, and a soft-boiled egg as well.

16. **W: Kashikomarimáshita. Hoka ni náni ka?**
W: Certainly, sir. Would you like anything else?

17. **Y: Íya, sore de takusan.**
Y: No, that'll be all.

18. **Mrs. Y: Booi san, nápukin o motté kite kudasái ne.**
Mrs. Y: Waiter, may I have a napkin, please?

19. **Y: Sore kara fooku mo. Koko ní wa fóoku ga nái yoo da ze.**
Y: Would you also get a fork, please? I don't have one. [(It) seems (it) is not here.]

20. **Mrs. Y: Osatoo mo negaimásu yo.**
Mrs. Y: And some sugar, too, please.

21. **W: Omatase itashimáshita.**
W: Here you are, madam.

22. **Mrs. Y: Kono kohíi wa sukkári tsumetaku nátte iru wa. Atsúi no to torikaete kudasái na.**
    Mrs. Y: My coffee is cold. Please bring me another cup.

23. **W: Kashikomarimáshita.**
    W: Gladly.

24. **Y: Booi san. Kanjoogaki o motté kite kudasái.**
    Y: Waiter, may I have the check?

25. **W: Omatase itashimashita.**
    W: Here you are, sir. [Sorry to have kept you waiting.]

26. **Y: Ja kore de tótte kudasái. Otsuri wa íi desu.**
    Y: Here, keep the change.

27. **W: Maido arígatoo gozaimásu.**
    W: Thank you very much, sir.

28. **Y: Ja sayonara.**
    Y: Good-by.

NOTES

Title: *Asahan* = Breakfast

1. The conversation here is first carried on between husband and wife; later it is continued between the couple and the waiter. Notice how freely the plain forms instead of the usual *-másu* or *-désu* forms of verbs and adjectives are used in such a conversation.

   Onaka ga suitaroo (from *suku*) = gets hungry. [The stomach gets empty.]

2. *Itadakitai* (extra polite) (from *itadaku*) = want to eat, drink, receive.

Wa: a particle used exclusively by women in casual conversation. It appears at the end of a sentence and adds a feminine touch.

8. *No:* another particle used almost exclusively by women which takes the place of *no desu* or *n desu* at the end of a sentence. With a rising intonation, it is, like the particle *ka,* a spoken question mark.

12. *Tsukanai* from tsuku) = goes with; is served with.

13. *Otsuke shimasoo* (from *suru*): *otsuke* comes from *tsukéru* = one serves something with, a transitive verb to be paired with *tsuku* (see #12, above). The construction employed here—that is, *o* plus the radical plus *suru* (or *itásu*) is that used in extra-polite speech when the speaker discusses doing something for the person with whom he is talking. Almost any plain verb can be used in this construction.

14. *Ni shimashoo* (from *suru*) = one makes (his choice or decision) to be; one decides on (taking).

15. *Kochira* = this side, this way; sometimes used in place of *watakushi* [I]. Similarly, *sochira* or *sochira sama* can be used for "you," "he," "she," or "they."

19. *Ze:* a terminal-particle for sentences used exclusively by men in casual conversations, meaning in effect, "I'm telling you," or "Don't you know that . . . ?"

20. *Negaimásu:* from *negáu* = beg, beseech, often used lightly when the speaker requests someone to do something for him.

22. *Tsumetaku natte iru* = is cold, is chilled [is in the state of having become cold].
    Na: another feminine particle added to a request, as in *te kudasái na* = You will do it, won't you?

26. *Ja:* a variant of *dé wa* = Well, then, if that is the case, when used at the beginning of a sentence. *Kore de tótte kudasai* = Using this (money), take (what I owe you). *Otsuri wa ii desu* = Keep the change. [As for the change (it) will be all right (for you to keep it).]

A SAMPLE MENU

Kondate		**Menu**	
Suimono	*Sáyori, Hawarabi, Namayuba*	Clear Soup	Snipe fish, Brackens, Fresh bean curds
Sashimi	*Maguro*	Sashimi	Tuna
Sunómono	*Sázae, Údo, Karashi-sumiso*	Salad	Turbo and udo (Japanese asparagus) dressed with vinegar, mustard, and bean paste

Donburi	*Kuwai, Sayaéndoo, Takenoko, Údo, Tori*	Vegetables	Arrowhead bulbs, Snowpeas, Bamboo shoots, Udo, Chicken
Yakimono	*Kói-teriyaki, Nagaimo-tsukeawase*	Fish	Broiled carp served with fancy relish
Kodonburi	*Tsukushi-tamagótoji*	Side Dish	Omelet with savory herbs
Góhan	*Yomena-meshi*	Rice	Rice cooked with spicy herbs
Shíru	*Sumashi-jítate-misoshíru, Toofu, Ninjin*	Bean Soup	Bean soup, Sumashi-style, Bean curds, Carrots
Koonomono	*Shintakúan, Narazuke, Shinshóoga, Komatsuna*	Relishes	Fresh pickled white radish, Pickles seasoned in Sake, Ginger shoots, Komatsuna

REVIEW QUIZ 6

1. *Onaka ga* _____ (must be hungry).
   a. *tsúitaroo*
   b. *suitaróo*
   c. *káitaroo*

2. _____ (Butter) *wa tsukánai n desu ka?*
   a. *Bíiru*
   b. *Báta*
   c. *Básu*

3. *Kono hóteru ni wa íi résutoran go* _____ (there is).
   a. *arimásu*
   b. *imásu*
   c. *shimásu*

4. *Kono koohíi wa* _____ (cold) *nátte iru wa.*
   a. *wáruku*
   b. *átsuku*
   c. *tsumetaku*

5. *Kochira mo sore to* _____ (the same) *ni shite kudasái.*
   a. *nita*
   b. *onaji*
   c. *chigau*

6. *Booi-san,* _____ (jelly) *o motté kite kudasái ne.*
   a. *jámu*
   b. *osatoo*
   c. *ocha*

7. *Sore kara fóoku* _____ (also).
   a. *moo*
   b. *to*
   c. *mo*

8. *Booi-san,* _____ (check) *o motté kite kudasái.*
   a. *kanjoogaki*
   b. *kippu*
   c. *tanjóobi*

9. *Fóoku ga* _____ (missing) *yoo da.*
   a. *nái*
   b. *inai*
   c. *ikanai*

10. _____ (Change) *wa ii desu.*
    a. *Kanjoogaki*
    b. *Okane*
    c. *Otsuri*

ANSWERS

1-b; 2-b; 3-a; 4-c; 5-b; 6-a; 7-c; 8-a; 9-a; 10-c.

LESSON 38

DÁI SÁNJUU
HACHI KA

IN, ON, UNDER

▭▭ ▭▭

1. *Ni, De, E, No* = In, Into

Sore wa jibikí ni arimásu.	It's in the dictionary.
Pokétto ni iremáshita.	He put it in his pocket.
Ano híto no heyá ni arimásu.	You'll find it in his room.
Hikidashi ni irete kudasái.	Put it into the drawer.
Mé ni náni ka hairimáshita.	I have something in my eye. [Something got into my eyes.]

Tookyoo de kaimáshita.	I bought it in Tokyo
Tookyoo no hakubútsukan de mimáshita.	I saw it in the museum in Tokyo.

2. *No naka ni (. . . de, . . . e, . . . no, . . . o)* = Inside

Sono kaban no náka o míte kudasái.	Please look in that brief case. [Please look in the within of that brief case.]
Gakkoo no náka no shokudoo de góhan o tabemáshita.	We ate [had our meal] in the dining room of [in the within of] the school.
Yamada-san to issho ni tatemóno no náka e hairimáshita.	Together with Mr. Yamada, we saw the inside of the building.
Kusuriya wa sono tatemóno no náka ni arimásu.	The drugstore is in [inside] that building.

3. *No ue ni (. . . de, . . . no, . . . e)* = On

Kono tegami o sono hito no tsukue no ué ni oite kudasái.	Put this letter on his desk.
Sonó hito no namae wa to no ué ni káite arimásu.	His name is written on the door.
Joobukuro no ué ni káite kudasái.	Write it on the envelope.

4. *No shita ni (. . . de, . . . no, . . . e)* = Under

Isu no shitá ni arimásu.	It's under the chair.

Sono hón wa hoka no hón no shita ni arimásu.	You'll find the book under the others.
Shindai no shita ni okimáshita.	He put it under the bed.
Takusan tsumikasanátte iru kami no shitá ni arimáshita.	I found it under a pile of papers.

5. *Ue* = Top, Surface

Ue ni oite kudasái.	Put it on top.
Ue o míte kudasai.	Look on the top.
Hón o sore no ué ni oite kudasái.	Put the book on that.

6. *Shita* = Bottom, Place under, Place below

Sore o shita ni oite kudasái.	Put that underneath.
Kono shita o mite kudasái.	Look under here.

7. *Moshi*[1] ... *-eba* = If

Notice that the *-(r)eba*[2] ending form of a verb, the *-kereba*-ending form of an adjective, and *nara* form of a copula express the idea, "if (something) happens," or "if (something) is the case." These forms are called the "provisional" and are used *only* for a present or future hypothetical condition.

móshi dekíreba	if I can
móshi juubun okane ga areba	if I have enough money

[1] *Moshi* is optional.
[2] Use *-eba* with consonant verbs; use *-reba* with vowel verbs.

móshi kúreba	if he comes
móshi onozomi nára	if you wish
móshi osukí nara	if you like that
móshi sámukereba	if it is cold
móshi yásukereba	if it is cheap

8. *-Tara* = If, When

Notice that the *-tara* form is made by adding *-ra* to the *-ta* form. It is used to express a condition of the past, present, or future. The *-tara* form is called the "conditional."

Ashita áme ga futtára ikimasén.	If it rains tomorrow I won't go.
Ashita átsukattara ikimasén.	If it's hot tomorrow I won't go.
Okane ga nákattara kaemasén.	If you don't have the money, you can't buy it.
Anmari takái to ittára yásuku shimáshita.	When I said it was too expensive, he lowered the price [he made it cheap].
Tabetákattara tábete mo íi desu.	If you want to eat it, you can [eat it].
Tákakattara honmono désu.	If it is expensive, it is [a] genuine [thing].
Sono kusuri o nóndara súgu yókunarimáshita.	When I took [drank] that medicine, I got well right away.

9. *To* = If, When, Whenever

Notice that *to* is used only when what follows it is a natural consequence to what is stated in the clause that precedes it. *To* is always preceded by the present form of a verb or adjective; it cannot be used when the terminal clause ends in *-te kudasai*.

Kono michi o massúgu yuku to bijútsukan no máe ni demásu.	If you follow [go] this road straight ahead, you will come to the front of the Fine Arts Museum.
Básu de yuku to gojíkan kakarimásu.	If you go by bus, it takes five hours.
Wakaránai kotó ga áru to Yamada-san ni kikimásu.	When there are things that I don't understand, I ask Mr. Yamada.
Áme ga furu to kúru hito ga sukunáku narimásu.	When it rains, fewer persons come [persons who come get fewer].
Máinichi káku to joozu ni narimásu.	When you write it every day, you become more skillful [in it].

10. *Nashi ni* = **Without**

ókane náshi ni	without money
nani mo náshi ni	without anything
machigái nashi ni	without fail
kónnan náshi ni	without difficulty
Kónnan náshi ni dekimásu.	You can do it without any difficulty.

QUIZ 27

1.	*Sore o shita ni oite kudasái.*	1.	It's in the dictionary.
2.	*Pokétto ni iremáshita.*	2.	Put that underneath.

3. *Sore wa jibikí ni arimásu.*

3. He put it in his pocket.

4. *Joobúkuro no úe ni káite kudasái.*

4. His name is on the door.

5. *Sonó hito no namae wa to no ué ni káite arimásu.*

5. Write it on the envelope.

6. *Ue o míte kudasái.*

6. You will find the book under the others.

7. *osuki nára*

7. Put it on top.

8. *móshi juubun okane ga áreba*

8. Look on the top.

9. *anmari takái to ittára*

9. if you wish

10. *machigái nashi ni*

10. if you like that

11. *kónnan náshi ni*

11. if I have enough money

12. *okane náshi ni*

12. when I said it was too expensive

13. *onozomi nára*

13. without money

14. *Ue ni oite kudasái.*

14. without fail

15. *Sono hón wa hoka no hón no shita ni arimásu.*

15. without difficulty

ANSWERS
1-2; 2-3; 3-1; 4-5; 5-4; 6-8; 7-10; 8-11; 9-12; 10-14; 11-15; 12-13; 13-9; 14-7; 15-6.

REVIEW QUIZ 7

1. _____ (That one) *ga hoshíi desu.*
   a. *Asoko*
   b. *Are*
   c. *Anna*

2. _____ (This) *wa ikága desu ka?*
   a. *Kore*
   b. *Kono*
   c. *Koko*

3. *Nihongo de* _____ (how) *iimásu ka?*
   a. *dóre*
   b. *dónna*
   c. *dóo*

4. *Soko e itta* _____ (never).
   a. *tsumori desu.*
   b. *kotó ga arimasén.*
   c. *hazu desu.*

5. _____ (Nothing) *kaimasén deshita.*
   a. *Nán demo*
   b. *Náni ka*
   c. *Nani mo*

6. *Kono hon wa* _____ (his) *desu.*
   a. *dóno hito no*
   b. *konó hito no*
   c. *anó hito no*

7. *Ome ni kakaru kotó ga dékite* _____ (fortunate) *desu.*
   a. *saiwai*
   b. *hajímete*
   c. *oki no doku*

8. _____ (One week) *kakarimásu.*
   a. *Ikkágetsu*
   b. *Isshúukan*
   c. *Ichínen*

9. _____ (Next) *kishá de ikimashóo.*
   a. *Ashita no*
   b. *Tsugí no*
   c. *Asátte no*

10. *Dóo mo* _____ (thanks).
    a. *wakarimasén.*
    b. *arígatoo gozaimásu.*
    c. *dekimasén.*

11. *Ni san* _____ (days) *shitára denwa o kákete kudasai.*
    a. *jíkan*
    b. *nichi*
    c. *nen*

12. *Kono káta o* _____ (know) *ka?*
    a. *gozónji de irasshaimásu*
    b. *sagashite imasu*
    c. *goshookai itashimásu*

13. *Iie, soo* _____ (don't think).
    a. *ikimasén.*
    b. *omoimasén.*
    c. *kimasén.*

14. *Kyóoto de* _____ (bought).
    a. *tsukurimáshita.*
    b. *kikimáshita.*
    c. *kaimáshita.*

15. *Sono tegami wa* _____ (wrote) *ka?*
    a. *mimáshita*
    b. *kakimáshita*
    c. *uketorimáshita*

16. Watakushi wa _____ (morning) *wa koohíi o nomimásu.*
    a. *hirú*
    b. *yóru*
    c. *ása*

17. Éki de tomodachi ni _____ (met).
    a. *hanashimáshita.*
    b. *aimáshita.*
    c. *kikimáshita.*

18. *Anáta no denwa bangoo o* _____ (give me).
    a. *goran nasái.*
    b. *kudasái.*
    c. *agemashóo.*

19. *Sore wa taihen* _____ (good) *desu.*
    a. *kékkoo*
    b. *omoshirói*
    c. *yasúi*

20. _____ (Soon) *kimásu.*
    a. *Súgu*
    b. *Ashita*
    c. *Áto de*

ANSWERS

1-b; 2-a; 3-c; 4-b; 5-c; 6-c; 7-a; 8-b; 9-b; 10-b; 11-b; 12-a; 13-b; 14-c; 15-b; 16-c; 17-b; 18-b; 19-a; 20-a.

SHAKUYA SAGASHI

HOUSE HUNTING

Study the notes at the end of this section for greater comprehension.

1. **Kashiya ga áru soo desu ga.**
   I hear you have a house to rent.

2. **Dóchira deshoo ka? Futatsu áru n desu ga.**
   Which one? We have two.

3. **Shinbun no kookoku o míte shittá no desu ga.**
   It's the one advertised in the paper.

4. **Hái, wakarimáshita.**
   Oh, that one.

5. **Dónna ie ka sukóshi setsumei shite moraemásen ka?**
   Can you describe them?

6. **Ookíi hoo wa itsúma gozaimásu.**
   The larger of the two has five rooms.

7. **Chiisái hoo wa dóo desu kam**
   How about the smaller one?

8. **Yóma de gozaimásu.**
   (It has) four rooms.

9. **Ookíi hoo wa suidoo ya gásu ga tsúite imásu ka?**
   Does the larger house have running water and gas?

10. **Hái, tsúite imásu. Benjó mo suisenshiki ni nátte orimásu.**
    Yes, it does. And it has a flush toilet.

11. **Niwa ga arimásu ka?**
    Is there a garden there?

12. **Hái, gozaimásu. Nihonshiki no rippa na niwa de gozaimásu.**
    Yes, there is. It's a fine, Japanese-style garden.

13. **Chiisái hoo wa?**
How about the smaller house?

14. **Niwa to iu hodo no niwa wa gozaimasén ga miharashi no íi takadai ni gozaimásu.**
There isn't any garden to speak of, but the house is situated on top of a hill and has a nice view. [(It)'s not much of a garden that there is . . .]

15. **Shízuka na tokoro désu ka?**
Is it in a quiet neighborhood?

16. **Hái, oodóori kara hanárete imásu kara taihen shízuka desu.**
Yes, it is away from big streets and it's very quiet there.

17. **Yáchin wa dono kurai desu ka?**
What's the rent?

18. **Ookíi hoo wa tsuki niman en desu.**
The rent for the larger house is twenty thousand yen per month.

19. **Chiisái hoo wa?**
And the smaller house?

20. **Tsuki ichimán gosen en de gozaimásu.**
Fifteen thousand yen per month.

21. **Kágu zoosaku wa dóo n an desu ka?**
What about furniture?

22. **Mina tsúite orimásu. Tatami mo harikáeta bákari de gozaimásu.**
(It)'s well furnished. The floor mats have been completely replaced.

23. **Reizóoko nado wa nái deshoo ne?**
I suppose a refrigerator is not included?

24. **Iie, saishinshiki no denki reizóoko ga tsúite orimásu.**
There is a late-model electric refrigerator. [There is an electric refrigerator of the latest style.]

25. **Ichínen no keiyaku de karitái to omótte iru n desu ga, sore de íi desu ka?**
I would like to get a lease for a year. Do you think that's possible [agreeable]?

26. **Sono ten wa yánushi to gosoodan itadakitái to omoimásu.**
You'd have to see the owner for that.

27. **Shikíkin wa irú n desu ka?**
Do I have to pay key money? [Is key money necessary?]

28. **Hái, sankagetsúbun itadaku kóto ni nátte orimásu.**
Yes, we ask three months' rent (for it).

29. **Hoka ní wa?**
Nothing else?

30. **Hoshóonin ga irimásu.**
You have to have references.

31. **Tsuide ni okiki shimásu ga denwa wa tsúite imasu ka?**
Is there a telephone already installed?

32. **Ainiku tsúite orimasen.**
No, there isn't. [Sorry, but it isn't installed.]

33. **Áa sóo desu ka.**
I see.

34. **Chikatetsu ya Kokutetsu no éki ni mo chiká-kute taihen bénri na tokoro de gozaimásu.**
The house is located not too far from the subway and the Kokutetsu-line station. So it's quite convenient.

35. **Áa sóo desu ka. Soko kara Marunouchi made wa dono kurai kakarimásu ka?**
I see. How much time does it take from there to Marunouchi?

36. **Yáku nijúppun gurai de gozaimásu.**
I would say about twenty minutes.

37. **Básu mo chikáku o tóotte imásu ka?**
Is there any bus line running nearby?

38. **Hái, Tookyoo-eki yuki ga ítchoo saki o tóotte imásu.**
Yes, there is one a block away. The bus goes to Tokyo Station.

39. **Sono uchí wa íma itte miraremásu ka?**
May we see the house now?

40. **Oki no dóku desu ga gozen-chuu shíka ome ni kakerárénai n desu ga.**
I'm sorry, but it is open for inspection only in the morning.

41. **Áa sóo desu ka. Sore ja ashita no ása kimashóo. Iroiro oséwasama deshita.**
Very well, I'll come tomorrow morning. Thanks a lot.

42. **Dóo itashimáshite. Kochira kóso shitsúrei itashimáshita.**
Not at all. Glad to be able to help you.

NOTES

Title: *Shakuya Sagashi* = Searching (for) a House to Rent.

1. *Áru soo desu* = I understood that there is.

2. *Dóchira* = which (of the two).

3. *Kookoku* = advertisement.

5. *Setsumei shite moraemasén ka* = can't I have you explain the details for me?

6. *Itsúma* = five rooms (*itsu* comes from *itsutsu* [5]; *ma* is a counter for rooms).

9. *Tsuite imásu* = are attached; are equipped.

10. *Shiki* = style; *suisenshiki* = flush-style. *Ni natte imásu* = has been made and is. *Orimásu:* a synonym for *imásu* but more formal.

14. *Niwa to iu hodo no niwa* = a garden (worthy of) calling it a garden; (there isn't any) garden to speak of.
    Miharashi = view.
    Takadai = top of a hill (within a city area).

16. *Hanárete imásu* = is away from.

17. *Yáchin* = house rent.

18. *Tsuki* = per month.

21. *Kagu zoosaku* = furniture and other equipment(s).

22. *Tatami* = Japanese-style floor mat.
    Harikáeta bákari desu = We have just replaced the mat covers with new ones (the *-ta* form of a verb plus *bákari desu* = just finished doing . . .).

23. *Reizóoko nádo* = a refrigerator and things like that.

24. *Iie* = no. Notice that this is used where "yes" would be used in English, for the thought is, "No, what you have mentioned is not correct." *Saishinshiki no denki reizóoko* = latest model electric refrigerator.

25. *Keiyaku* = contract; lease.

26. *Yánushi* = landlord.
Gosoodan itadakitái = I would like to have you consult.

27. *Shikíkin* = key money, security: applied to the last rent payments or refunded (on moving).

28. *Sankagetsúbun* = the equivalent of three months' (rent). (*-bun* = the portion for.)
Koto ni nátte orimásu = It is arranged that, it is fixed that (we receive).

30. *Hoshóonin* = reference (i.e., one who guarantees).

34. *Chikatetsu* = subway.
Kokutetsu = government-owned railroad.

35. *Marunóuchi* = the heart of the business section in Tokyo.

38. *Tookyoo-eki yuki* = bound for Tokyo: *yuki* = bound for, when used after a place name.

39. *Miraremásu* = can see. The same form—made by adding *-(r)areru* to the stem—is used for both the passive voice and polite expressions.

40. *Ome ni kakerarénai* = can't show (you); *ka-kerarénai*: a negative form of *kakeraréru*, which is a potential form made from *kakéru* by adding *-rareru* to the stem.

41. *Oséwasama deshita* = thanks: a common way of expressing thanks for services rendered.

QUIZ 28

1. _____ (Five rooms) *gozaimásu.*
   a. *Yóma*
   b. *Itsúma*
   c. *Góma*

2. *Oodóori kara* _____ (away from) *imásu.*
   a. *hanárete*
   b. *hanáshite*
   c. *tooi*

3. _____ (Rent) *wa dono kurai désu ka?*
   a. *Yáchin*
   b. *Nedan*
   c. *Shikíkin*

4. *Sankagetsúbun* _____ (receive) *kóto ni nátte orimásu.*
   a. *haráu*
   b. *itadaku*
   c. *tazunéru*

5. _____ (Furniture) *wa tsúite imásu ka?*
   a. *Tatami*
   b. *Reizooko*
   c. *Kágu zoosaku*

6. _____ (Running water) *ga tsúite imásu ka?*
   a. *Suidoo*
   b. *Gásu*
   c. *Mizu*

7. _____ (Garden) *ga arimásu ka?*
   a. *Heyá*
   b. *Niwa*
   c. *Takadai*

8. *Gozenchuu* _____ (only) *ome ni kakeraremasén.*
   a. *démo*
   b. *hoka*
   c. *shíka*

9. _____ (Tomorrow) *no ása kimashóo.*
   a. *Kinoo*
   b. *Ashita*
   c. *Asátte*

10. *Iroiro* _____ (thanks for your service) *deshita.*
    a. *omachidoosama*
    b. *oki no doku sama*
    c. *oséwasama*

ANSWERS

1-b; 2-a; 3-a; 4-b; 5-c; 6-a; 7-b; 8-c; 9-b; 10-c.

LESSON 39

DÁI SÁNJUU KYÚU KA

TO COME, TO SAY, TO DO

1. **Kuru To come**

Kimásu.	I (you, he, she, we, they) come.
Kité kudasái.	Come!
Koko e kité kudasái.	Come here.
Watakushi to issho ni kité kudasái.	Come with me.

Mata kité kudasái.	Come again.
Uchi máde kité kudasái.	Come to the house.
Ítsu ka yóru kité kudasái.	Come some evening.
Kónaide kudasái.	Don't come.
Dóko kara kimásu ka?	Where are you coming from?
Tookyoo kara kimásu.	I am coming from Tokyo.
Gekijoo kara kimásu.	I am coming from the theater.
Súgu kimásu.	I am coming right away.

-ta bákari desu = to have just completed an action.

| *Amerika kara kitá bákari desu.* | I have just come from the United States. |
| *Sono tegami wa íma kitá bákari desu.* | That letter has just arrived. |

-te kuru = to have just started to, to have started and continued to the present doing.

Áme ga futte kimáshita.	The rain has started to fall.
Nihongo ga wakátte kimáshita.	I have started to understand Japanese. [Japanese has begun to be clear to me.]
Nihongo o rokkágetsu benkyoo shite kimáshita.	I have been studying Japanese for six months.
Nihongo no hón bákari yónde kimáshita.	I have been reading nothing but books in Japanese.

2. *Iu (yuu)* To say

Iimásu.	I (you, he, she, we, they) say

to iu = to say that . . .

Ikanai to iimáshita.	I said that I wouldn't go. [(I) said, "(I) will not go."]
Ikanái ka to iimáshita.	I said, "Aren't you going?" He said, "Aren't you going?"

tó ka iu = to say something to the effect that, to say something like.

Ikanái ka tó ka iimáshita.	He said something like, "Aren't you going (but I am not exactly sure what he said)?"
Hitóri de ittá to ka iimáshita.	He said something to the effect that he went alone.
Iinikúi desu.	It's hard to say.
Itte kudasái.	Say (it)! Tell (it)!
Moo ichido itte kudasái.	Say it again.
Nihongo de itte kudasái.	Say it in Japanese.
Yukkúri itte kudasái.	Say it slowly.
Iwanáide kudasai.	Don't say that.
Sonó hito ni itte kudasái.	Tell (it) to him.

yoo ni iu = to tell someone to

Kúru yoo ni itte kudasái.	Tell him to come.

Kónai yoo ni itte kudasái.	Tell him not to come.
Kau yóo ni itte kudasái.	Tell him to buy (it).
Kawanai yóo ni itte kudasái.	Tell him not to buy (it).
Sonó hito ni iwanáide kudasái.	Don't tell it to him.
Sonó hito ni nani mo iwanáide kudasái.	Don't tell him anything.
Dare ni mo iwanáide kudasái.	Don't tell that to anybody.
Nán to iimáshita ka?	What did you say?
Nán to osshaimáshita ka?	What did you say (*extra polite*)?
Hóteru wa dóko ni áru ka oshiete kudasaimasén ka?	Can you tell me where there is a hotel? [Would you not teach me . . . ?]
Nani mo iimasén deshita.	He hasn't said anything.

QUIZ 29

1. *Gekijoo kara kimasu.*	1. Come with me.
2. *Hitóri de ittá to ka iimáshita.*	2. Where are you coming from?
3. *Súgu kimasu.*	3. Come some evening.
4. *Dóko kara kimásu ka?*	4. I'm coming right away.
5. *Itte kudasái.*	5. I'm coming from the theatre.
6. *Nihongo de itte kudasái.*	6. Say it in Japanese.

7. *Áme ga futte kimáshita.*

7. I have just come from the United States.

8. *Ítsu ka yóru kite kudasái.*

8. The rain has started to fall.

9. *Watakushi to issho ni kite kudasái.*

9. He said something to the effect that he went alone.

10. *Amerika kara kita bákari desu.*

10. Tell me.

ANSWERS

1-5; 2-9; 3-4; 4-2; 5-10; 6-6; 7-8; 8-3; 9-1; 10-7.

3. *Suru* **To do**

Shimásu.	I (you, he, she, we, they) do.
Shimásu.	I do it.
Shite imásu.	I'm doing it.
Náni o shite imásu ka?	What are you doing?
Dóo shimásu ka?	How do you do that?
Náni o shite imáshita ka?	What have you been doing?
Shináide kudasái.	Don't do it!
Moo shináide kudasái.	Don't do it any more.
Shinákereba narimasén.	You must do it.
Shité wa ikemasén.	You mustn't do it.
Moo shité wa ikemasén.	You mustn't do it any more.
Shite shimaimáshita.	It's done. [(I)'ve finished doing (it).]
Nani mo shite imasén.	I'm not doing anything.

Nani mo shináide kudasái.	Don't do anything.
Moo ichido shite kudasái.	Do it once more.
Háyaku shite kudasái.	Do it quickly!
Chúui shite kudasái.	Pay attention!
Benkyoo shite kudasái.	Please study it.
Íma shita bákari desu.	I've just done it now.
Moo oai shimáshita.	I've already met him *(extra polite).*
Dóo shimashóo ka?	What's to be done? What shall we do? What can be done? [How shall we do?]
Dáre ga shimáshita ka?	Who did that?
Doo shitara íi ka wakarimasén.	I don't know what to do.
Óokiku shimashita.	We enlarged (it).
Iku kóto ni shimáshita.	We've decided to go. [(We)'ve acted on (our) going.]

QUIZ 30

1.	*Dóo shimásu ka?*	1.	You mustn't do it.
2.	*Shinai de kudasái.*	2.	Do it quickly.
3.	*Shite shimaimáshita.*	3.	What are you doing?
4.	*Doo shimashóo ka?*	4.	How do you do that?

5. *Chúui shite kudasái.*

5. Don't do it.

6. *Óokiku shimáshita.*

6. It's done.

7. *Moo ichido shite kudasái.*

7. You must do it.

8. *Dáre ga shimáshita ka?*

8. What's to be done?

9. *Íma shita bákari desu.*

9. What have you been doing?

10. *Iku kóto ni shimáshita.*

10. Do it once more.

11. *Shinákereba ikemasén.*

11. Pay attention.

12. *Shité wa ikemasén.*

12. We've decided to go.

13. *Náni o shite imásu ka?*

13. I've just done it now.

14. *Háyaku shite kudasái.*

14. We made it large.

15. *Náni o shite imáshita ka?*

15. Who did that?

ANSWERS

1-4; 2-5; 3-6; 4-8; 5-11; 6-14; 7-10; 8-15; 9-13;
10-12; 11-7; 12-1; 13-3; 14-2; 15-9.

REVIEW QUIZ 8

1. *Sugu* _____ (I'm coming).
   a. *kite imasu.*
   b. *kimasu.*
   c. *kimashita.*

2. _____ (Hard to say) *desu.*
   a. *Inikúi desu.*
   b. *Ikinikúi desu.*
   c. *Iinikúi desu.*

3. *Náni o* _____ (do) *imásu ka?*
   a. *shitte*
   b. *shite*
   c. *shiite*

4. *Dóo* _____ (do) *íi ka wakarimasén.*
   a. *ittára*
   b. *shitára*
   c. *shitára*

5. *Anó hito wa rippa na uchí o* _____ (have).
   a. *tsukútte imásu.*
   b. *mótte imásu.*
   c. *sagashite imásu.*

6. _____ (Don't take) *kudasaí.*
   a. *Toránaide*
   b. *Mínaide*
   c. *Nománaide*

7. *Súgu* _____ (stop) *kudasái.*
   a. *tomatte*
   b. *tátte*
   c. *tábete*

8. *Ashita wa íi otenki ni náreba ii to* _____
   (hope).
   a. *iimásu.*
   b. *omoimásu.*
   c. *kakimáshita.*

9. *Watakushi wa* _____ (did not see).
   a. *ma ni aimasén deshita.*
   b. *mairimasén deshita.*
   c. *mimasén deshita.*

10. *Moo ichido* _____ (see) *kudasái.*
    a. *míte*
    b. *nite*
    c. *shite*

11. *Ano hito no banchi wa* _____ (do not know).
    a. *arimasén.*
    b. *shirimasén.*
    c. *chigaimásu.*

12. *Sono kóto wa máe kara yóku* _____ (know).
    a. *zonji ágete orimásu.*
    b. *shitte orimásu.*
    c. *benkyoo shite orimásu.*

13. *Íma denwa de* _____ (is talking).
    a. *kotáete imásu.*
    b. *kiite imásu.*
    c. *hanáshite imásu.*

14. *Íma súgu iku* _____ (can).
    a. *tsumori desu.*
    b. *kotó ga dekimásu.*
    c. *hazu désu.*

15. *Anó hito wa watakushi no iu koto ga yóku*
    _____ (understands).
    a. *dekimásu.*
    b. *wakarimásu.*
    c. *kikoemásu.*

16. *Booshi o* _____ (please buy).
    a. *tótte kudasái.*
    b. *katte kudasái.*
    c. *mótte kudasái.*

17. *Kono machí ni* _____ (person I know) *wa hitori mo orimasén.*
    a. *yónde iru hito*
    b. *shite iru hito*
    c. *shitte iru hito*

18. *Moo sukóshi* _____ (want) *desu.*
    a. *hóshikatta*
    b. *hóshikunai*
    c. *hoshíi*

19. *Íkutsu* _____ (left) *imásu ka?*
    a. *nokótte*
    b. *katte*
    c. *mótte*

20. *Ítsu* _____ (must you go) *ka?*
    a. *ikanákute mo íi desu*
    b. *ikanákereba narimasén*
    b. *itté wa ikenái desu*

ANSWERS

1-b; 2-c; 3-b; 4-c; 5-b; 6-a; 7-a; 8-b; 9-c; 10-a; 11-b; 12-a; 13-c; 14-b; 15-b; 16-b; 17-c; 18-c; 19-a; 20-b.

I'M A STRANGER HERE

Gomen kudasái.
Hello. [Pardon.]

Aa Súmisu-san desu ka. Omachi shite orimáshita.
Oh, Mr. Smith. I've been waiting for you.

Kyóo wa dóo mo oisogashíi tokore o arígatoo gozaimásu.

I certainly appreciate your taking time out for me. [Thank you (for taking the time for me) when you are so busy.]

Doo itashimáshite. Oyasui goyóo desu. Dé wa súgu dekakemashóo.

Don't mention it. Shall we get going?

Watakushi wa máda migi mo hidari mo wakarimasén kara yoroshiku onegai itashimásu.

I'm a total stranger here. [(I) can't even tell right from left, and would appreciate (your) taking me around.]

Hái, kashikomarimáshita. Yuubínkyoku ni goyóo ga aru to osshaimáshita ne.

Surely. You said you wanted to go to the post office, didn't you?

É, sóo na n desu.

Yes, that's right.

Dé wa kono michi o ikimashóo.

Then lets take this street.

Kono michi no namae wa nán to yuu n desu ka?

What's the name of this street?

Shoowa Doori to iimásu. Ómo na misé wa taitei koko ni arimásu.

(It)'s Showa Street. Most of the important stores are here.

Nakanaka nigíyaka na tokoro désu ne.
It's quite busy here, isn't it?

E, ítsu mo kóo desu.
Yes, it is always crowded here, day and night.

Áa, ano ookíi tatemóno wa nán desu ka?
Oh, yes. What's that big building over there?

Aa, aré desu ka?
You mean that one?

E.
Yes (that one).

Are wa depáato desu.
Oh, a department store.

**Hoo, asoko ní wa Amerika no shokuryóohin
nado mo arimásu ka?**
[Oh, I see.] Do they sell any American food?

Ikura ka arimásu.
Not much but some.

**Sore kara íma no depáato no tonari no
tatemóno wa nán desu ka?**
What's that building next to the department store?
[And then . . .]

**Shiyákusho desu. Súgu ushiro ni Keisatsusho ga
arimásu.**
That is City Hall. The Police Station is right back
of it.

Hoo, kore wa zúibun ookíi kusuriya desu ne.
Isn't that a big drugstore! [Oh I see . . .]

Ée, kore wa Amerikan Fáamashii to itte Nippon no kusuri mo gaikoku no kusuri mo utte imasu.

Yes, this is called (the) American Pharmacy and carries both Japanese and foreign drugs.

Sóo desu ka? Kono machí ni wa íi byooin ga arimásu ka?

Is that right? Is there a good hospital in this city?

Hái, íkutsu mo arimásu ga, ma, Daigaku Byóoin ga ichiban íi deshoo.

Yes, there are quite a few of them, but—well— perhaps the best is the University Hospital.

Aa sóo desu ka.

Oh, I see.

Daigaku Byóoin ni wa Eigo no yóku dekíru isha ga takusan imásu.

There are many doctors there who speak English.

Soo desu ka? Dóko ni áru n desu ka?

Is that right? Where is it?

Daigaku no kóonai desu ga, koko o hashítte iru básu de iku to nijúppun gurai desu.

It's on the university campus. If you take the bus from here, you can get there in twenty minutes.

Mmm? Kore wa rippa na hóteru desu ne.

Hmm? This is a fine hotel, isn't it?

Sóo desu née. Gaikokújin wa taitei koko ni tomarimásu.

Yes. Foreigners usually stay here.

Haa? Sore kara éki wa dóko desu ka?
I see. Then where is the railroad station?

Tsugí no kádo o migi ni magatte ítchoo desu.
You turn right at the next corner. It's one block
    from there.

Al Kisha no jikokuhyoo ga hoshíi n desu ga . . .
[Oh, (I remember).] I wanted to get a timetable.

**E! Sore nára éki made ikanákute mo te ni
    hairimasu. Sono kádo no hón'ya de utte
    imásu.**
[Yes,] if that's the case, you don't have to go to the
    station. You can buy [get hold of] (one) at the
    bookstore on the corner.

Kisha no jikokuhyoo wa kaú n desu ka?
So you have to pay for it, do you?

**Ée, sóo na n desu. Kono kuni dé wa jikokuhyoo
    wa kawanákereba narimasén.**
That's right. In this country you have to buy train
    timetables.

Sóo desu ka. Sore wa shirimasén deshita.
Oh, I see. I didn't know that.

**Yuubínkyoku wa súgu soko désu ga, jikokuhyoo
    o kaú no wa íma ni shimásu ka soretomo ato
    ni shimásu ka?**
The post office is right there but do you want to
    buy the timetable now or [otherwise] later?

**Sóo desu née. Áto ni shimashoo. Saki ni denpoo
    o útte shimaitái desu kara.**
Let me see. I'll buy it later. I would like to send a
    telegram first.

Aa sóo desu ka. Sore ja súgu ikimashóo.
Oh, I see. Then let's go right away.

Onegai itashimásu.
That'll be fine.

Kore ga yuubínkyoku desu.
This is the post office.

Zúibun kónde imásu ne.
It's quite crowded, isn't it?

Denpoo no madóguchi wa hidari no hóo desu.
The telegraph window [window for telegraph] is to the left.

Aa wakarimáshita. Asoko desu ne.
Oh, yes. I see it. That's it, isn't it?

Sóo desu. Watakushi wa koko no bénchi de omachi shimashóo.
Right. I'll be waiting for you at the bench here.

Sóo desu ka. Dé wa onegai itashimásu.
Fine! I would appreciate that.

Goyukkúri dóozo.
Don't hurry.

QUIZ 31

1. _____ (Don't mention it.)
   a. *Gomen kudasái.*
   b. *Dóo itashimáshite.*
   c. *Kashikomarimáshita.*

2. _____ (The post office) *ni ikimashóo.*
   a. *yuubínkyoku*
   b. *denshínkyoku*
   c. *jimúsho*

3. *Migi mo hidari mo* _____ (can't tell).
   a. *miemasén*
   b. *wakarimasén*
   c. *kakimasén*

4. *Kono machí ni wa* _____ (hospital) *ga arimásu
   ka?*
   a. *byooin*
   b. *byooki*
   c. *biyóoin*

5. *Kono* _____ (street) *no namae wa nán to iimásu
   ka?*
   a. *machí*
   b. *michi*
   c. *uchi*

6. *Ano ookíi* _____ (building) *wa nán desu ka?*
   a. *tabemóno*
   b. *uchi*
   c. *tatemóno*

7. *Depáato no* _____ (next) *ni Shiyákusho ga
   arimásu.*
   a. *tonari*
   b. *ushiro*
   c. *máe*

8. *Gaikokújin wa taitei kono hóteru ni* _____
   (stay).
   a. *sumimásu*
   b. *yasumimásu*
   c. *tomarimásu*

9. _____ (Telegram) *o útte shimotái desu.*
   a. *Denwa*
   b. *Densha*
   c. *Denpoo*

10. _____ (The railway station) *wa dóko desu ka?*
   a. *Éki*
   b. *Kishá*
   c. *Shiyákusho*

ANSWERS

1-b; 2-a; 3-b; 4-a; 5-b; 6-c; 7-a; 8-c; 9-c; 10-a.

LESSON 40   DAI YONJUKKA

THE MOST COMMON VERB FORMS

I EAT, FINISH, COME, DO

1. **Plain Forms**

	I EAT (VOWEL VERB)	I FINISH (CONSONANT VERB)	I COME (IRREGULAR VERBS)	I DO
PRESENT	*tabéru*	*owaru*	*kúru*	*suru*
-*ta* FORM (PAST)	*tábeta*	*owatta*	*kitá*	*shita*
-*te* FORM (GERUND)	*tábete*	*owatte*	*kité*	*shite*
TENTATIVE	*tabeyóo*	*owaróo*	*koyóo*	*shiyóo*
INFINITIVE	*tabe*	*owari*	*ki*	*shi*

Verbs ending in -*eru* or -*iru,* with some exceptions, take all the forms listed above for *taberu.*

For example:

| *haréru* | the sky clears |
| *atsuméru* | gathers (something) |

hajimeru	starts (something)
ochíru	falls

All other verbs, except *kúru* [comes] and *suru* [does], which are irregular, are declined like *owaru*. For construction of the *-te* and *-ta* forms, see Lesson 12, page 57.

For example:

agaru	rises
arau	washes
atsumáru	gathers
hakáru	measures

a. To make the various forms, you add the following endings to the stem *(tabe-, owar-)*:

	VOWEL VERBS	CONSONANT VERBS
PRESENT	*-ru*	*-u*
PAST (*-ta* FORM)	*-ta*	*-ta, -tta, -ita, -nda*[1]
GERUND (*-te* FORM)	*-te*	*-te, -tte, -ita, -nda*[1]
TENTATIVE	*-yoo*	*-oo*
INFINITIVE	—	*-i*

b. Some irregular *-te* and *-ta* forms:

	PRESENT	*-te* FORM	*-ta* FORM
I go	*iku*	*itte*	*itta*
You go, he goes (extra polite)	*irassháru*	*irasshátte* (regular) *iráshite* *iráshitte*	*irasshátta* *iráshita* *iráshitta*

c. Some irregular infinitive forms used in extra-polite speech:

[1] See Lesson 12, page 56.

	PRESENT	INFINITIVE
there is	*gozáru*[1]	*gozai (másu)*
you go, he goes	*irassháru*	*irasshai (másu)*
he says	*ossháru*	*osshai (másu)*
he gives	*kudasáru*	*kudasai (másu)*
he does	*nasáru*	*nasai (másu)*

2. Polite Forms

tabemásu	I eat, I'll eat
tabemáshita	I ate
tábete, tabemáshite	I eat and . . .
Tabemashóo.	I think I'll eat.
owarimásu	I finish, I'll finish
owarimáshita	I finished
owatte, owarimáshite	I finish and . . .
owarimashóo	I finish and . . .
kimásu	I come
kimáshita	I came
kite, kimáshite	I come and . . .
Kimashóo.	I think I'll come.
shimásu	I do, I'll do
shimáshita	I did
shite, shimáshite	I do and . . .
shimashóo	I think I'll do

3. Future

Taberu Eat	*Owaru* Finish	*Kuru* Come	*Auru* Do
tabemásu	*owarimásu*	*kimásu*	*shimásu*
tabemashóo	*owarima-shóo*	*kimashóo*	*shimashóo*

[1]This present plain form is not used in modern spoken Japanese.

tabéru	*owarú*	*kúru deshoo surú deshoo*
deshóo	*deshoo*	

Notice that the forms used to express the future vary. If the event under discussion is definite, you use *-masu,* the same form used for the present. If it is not definite, you use *-mashoo* or *-(r)u deshoo.* Use *-mashoo* when it depends on you, the speaker, whether the event will take place or not; use *-(r)u deshoo* when it does not depend on you. Compare these forms:

Tabemásu.	I shall eat it.
	I will eat it.
	I eat it.
	[Eating takes place definitely, in the present, the future, or the past.]

Tabemashóo.	I think I'll eat it.
	Let's eat it.
	[(It)'s not definite but (I) think (I)'ll eat; (the choice) is up to me (us).]

Tabéru deshoo.	I think he will eat it.
	[(It)'s not definite, but he will probably eat it; it's not up to me.]

Denwa o kakemashóo.	Let's phone.
Kawáku deshoo.	It'll dry, I think.
Júppun de kawakimásu.	It will dry in ten minutes (definitely).
Kutsú o migakimashóo.	I think I will polish my shoes.

Koko ni oitára nakunaru deshóo.	If you leave it here, it will get lost (I think).
Súgu naóru deshoo.	He'll get well soon.
Tanaka-san ni tanomimashóo.	Let's ask Mr. Tanaka to do it.
Yamada-san ga tetsudáu deshoo.	Mr. Yamada will probably help you.
Sonna ni hataraitára tsukaréru deshoo.	If you work so hard, you will probably get tired.
Tsuzukemashóo.	Let's continue it.

4. Past

tabemáshita	*owari-máshita*	*kimáshita*	*shimáshita*
(from *tabéru*)	(from *owaru*)	(from *kúru*)	(from *suru*)

The -*máshita* form expresses an action or state that is already completed, and in most cases is equivalent to the past and present perfect tenses in English.

For example:

Tsutsumimáshita.	I wrapped it up.
Ugokashimáshita.	I moved it.
Ugokimáshita.	It moved.
Urimáshita.	I sold it.
Utaimáshita.	I sang it.
Wakemáshita.	I divided it.
Waraimáshita.	I laughed.
Warimáshita.	I broke it.
Watashimáshita.	I handed it.
Yaburimáshita.	I tore it.

5. I Used to . . .

Tábeta monó deshita.
Tábeta monó desu. } I used to eat.

Owatta monó deshita.
Owatta monó desu. } I used to finish.

Kitá monó deshita.
Kitá monó desu. } I used to come.

Shita monó deshita.
Shita monó desu. } I used to do.

Use the -ta form plus monó deshita (or desu) when referring to an action or state that used to take place but no longer does.

For example:

Bikkúri shita monó deshita.   I used to be surprised.

Té de hakonda monó deshita.   I used to carry it by hand.

Maitoshi hikkóshita monó deshita.   I used to move every year.

Ichínen ni nijippóndo mo futótta monó deshita.   I used to gain as much [weight] as twenty pounds every year.

6. I Have . . .

Tábeta kotó ga arimásu.   I have eaten it.

Yónda kotó ga arimásu.   I have read it.

Kitá koto ga arimásu.   I have come.

Shita kotó ga arimásu.   I have done (it).

Most of the ideas expressed in English by the present perfect ("have" plus the past participle) are expressed in Japanese by the use of the -*máshita* form. However, when you mean that you have had the experience of doing something one or more times in the past, you use the -*ta* from plus *koto ga arimásu*.

For example:

Eigo ni yakúshita koto ga arimásu.	I [have] once translated it into English.
Eigo ni yakushimáshita.	I [have] translated it into English.
Tabako wa máe ni yameta kotó ga arimásu.	I have once before stopped [discontinued] smoking.
Hyaku póndo made yaseta kotó ga arimásu.	Once my weight was down to one hundred pounds. [I have once lost my weight down to one hundred pounds.]
Sono kotó ni tsúite shirábeta koto ga arimásu.	I have [once] made an investigation concerning that matter.

7. I Had ...

Tábete arimáshita.	I had eaten it. [(It) had been eaten.]
Yónde arimáshita.	I had read it. [(It) had been read.]
Kité imáshita.	I had come.
Shite arimáshita.	I had done it. [(It) had been done.]

In most cases the ideas expressed in English by the past perfect ("had" plus the past participle) can be expressed in Japanese by *-te arimáshita* for transitive verbs and *-te imáshita* for intransitive verbs. Note that in the case of transitive verbs, however, the object of the verb in Japanese becomes the subject in English.

For example:

Kudámono wa katte arimáshita.	I had purchased the fruit (when he arrived). [The fruit had been purchased . . .]
Haná wa móo chitte imáshita.	The flowers had already fallen off (the trees when we went there).
Purogúramu wa móo hajimatte imáshita.	The program had already started (when we arrived there).
Zaseki wa tótte arimáshita.	He had already taken the seats (for us when we arrived).

8. Imperatives and Requests

Each verb has a form called the "imperative" which is very brusque and is used almost exclusively in a conversation between men. This form should not be used in a normal, quiet situation. To form the imperative, add *-ro* to the stem for vowel verbs and *-e* to the stem for consonant verbs.

Tabéro!	Eat!
Déteike!	Leave!
Damáre!	Shut up!

Kói![1]	Come!
Háyaku shiro![2]	Do it quickly!

Notice that an ordinary polite request ends in *-te kudasái* for the affirmative. To form the negative, add *-anáide kudasái* to the stem of a consonant verb and *-náide kudasái* to the stem of a vowel verb.

Yománaide kudasái.	Please don't read.
Tabénaide kudasái.	Please don't eat.

To form an even more polite expression of request, prefix the infinitive of the verb with *o-* and add *kudasái* or *ni nátte kudasái* for the affirmative. Form the negative as in the paragraph above.

Otori kudasái. ⎫	Take it.
Otori ni nátte kudasái. ⎭	
Otori ni naránaide kudasái.	Please do not take it.
Tetsudátte kudasái.	Help me! [Give hand, please.]
Moo sukóshi motté kite kudasái.	Bring me some more.
Watakushi no tokoro e motté kite kudasái.	Bring it to me. [Bring it to my place.]
Tomatte kudasái!	Stop!
Súgu tomatte kudasái!	Stop right here!
Sonó hito o tomete kudasái!	Stop him.
Koshikákete kudasái. ⎫	Sit down. Have a seat.
Okoshikake kudasái. ⎭	
Shínjite kudasái.	Believe me!
Kiite kudasái.	Listen.

[1]Irregular: from *kúru*
[2]Irregular: from *suru*

Watakushi no iu kóto o kiite kudasái.	Listen to me. [Listen to what I say.]
Kore o kiite kudasái.	Listen to this.
Chúui shite kiite kudasái.	Listen carefully.
Anó hito no iu kóto o kiite kudasái.	Listen to him *(firmly)*.
Anó hito no iu kóto o kikanáide kudasái.	Don't listen to him.
Háitte kudasái.	Come in! Enter!
Ohairi kudasai.	Come in. Enter *(extra polite)*.
Sonó hito no tokoró e okutte kudasái.	Send it to him.
Watakushi no tokoró e okutte kudasái.	Send them (it) to me.
Sonó hito no tokoro e íkuraka okutte kudasái.	Send him some.
Watakushi no tokoró e íkuraka okutte kudasái.	Send me some.
Taméshite kudasai.	Try. [Please check!]
Tamesánaide kudasai.	Don't try!
Tábete mite kudasái.	Try eating it.
Yónde mite kudasái.	Try reading it.
Kao o aratte kudasái.	Wash yourself! [Wash your face.]
Tátte kudasái.	Please stand up! Please get up!
Otachi kudasái.	Please stand up. Kindly rise *(extra polite)*.
Yónde kudasái.	Read that!
Watakushi o soko e tsurete ítte kudasái.	Take me there!

Moo hitótsu otori kudasái.	Take another one *(extra polite)*. [Please take one more.]
Kishá de itte kudasái.	Take the train. [Go by train.]
Kishá de oide kudasái.	Take the train *(extra polite)*. [Please go by train.]
Tákushii de itte kudasái.	Take a taxi.
Míte kudasai.	Look!
Goran ni nátte kudasái.	Please look *(extra polite)*!
Moo ichido míte kudasái.	Look again!
Koko o míte kudasái.	Look here!
Watakushi o míte kudasái.	Look at me!
Kore o míte kudasái.	Look at this!
Mínai de kudasái.	Don't look.
Goran ni naránaide kudasái.	Don't look *(extra polite)*.
Káeshite kudasái.	Return it to me.
Okaeshi ni nátte kudasái.	Return it to me *(extra polite)*.
Soko o agatte kudasái.	Go up there.
Mísete kudasái.	Show me!
Misénaide kudasái.	Don't show it!
Wasurenáide kudasái.	Don't forget.
Déte itte kudasái.	Leave!
Súgu déte itte kudasái.	Leave quickly! Go right away!
Déte ikanáide kudasái.	Don't leave!
Kore o asoko e motté itte kudasái.	Carry this over there!
Tótte kudasái.	Take it.

Otori kudasái.	Please take it *(extra polite)*.
Otori ni nátte kudasái. *Torinasái.*	Take it. [I'm ordering you.]
Toránaide kudasái.	Don't take it.
Otori ni naránaide kudasái.	Please don't take it *(extra polite)*.
Uchi e káette kudasái.	Go home!
Háyaku uchi e káette kudasái.	Go home early!
Moo ichido itte kudasái.	Say it again.
Moo ichido osshátte kudasái.	Please say it again *(extra polite)*.
Ite kudasái.	Stay.
Koko ni ite kudasái.	Stay here.
Shízuka ni shite kudasái.	Be quiet.
Ugokánaide kudasái.	Be still. Don't move.
Tsúite kite kudasái.	Follow. Follow me.
Anó hito ni tsúite itte kudasái.	Follow him.
Sawaranáide kudasái.	Don't touch!
Koohíi o tsuide kudasái.	Pour me some coffee.

KYUUYUU TO NO SAIKAI

MEETING AN OLD FRIEND

Study the notes at the end of this section for greater comprehension.

1. **Y:**[1] **Zuibun hisashiburi désu ne? Ogénki desu ka?**

   Y: Well! (Long time no see!) How are you?

2. **S:** **Okage sama de. Otaku wa?**

   S: Fine, thanks. (And) you and your family?

3. **Y:** **Arígatoo. Minna tassha desu. Nagái goryokoo de otsukare deshóo.**

   Y: Thanks, we're all well. (You're) not too tired from your trip?

4. **S** **Íya. Betsu ni.**

   Not at all.

5. **Y:** **A! Kánai o goshookai itashimashóo.**

   Y: [Oh, yes.] I'd like you to meet my wife.

6. **S:** **Dóozo.**

   I'd be very happy to.

7. **Y:** **Kochira wa Sátoo-san.**

   Y: This is (my friend) Sato.

8. **S:** **Hajimemáshite. Dóozo yoroshiku.**

   S: I am very happy to know you.

9. **Mrs. Y:** **Kochira kóso.**

   Mrs. Y: Glad to know you.

10. **S:** **Yaa. Hisashiburi de yúkai desu ne.**

    S: Yes, indeed. It's really good to see you again.

11. **Y:** **Yáa. Mattaku dookan desu. Tokí ni Satoo-san anata wa chittó mo kawarimasén ne.**

   Y: Yes, indeed. By the way, you haven't changed a bit.

12. **S:** **Iyaa. Sono ten ja anáta mo sukoshi mo kawatte imasén yo.**

   S: Neither have you. [No, in that respect you haven't changed a bit.]

13. **Mrs. Y:** **Ókusama wa Amerika no goseikatsu o otanoshimi désu ka?**

   Mrs. Y: How does Mrs. Sato like the United States?

14. **S:** **Ée. Hijoo ni tanoshínde orimásu.**

   S: [Yes.] She likes it a lot.

15. **Mrs. Y:** **Achira wa Tookyoo tó wa daibu chigaú no de gozaimashóo ne?**

   Mrs. Y: It must be very different from Tokyo.

16. **S:** **Táshika ni chigau tokoró wa arimásu ne.**

   S: There certainly are lots of very curious things in the United States!

17. **Mrs. Y:** **Tatóeba dóo iu tokoró na no de gozaimásu no?**

   Mrs. Y: For example?

18. **S:** **Tatóeba desu ne, so, kusuriya de shokuji o surú nado to itté mo chótto gosoozoo ni narénai deshoo?**

   S: For example [so, (here is a good one)], it certainly wouldn't occur to you to have lunch in a pharmacy.

19. **Y:** **Joodán deshoo.**
    Y: You're joking!

20. **S:** **Íya. Majime na hanashí desu yo.**
    S: Not at all. I'm very serious.

21. **Mrs. Y: Máa! Kusuriya de oshokuji o na-sáru!**
    Mrs. Y: (Imagine) eating [having a meal] in a pharmacy!

22. **S:** **Sóo na n desu yo. Bifuteki dátte aru n desu yo, ókusan.**
    S: Yes, you can even have a steak.

23. **Y:** **Kusuriya ní?**
    Y: In a pharmacy?

24. **S:** **Sóo na n desu. Dezáato ni wa oishii aisukuríimu ga arimásu shi ne.**
    S: Yes, in a pharmacy—with excellent ice cream for dessert.

25. **Mrs. Y: Démo kusuri no niói ga oki ni nari-masén?**
    Mrs. Y: But the smell of the pharmacy—doesn't that bother you?

26. **S:** **Niói nanka shimasén yo.**
    S: There isn't any smell.

27. **Y:** **Hee? Kusuri o utte ité mo desu ka?**
    Y: Really? Even when they sell drugs?

28. **S:** **Ee. Sore ga shinái n desu yo. Amerika no Doragu Sutoa wa.**
    S: No [yes, (what you said is right)] there isn't any in American "drug-stores."

29. **Y:**   **Hoo . . . á, wakátta. Iwayuru Nihon de yuu kusuriya to chigaú n desu ne.**

    Y: [Hmm . . .] Oh! That's the trick! It's a different place from the kind of place we call pharmacy in Japan, isn't it?

30. **Y:**   **Dakara yakkyoku ja nái to iu wáke na n desu ne.**

    Y: Therefore it's no longer a pharmacy.

31. **S:**   **E. Doragu Sutoa dé wa omócha tó ka, kitte tó ka, tabako tó ka okáshi no yóo na monó made mo utterú n desu.**

    S.   You also find many other things in a drugstore: toys, stamps, cigarettes, candy . . .

32. **Y:**   **Hoo . . . ! Kawatte irú n desu ne?**
    Y: Hmm! That's really very funny.

33. **S:**   **Máda sono ué ni hón mo áru, bunbóogu mo áru, daidokoro yóogu mo áru, keshóohin mo áru, maa, náni mo ká mo áru to itta katachi désu yo.**

    S: . . . books, stationery, cooking utensils, toilet articles, and what-have-you.

34. **Y:**   **Hmm! Ma, yorozuya to iu wáke desu ne.**

    Y: Hmm? [So to speak] it's a general store, then?

35. **S:**   **Ee, démo kusuri wa chan to utterú n desu yo.**

    S: No, it's (still) a pharmacy!

NOTES

Title: *Kyuuyuu tó no Saikai* = Meeting an Old Friend

1. *Hisashiburi désu* = It has been a long time since (I saw you last).

2. *Otaku wa* = your family, you.

3. *Goryokoo de* = on account of a long trip. *Otsukare deshóo* = you must be tired.

4. *Íya* (same as *iie*) = no. *Betsu ni* = (not) especially.

7. *Sátoo-san:* Note the use of *san* in spite of Sato's being Yamada's old friend. Adding a *san* is a common practice regardless of the extent of the friendship. The first name is not usually mentioned in a situation like this.

11. *Mattaku dookan desu* = I'm in complete agreement with you. [The] same here. *Toki ni* = by the way. *Satoo-san:* Notice the use of the surname of the person with whom you are speaking. *Kawarimasen* = (you) don't change.

12. *Kawatte imasén* = You haven't changed. [You are not in the state of having changed.]

13. *Tanoshímu* = enjoy; *otanoshimi de irasshaimásu: o* plus the infinitive plus *de irasshaimásu* (or *de gozaimásu*) = an extra-polite expression often used by women in somewhat formal speech.

17. *Tatóeba* = for instance.

18. *Desu ne* = a meaningless expression similar to the American phrase, "you know."

Gosoozoo ni narénai = you cannot imagine
(extra polite); *naréru* = potential form derived
from the consonant verb *náru*.

22. *Dátte* (same as *dé mo* = even (used in everyday speech).

24. *Shi:* adds the feeling of, "and it's in addition to
what I've said."

25. *Oki ni narimasén* (when spoken with a rising
intonation) = doesn't it bother you? (an extra-
polite form of *ki ni náru* [something bothers]).

26. *Nánka* = and things like that (used in everyday
speech); *nánka* is usually mutually exclusive
with the particles *ga, wa,* and *o*.

27. *Utte ité mo desu ka* = is it so even when they
are selling medicines?

28. Notice the inverted word order used in informal conversation.

29. *Wakátta* = I've got it. [(It) has become clear.]

30. *Yakkyoku* = pharmacy

31. ... *tó ka* ... *tó ka* ... *tó ka* (comparable to
... *ya* ... *ya* ... *ya*) = and ... and ... and
(with the implication that the listing is incomplete).

32. *Kawatte iru* = is different.

33. *Sono úe ni* = on top of that.
Náni mo ká mo = and what-have-you; everything.

34. *To iu wáke desu* = it amounts to saying; it
means. *Yorozuya* = ten-thousand-variety
shop; general store.

QUIZ 32

1. _____ (Long time no see) *desu ne.*
   a. *Omoshirói*
   b. *Atatakái*
   c. *Hisashiburi*

2. _____ (Fine, thanks) *sama de.*
   a. *Oki no doku*
   b. *Okage*
   c. *Omachidoo*

3. *Nagái goryokoo de* _____ (tired) *deshoo.*
   a. *omoshírokatta*
   b. *otanoshimi*
   c. *otsukare*

4. _____ (Wife) *o goshookai itashimashóo.*
   a. *Kánai*
   b. *Kodomo*
   c. *Tomodachi*

5. *Hisashiburi de* _____ (pleasure) *desu ne.*
   a. *arigatái*
   b. *yúkai*
   c. *saiwai*

6. _____ (Not at all) *kawarimasén ne.*
   a. *Anmari*
   b. *Sukóshi shika*
   c. *Chittó mo*

7. _____ (Serious) *na hanashí desu.*
   a. *Majime*
   b. *Kantan*
   c. *Hén*

8. _____ (Delicious) *aisukuríimu ga arimásu.*
   a. *Oishii*
   b. *Takái*
   c. *Yasíi*

9. _____ (Bother) *ni narimasén ka?*
   a. *Oki*
   b. *Okaki*
   c. *Oiya*

10. _____ (On top of that) *hón mo bunbóogu mo arimásu.*
    a. *Sono kawari ni*
    b. *Sono ué ni*
    c. *Sono misé ni*

ANSWERS

1-c; 2-b; 3-c; 4-a; 5-b; 6-c; 7-a; 8-a; 9-a; 10-b.

THE MOST COMMON VERBS AND VERB PHRASES

1. *Miru* To see

míru	*mimásu*	I see
míta	*mimáshita*	I saw
míte	*míte*	I see (saw) and . . .
miyóo	*mimashóo*	I think I'll see.
mínai	*mimasén*	I don't see

Mimashóo.	Let's see. Let's take a look.
Mimasén.	I don't see.
Nan de mo mimásu.	He sees everything.

Notice that *míru* means "to see" only in the sense of perceiving by the eye. Study the following:

Níkkoo o míta koto ga arimásu ka?	Have you ever seen the Nikko (Shrine)?
Yamada-san ni átta koto ga arimásu ka?	Have you ever seen Mr. Yamada?
Íma atta bákari desu.	I've just seen him.
Watakushi wa éiga o mimasén.	I don't go to the movies. [I don't see movies.]
Anata no iu kóto ga wakarimasen.	I don't see what you mean.
Dónata ni oai ni narimásu ka?	Whom do you see?
Íma átte itadakemásu ka?	Can you see me now *(extra polite)*? [Can (I) have (you) see me now?]
Ítsu ka yóru asobi ni oide kudasái.	Come to see us some evening *(extra polite)*.

2. Shitte iru To know
Shiru To learn, To get to know

shitte iru	*shitte imásu*	I know
shitte ita	*shitte imáshita*	I knew
shitté ite	*shitté ite*	I know (knew) and . . .
shitte iyóo	*shitte imashóo*	I think I'll know
shitte inai	*shitte imasén*	I don't know
shiranai	*shirimasén*	I don't know
shiru	*shirimásu*	I learn
shitta	*shirimáshita*	I learned
shitte	*shitte*	I learn (learned) and . . .
shiróo	*shirimashóo*	I think I'll learn
shiranai	*shirimasén*	I don't learn

Shitte imásu.	I know it. [I'm in the state of having learned it.]
Shirimasén.	I don't know. [I haven't learned.]
Yóku shitte imásu.	I know it well.
Nani mo shirimasén.	He doesn't know anything.
Sono kóto ni tsúite wa nani mo shirimasén.	I don't know anything about it.
Koko ni iru kóto o shitte imásu.	I know that he is here. [I know the fact that he is here.]
Sore o shitte imásu ka?	Do you know that?
Dóko ni irú ka shitte imásu ka?	Do you know where he is?
Sono kóto ni tsúite wa kore íjoo shirimasén.	He doesn't know any more [than this] about it.
Sono kóto ni tsúite wa anáta ga shitte iru yóo ni wa shirimasén.	He doesn't know any more about it than you do [know].
Sono kóto wa shinbun de shirimáshita.	I learned (of) it through the newspaper.

3. *Mótsu* To hold

mótsu	*mochimásu*	I hold
mótta	*mochimáshita*	I held
mótte	*mótte*	I hold (held) and . . .
motóo	*mochimashóo*	I think I'll hold
motánai	*mochimasén*	I don't hold

Kore o chótto mótte kudasái.	Hold this for me a moment.
Té ni booshi o mótte imásu.	He's holding a hat in his hand.

Íma wa mótte imásu.	I have it now.
Shikkári mótte kudasái.	Hold firm.

Notice that the ideas expressed by the English word "have" and "possess" are expressed in Japanese by using the *-te* form of the verb *mótsu* [to hold] plus *imásu*. Compare the following:

Okane wa íkura mótte imásu ka?	How much money have you?
Nisen en mótte imasu.	I have two thousand yen.
Sore wa omosugimásu kara hitóri de mótsu koto wa dekimasén.	It's too heavy [and] so I can't hold it alone.

Notice also that the ideas expressed in English by "take (to)," "bring," and "carry around," are expressed in Japanese by using the *-te* form of the verb *mótsu* together with the verb *iku* [go], *kúru* [come], *arúku* [walk]. Compare the following:

Kása o motte ítte kudasái.	Take your umbrella (with you).
Kása o motté kite kudasái.	Bring over (your) umbrella.
Anó hito wa ítsu mo kása o mótte arukimásu.	He always carries his umbrella around.

4. *Dekiru* To be able

dekíru	*dekimásu*	I can
dékita	*dekimáshita*	I could
dékite	*dékite*	I can (could) and . . .
dekiyóo	*dekimashóo*	I think I can
dekínai	*dekimasén*	I can't

Dekimasén.	I can't.
Suru kotó ga dekimásu.	I can't do it.
Kúru koto ga dekimásu ka?	Can you come?
Sono shitsumon ní wa kotaéru koto ga dekimasén.	I can't answer the question.
Mendoo náku dekimásu.	You can do it without any difficulty.
Soko e iku kóto ga dekimasén.	I can't go there.
Ítsu déru koto ga dekimásu ka?	When can we leave?
Tetsudátte kudasáru koto ga dekimásu ka?	Can you help me?
Anó hito wa karada ga warúi desu kara ryokoo dekimasén.	Since he is sick, he can't travel.
Rainen máde sotsugyoo dekimasén.	He can't graduate till next year.

Notice that *dekimasén* can follow some nouns without employing a particle. In such a case, it means, "can (do something)."

The idea "to be able to (do something)" or "can (do something)" can be expressed in several ways. The most common is by the use of *koto ga dekíru,* demonstrated above. Some other ways follow:

a. For consonant verbs only.

Drop the final *-u* of the plain present and add *-eru.* The resulting form is a vowel verb which means "capable of doing something."

For example:

CONSONANT VERB		DERIVED VOWEL VERB	
iku	go	*ikeru*	can go
kau	buy	*kaeru*	can buy
hanásu	speak	*hanaséru*	can speak

Ashita ikemásu ka?	Can you go tomorrow?
Shirokiya de kaemásu ka?	Can you buy it at Shirokiya's (department store)?

b. For both consonant and vowel verbs:

In the case of a consonant verb, drop the final *-u* and add *-areru* in its place. In the case of a vowel verb, drop the final *-eru* or *-iru,* and add *-rareru* in its place. In the case of the two irregular verbs *kúru* and *suru* the parallel forms are *koraréru* [can come] and *sareru* [can do].

For example:

CONSONANT VERB	POTENTIAL FORM WITH -*(r)areru* DERIVED FROM ANOTHER VERB FORM	
iku	*ikareru*	can go
kau	*kawareru*	can buy

VOWEL VERB		
tabéru	*taberaréru*	can eat
míru	*miraréru*	can see

Notice that in the case of a consonant verb like *kau,* which has a plain present ending in two vowels, you add *-wareru* instead of *-areru.*

Tookyoo é wa juujíkan de ikaremásu.	You can go to Tokyo in ten hours.

Nára e iku to furúi tatemóno ga takusan miraremásu.	If you go to the city of Nara, you can see many ancient buildings.

5. *Wakaru* To understand

wakáru	*wakarimásu*	I understand
wakátta	*wakarimáshita*	I understood
wakátte	*wakátte*	I understand (understood) and . . .
wakaróo	*wakarimashóo*	I think I'll understand
wakaránai	*wakarimasén*	I don't understand

Anó hito wa kore ga wakarimasén.	He doesn't understand this.
Yóku wakarimásu.	I understand very well.
Watakushi no iu kóto ga wakarimásu ka?	Do you understand me [what (I) say]?
Watakushi no iu kóto ga wakarimasén ka?	Don't you understand me?
Wakarimásu ka?	Do you understand?
Nihongo ga wakarimásu ka?	Do you understand Japanese?
Eigo ga wakarimásu ka?	Do you understand English?
Anó hito ga anáta ni itte iru kóto ga minna wakarimásu ka?	Do you understand everything he's saying to you?
Wakarimasén.	I don't understand.
Wakarimáshita ka?	Did you understand?
Watakushi no iu kóto ga wakátte moraemasén.	I can't make myself understood. [(I) can't have what (I) say understood.]

Anó hito wa shóobai no koto wa sukoshi mo wakarimasén.		He doesn't understand [not a bit] about business.
Zenzen wakarimasen. *Kaimoku wakarimasén.* *Sukoshi mo wakarimasen.* }	.	I don't understand it at all. I don't understand anything about it. It's a mystery to me. I'm completely in the dark.

6. *Oku* To put, To Place

oku	*okimásu*	I put
oita	*okimáshita*	I put *(past)*
oite	*oite*	I put and . . .
okóo	*okimashóo*	I think I'll put
okanai	*okimasén*	I don't put

Soko ni oite kudasái.	Put it there.
Dóko ni okimáshita ka?	Where did you put it?
Ano híto wa jibun de monó o oita tokoró o súgu wasuremásu.	He never knows where he puts (his) things. [He forgets right away the place where he has put (his) things himself.]

You use *oku* when you are talking about "putting" or "placing" a thing some place. To express the thought of "putting on" wearing apparel, you may use several different words. For example:

kabúru	to put on one's head; to put a thing over one's head
Booshi o kabútte kudasái.	Put your hat on.

kiru	to wear on the body
Nihon no kimono o kimáshita.	She wore a Japanese kimono.
haku	to wear on the foot or leg
Kurói kutsú o haite ikimáshita.	He was wearing black shoes (when) he went.

When *oku* follows another verb using the *-te* form, it implies that the action of the verb preceding *oku* takes place in anticipation of some future situation. For example:

Sono kóto wa Yamada-san ni denwa de shirasete okimáshita.[1]	I [have] notified Mr. Yamada in advance over the telephone.
Konshuu wa Doyóobi ni kaimono ga dekínai node Suiyóobi ni kaimono o shite okimáshita.	Since I can't do any shopping on Saturday, I did the shopping on Wednesday.

7. *Kúru* To come

kúru	*kimasu*	I come
kita	*kimáshita*	I came
kite	*kite*	I come and . . .
koyóo	*kimashóo*	I think I'll come
kónai	*kimasén*	I don't come

Hitóri de kimáshita.	I came alone. I came by myself.
Hitóri de kúru deshoo.	I think he is coming alone.

[1]The statement implies, "I have the intention of explaining it in detail when I see him, but for now . . ."

Moo kité imásu.		He is already here. [He is in the state of having come already.]
Sánji made ni kóna-kattara saki ni ikimashóo.		If he doesn't come by three, let's go ahead of him.

8. *Mátsu* To wait

mátsu	*machimásu*	I wait
mátta	*machimáshita*	I waited
mátte	*mátte*	I wait (waited) and . . .
matóo	*machimashóo*	I think I'll wait
matánai	*machimasén*	I don't wait

Koko de mátte kudasái.	Wait here.
Watakushi o mátte kudasái.	Wait for me.
Sukóshi mátte kudasái.	Wait a little.
Chótto mátte kudasái.	Wait a minute.
Matánaide kudasái.	Don't wait.
Sonó hito o mátte imásu.	I'm waiting for him.
Hoka no hitótachi o mátte irú no desu.	She (he) is waiting for the others.
Dáre o mátte irú no desu ka?	Whom are you waiting for?
Náze mátte irú no desu ka?	Why are you waiting?
Omatase[1] shite sumimasén deshita. *Omachidoo sama déshita.*	I'm sorry I kept you waiting. [I caused you to wait; I'm sorry.]

[1]*matsu* plus *-aseru* (causative ending) = *mataséru:* cause someone to wait, make (have, let) someone wait.

9. *Kiku* To ask

Asoko de kiite kudasái.	Ask over there.
Asoko de sonó hito no koto o kiite kudasái.	Ask about him over there.
Náni o kiite irú no desu ka?	What's he asking?
Michi ga wakaránaku náttara hito ni kiite kudasái.	Ask your way if you get lost.
Sonó hito ni jikan o kiite kudasái.	Ask him the time.
Kiité kite kudasái.	Go and ask him. [Ask and come back (to this place).]
Dáre ka watakushi no kóto o kiitára súgu káette kúru to itte kudasái.	If someone asks for me [tell him that], I'll be back in a moment.
Dóko ni áru ka kikimáshita.	He asked where it is.
Denwa o kákete kiite kudasái.	Call him on the phone [and ask].

10. *-tai* To want to (do something)

Ikitái	*Ikitái desu*	I want to go.
Ikitákatta	*Ikitái deshita* *Ikitákatta desu* }	I wanted to go.
Ikitákute	*Ikitákute*	I want (wanted) to go and . . .
Ikitakaróo	*Ikitái deshoo*	I suppose he wants to go.
Ikitakunái	*Ikitakunái desu*	I don't want to go.

Kaitái desu.	I want to buy it.
Nani mo kaitáku arimasén.	I don't want to buy anything.
Dekíru no desu ga shitakunái no desu.	He can do it but he doesn't want to.
Kaeritái no desu ka?	Does he want to return?
Watakushítachi to issho ni ikitái[1] desu ka?	Do you want to come with us?

Notice that the expression *-tái desu* is used when you want to do something. When you want to have or get something you use *hoshíi desu*. For example:

Hoshíi desu.	I want it.
Hóshikunái desu. *Hóshiku arimasén.*}	I don't want it.
Nani mo hóshiku arimasén.	I don't want anything.
Sukóshi hoshíi desu.	I want some.
Náni ga hoshíi desu ka?	What do you want?

11. *-(a)nákereba narimasén* To have to

Use *-anákereba narimasén* for consonant verbs, and *-nákereba narimasén* for vowel and irregular verbs.

Ikanákereba narimasén.	I must go.
Kónakereba narimasen.	He should (has to) come.
Koko ni inákereba narimasen.	He should (has to) be here.

[1]Notice the use of *iku* [going away from where we are now].

Sonó hitotachi wa soko ni inákereba narimasen.	They have to be there.
Soko e ikanákereba narimasén ka?	Do you have to go there?
Watakushi wa náni o shinákereba naránai no desu ka?	What do I have to do?
Íkura okaeshi shinákereba naránai no desu ka?	How much do I owe you?
Nani mo harawánakute íi desu.	You don't owe me anything. [You need not pay anything.]
Kyóo wa kónakute mo íi desu.	You don't have to come today.
Sore wa kawanákute íi desu.	You don't have to buy it.

Notice that the idea of "don't have to" or "need not" is expressed by a sequence quite different from that for "have to" or "need to." For "don't have to," use *-anákute mo¹ íi desu* for consonant verbs, and use *-nákute mo íi desu* for vowel verbs and irregular verbs.

12. *Sukí desu*   To love, To like (something)

Anó hito ga sukí na no desu.	He loves her.
Anáta wa anó hito ga sukí desu ka?	Do you like him (her)?
Sore wa sukí ja arimasén.	I don't like it.
Moo hitótsu no hóo ga sukí desu.	I like the other better.

¹The use of *mo* is optional.

koto ga suki desu	to love, to like to do (something)
Sanpo suru kotó ga suki desu.	I love to [take a] walk.
Gaikokugo o naráu koto ga suki desu.	I like to learn foreign languages.
Jidóosha de ryokoo suru kóto ga sukí desu.	I like to travel by car.

13.

$\left. \begin{array}{l} \text{a.} \\ \text{b.} \\ \text{c.} \end{array} \right\}$

-(r)aréru

   a. For the Passive (to be, to get) plus a past participle
   b. For the Potential (to be able to)
   c. Extra polite

a. Passive

Use *-raréru* for vowel and irregular verbs; use *-aréru* for consonant verbs.

Júnsa ni tomerare-máshita.	I was stopped by a policeman.
Watakushi wa Yamada-san ni Tanaka-san to machigaeraremáshita.	I was mistaken by Mr. Yamada for Mr. Tanaka.
Iriguchi de namae o kikaremáshita.	I was asked my name at the entrance. [At the entrance, I was asked to state my name.]
Áme ni furaremáshita.	We were caught in the rain. [We underwent the falling of the rain.]
Tomodachi ni koraremáshita.	We were visited by a friend (when we didn't want anyone to come).

Notice that the subject of the verb appearing before -*(r)aréru* is designated by the particle -*ni,* the person who is affected by the action of the verb is marked with *wa* or *ga.*

b. Potential

Anó hito wa górufu ga sukí de yamerare-masén.	He likes golf and can't stop (playing) it.
Okane ga nái node tsuzukeraremasén.	As I do not have (enough) money, I can't continue it.
Kippu no nái hito wa toosaremasén.	We can't admit [pass] persons who have no tickets.
Toshókan ga shimátte iru node shirabe-raremasén.	The library is closed, so I can't check it.
Kore wa anmari hídoku kowáreta node moo naosaremasén.	This has been damaged so badly that we can't repair it any longer.

c. Extra polite

Note that all of the following sentences are spoken very politely.

Sensei wa ítsu káette koraremásu ka?	When is the teacher coming back?
Yamada sensei[1] wa Kyóoto ni súnde oraremásu.	Mr. Yamada, the teacher, lives in Kyoto.
Yóshino-san wa sakunen nakuna-raremáshita.	Mr. Yoshino died last year.
Tanaka-san wa sono tanomí o kotowarare-máshita.	Mr. Tanaka refused that request.

[1]See footnote to Grammar Section 12, page 300.

Sátoo-san wa súgu Shígeta-san ni denwa o kakeraremáshita.

Mr. Sato phoned Mr. Shigeta right away.

14. -(s)aseru To make (have, let, allow, force) one to (do something)

Use *-saseru* for vowel and irregular verbs; use *-aseru* for consonant verbs.

Mise no hitó ni erabasemáshita.

I had the clerk of the store choose them.

Akaboo ni nímotsu o hakobasemáshita.

I had the redcap carry the baggage.

Kyóo wa sánji ni uchi e kaerásete kudasái.

Please let me go home at three o'clock.

Sono tegami o watakushi ni yomásete kudasái.

Please let me read that letter.

Kono kusuri o yojikan óki ni nomásete kudasái.

Have him take this medicine every four hours.

QUIZ 33

1. *Mísete kudasái.*
2. *Ohairi kudasái.*
3. *Wasurenáide kudasái.*
4. *Moo ichido itte kudasái.*
5. *Tótte kudasái.*
6. *Otori kudasái*
7. *Kishá de itte kudasái.*

1. Look at this.
2. Look here.
3. Take the train.
4. Take another one.
5. Take it *(extra polite).*
6. Take it.
7. Don't forget.

8. *Moo hitótsu otori kudasái.*   8. Say it again.

9. *Koko o míte kudasái.*   9. Come in.

10. *Kore o míte kudasái.*   10. Show me.

ANSWERS

1-10; 2-9; 3-7; 4-8; 5-6; 6-5; 7-3; 8-4; 9-2; 10-1.

PUBLIC NOTICES AND SIGNS

Kooji	Public Notice	公示
Dánshi	Gentlemen	男子
Fujin	Ladies	婦人
Danshi(yoo) bénjo	Men's Room	男子(用)便所
Fujin(yoo) bénjo	Ladies' Room	婦人(用)便所
Benjo, Tearaijo	W.C.	便所、手洗所
Kin'en, Tabako goenryo kudasái	Non-Smokers	禁煙 煙草ご遠慮下さい。
Kin'en, Tabako goenryo kudasái	No Smoking	禁煙 煙草ご遠慮下さい。
Eigyoochuu	Open	営業中
(Hónjitsu) heiten, Kyuugyoo	Closed	(本日)閉店、休業
Iriguchi	Entrance	入口
Déguchi	Exit	出口
Hijóoguchi	Emergency Exit	非常口
Erebéetaa, Shookooki	Elevator	エレベーター 昇降機
Ikkai	Ground Floor	一階
Osu	Push	押す
Hiku	Pull	引く

Mawasu	Turn	廻す
Yobirin o narashite kudasái	Please Ring	呼鈴を鳴らして下さい。
Tachiiri kinshi *Toorinuke kinshi*	Keep Out! No Thoroughfare!	立入禁止 通り抜け禁止
Ohairi kudasái	Come In	お入り下さい。
Nókku muyoo *Nókku o shináide ohairi kudasái*	Enter Without Knocking	ノック無用 ノックをしないでお入り下さい。
Nókku o shite hudasái	Knock	ノックをして下さい。
Nókku o shité kara ohairi kudasái	Knock Before Entering	ノックをしてからお入り下さい。
Kaisoo ni tsuki kyuugyoo	Closed for Repairs	改装につき休業
Shinsoo kaiten	Under New Management	新装開店
Nyuujoo okotowari	No Admittance	入場お断り
Kínjitsu kaiten	Will Open Shortly	近日開店
Shuuya éigyoo	Open All Night	終夜営業
Tsúba o hakánaide kudasái *Tsúba o háku bekárazu*	No Spitting	つばを吐かないで下さい。 つばを吐くべからず
Hakimono o nugútte kudasái	Wipe Your Feet	履物を拭って下さい。

Inú o kusari kara hanasánaide kudasái	Leash Your Dog	犬をくさりから放さないで下さい。
Hokóosha okotowari	Pedestrians Keep Out	歩行者お断り
Tachiiri kinshi	No Trespassing	立入禁止
Kujoo soodanjo *Kujoo shoríbu*	Complaint Department	苦情相談所 苦情処理部
Madóguchi de omooshikomi kudasái	Apply at the Window	窓口でお申し込み下さい。
Ryoogaejo	Money Exchanged	両替所
Urimono	For Sale	売物
Chintai itashimásu *Chingashi itashimásu*	For rent	賃貸いたします。
Kashi apáato zoosaku náshi	Unfurnished Apartment for Rent	貸アパート家具なし
Kashi apaato zoosaku tsuki	Furnished Apartment for Rent	貸アパート家具付
Waribiki hánbai *Tokka hánbai*	Reduction	割引販売 特価販売
Uridashi	Sale	売り出し
Keitaihin azukarijo	Check Room, Cloakroom	携帯品預り所
Dookyúu shitsu	Billiard Room	撞球室

Kozukáishitsu	Janitor	小使室
Ukai	Detour	迂回
Koojichuu	Road Under Repair	工事中
Káabu kiken	Dangerous Curve	カーブ危険
Chuusha kinshi	No Parking	駐車禁止
Ippoo kóotsuu	One Way Street	一方通行
Sénro o yoko-giránaide kudasái *Sénro no oodan kinshi*	Don't Cross the Tracks	線路を横切らないで下さい。 線路の横断禁止
Fumikiri	Railroad Crossing	踏切
Tetsudoo	Railroad	鉄道
Gáado	Underpass	ガード
Tomare	Stop!	止まれ！
Chúui	Caution!	注意！
Oodanhódoo	Pedestrian Crossing	横断歩道
Koosáten	Crossroads	交差点
Básu teiryuujoo	Bus Stop	バス停留所
Harigami genkin	Post No Bills	貼紙禁止
Jisoku sanjukkiro íka	Max. Speed 30 K. P. H.	時速30キロ以下
Jokoo	Go Slow	除行
Gakkoo kúiki jokoo	School—Go Slow	学校区域除行
Kiken, Abunái	Danger!	危険！危い！
Penki nuritate	Fresh Paint	ペンキ塗りたて
Mádo kara kao ya té o dasánaide kudasái	Don't Lean Out of the Window!	窓から顔や手を出さないで下さい。

Keihooki	Alarm Signal	警報機
Kooatsusen chúui	High Voltage	高圧線注意
Chikatetsu iriguchi	Subway	地下鉄入口
Keitaihin ichiji azukarijo	Baggage Room, Check Room	携帯品一時預り所
Machiáishitsu	Waiting Room	待合室
Ittóo	First Class	一等
Nitóo	Second Class	二等
Santóo	Third Class	三等
Toochaku	Arrival ⎱ (Trains)	到着
Hassha	Departure ⎰	発着
Purattohóomu, Hóomu	Platform	プラットホーム、ホーム
Annaijo	Information	案内所
Kippu úriba	Box Office	切符売場
Yuubínkyoku	Post Office	郵便局
Posuto	Mailbox	ポスト
Nyuujooken úriba ⎱ *Kippu úriba* ⎰	Ticket Office	入場券売場 切符売場
Kasaihoochíki	Fire Alarm Box	火災報知機
Kooritsu toshókan	Public Library	公立図書館
Keisatsusho	Police Station	警察署
Gasorin sutándo	Gas Station	ガソリンスタンド
Shóten	Bookstore	書店
Shiyákusho	City Hall	市役所
Rihátsuten	Barber Shop	理髪店
Biyóoin	Hair Dresser	美容院
Íshi ⎱ *Íin* ⎰	Physician	医師 医院
Shiká	Dentist	歯科
Kutsu shúuri	Shoe Repairing	靴修理

Máchinee ⎫ *Chuukan-* ⎬ *kóogyoo* ⎭	Matinee	マチネー
Yakan kóogyoo *hachíji* *sanjúppun* *kaien*	Evening Performance at 8:30	夜間興業 8時30分開演
Seisoo *chakuyoo*	Formal Dress	正装着用
Heifuku *chakuyoo*	Informal Dress	平服着用
Renzoku *kóogyoo*	Continuous Performance	連続興業
Bangumi henkoo	Change of Program	番組変更
Kissáshitsu	Refreshments	喫茶店

FINAL REVIEW QUIZ

1. _____ (How) *desu ka?*
   a. *Íkura*
   b. *Ogénki*
   c. *Ítsu*

2. *Yukkúri* _____ (speak) *kudasái.*
   a. *hanáshite*
   b. *káite*
   c. *tábete*

3. *Tabako ga* _____ (have) *ka?*
   a. *hoshii desu*
   b. *kaitái desu*
   c. *arimásu*

4. *Ményuu o* _____ (show me) *kudasái.*
   a. *misete*
   b. *tótte*
   c. *motté kite*

5. *Koohíi o íppai* _____ (give me).
   a. *nomimáshita*
   b. *kudasái*
   c. *agemáshita*

6. _____ (Breakfast) *wa hachíji ni tabemáshita.*
   a. *Yuuhan*
   b. *Asahan*
   c. *Hiruhan*

7. *Chasaji o* _____ (bring).
   a. *motte ítte kudasái.*
   b. *motté kite kudasái.*
   c. *mótte kudasái.*

8. _____ (Station) *wa dóko ni arimásu ka?*
   a. *Denwa*
   b. *Éki*
   c. *Yuubínkyoku*

9. _____ (Which way) *desu ka?*
   a. *Sochira*
   b. *Kochira*
   c. *Dóchira*

10. *Taihen* _____ (near) *desu.*
    a. *tooi*
    b. *chikái*
    c. *ookíi*

11. *Okane o* _____ (does he have) *ka?*
    a. *hoshii desu*
    b. *uketorimáshita*
    c. *mótte imásu*

12. *Watakushi no tegami ga* _____ (are there) *ka?*
    a. *arimasén*
    b. *arimásu*
    c. *arimáshita*

13. _____ (Do you understand) *ka?*
   a. *Shitte imásu*
   b. *Wakarimásu*
   c. *Kiite imásu*

14. *Hajimete* _____ (glad to know you).
   a. *ome ni kakarimásu.*
   b. *anáta o shirimáshita.*
   c. *sore o kikimáshita.*

15. *Sukóshi hoshíi desu ka* _____ (want a lot) *desu ka?*
   a. *sukoshi mo hóshiku nái*
   b. *takusan hoshíi*
   c. *anmari hóshiku nái*

16. *Yamada-san ni* _____ (must see).
   a. *hanasánakereba narimasén.*
   b. *awánakereba narimasén.*
   c. *kikanákereba narimasén.*

17. *Sore wa Nihongo de dóo* _____ (does one say) *ka?*
   a. *kikimásu*
   b. *iimásu*
   c. *kakimásu*

18. *Denwa wa Nakano no* _____ (3307) *ban desu.*
   a. *sánjuu san shichi*
   b. *san san rei nana*
   c. *sansen sanhyaku shichí*

19. _____ (What time) *desu ka?*
   a. *Nan'yóobi*
   b. *Nánnichi*
   c. *Nánji*

20. _____ (Tomorrow morning) *kité kudasái.*
    a. *Ashita no yóru*
    b. *Ashita no ása*
    c. *Ashita no gógo*

21. *Ittá keredomo* _____ (couldn't meet).
    a. *atta koto ga arimasén deshita*
    b. *áu koto ga dekimasén deshita*
    c. *au tsumori ja arimasén deshita*

22. _____ (I want to go) *desu.*
    a. *Ikitái*
    b. *Hoshíi*
    b. *Iku kóto ga sukí*

23. *Tanaka-san wa íma Tookyoo ni inai* _____
    (I hear).
    a. *sóo desu*
    b. *rashíi desu*
    c. *no deshóo*

24. _____ (Check) *o motté kite kudasái.*
    a. *Otsuri*
    b. *Ocha*
    c. *Kanjoogaki*

25. *Kyooto e* _____ (I have been to).
    a. *iku kotó ga dekimasén.*
    b. *itta kóto ga arimásu.*
    c. *iku kóto ga sukí desu.*

ANSWERS

1-b; 2-a; 3-c; 4-a; 5-b; 6-b; 7-b; 8-b; 9-c; 10-b; 11-c;
12-b; 13-b; 14-a; 15-b; 16-b; 17-b; 18-b; 19-c; 20-b;
21-b; 22-a; 23-a; 25-c; 25-b.

SUMMARY OF JAPANESE GRAMMAR
1. THE ALPHABET AND ANGLICIZATION

The sounds of Japanese have been transcribed into the English alphabet and all letters of the English alphabet except "l," "q," and "x" are employed and known by their English names. Generally speaking, the *r*-sound replaces "l." Note that *c* is used only in the combination *ch*.

There are two major systems of anglicization: the Hepburn System and the Japanese National System. The Hepburn System has a longer history and wider acceptance than the Japanese National System. The National System is more logical and reflects the phonological structure of the language better.

A slightly modified form of the Hepburn System is used here to present Japanese words and sentences, but the standard Hepburn System without modification is used when a Japanese word (usually a proper noun) is included in the English translation. The system has been modified as follows:

a. So-called "long vowels" are written as double vowels instead of with a macron (-) over the vowel symbol (i.e., *Tookyoo* instead of *Tōkyō; kuuki* instead of *kūki)*.

b. The syllabic *n* is written as an *n* at all times instead of as an *m* when it precedes *p*, *b*, or *m*.

The following table illustrates the various ways in which consonants and vowels are combined in the Hepburn System to produce the sounds of Japanese. Chart I aligns *vertically* the five vowel sounds, and shows *horizontally* the basic (mostly voiceless) consonants with which they can be used to create the basic syllables of Japanese. Chart II shows the sounds[1] (the voiced counterparts) into which these consonants can change. The same relationship that exists between Charts I and II exists also between Charts III and IV.

A blank occurring in the charts (at the junction of a vertical and horizontal column) denotes that that combination of consonant and vowel is *never* used.

TABLE 1
SYLLABLES OF THE MODIFIED HEPBURN SYSTEM IN MODERN JAPANESE

			0	1	2	3	4	5	6	7	8	9	10
Chart I	V O W E L S	1	a	ka	sa	ta	na	ha	ma	ya	ra	wa	n (or m)
		2	i	ki	shi	chi	ni	hi	mi		ri		
		3	u	ku	su	tsu	nu	fu	mu	yu	ru		
		4	e	ke	se	te	ne	he	me		re		
		5	o	ko	so	to	no	ho	mo	yo	ro		
Chart II		1		ga	za	da		ba	pa			va	
		2		gi	ji	di		bi	pi			vi	
		3		gu	zu	du		bu	pu			vu	
		4		ge	ze	de		be	pe			ve	
		5		go	zo	do		bo	po			vo	
Chart III		1		kya	sha	cha	nya	hya	mya		rya		
		3		kyu	shu	chu	nyu	hyu	myu		ryu		
		5		kyo	sho	cho	nyo	hyo	myo		ryo		
		1		gya	ja			bya	pya				
		3		gyu	ju			byu	pyu				
		5		gyo	jo			byo	pyo				

[1]Notice that in vertical column 5, the *h* of Chart I is converted to either *b* or *p* in Chart II. (See Section 4 of the Grammar, page 279.)

TABLE 1

SYLLABLES OF THE MODIFIED HEPBURN SYSTEM IN MODERN JAPANESE

Chart IV	-kk-	-ss- -ssh(t)	-tt- -tch(i)-	-pp-				

The differences between the Hepburn and National Systems are limited to the syllables listed below:

HEPBURN SYSTEM	JAPANESE NATIONAL SYSTEM	HEPBURN SYSTEM	JAPANESE NATIONAL SYSTEM
shi	si	chu	tyu
chi	ti	cho	tyo
tsu	tu	ja	zya
fu	hu	ju	zyu
ji	zi	jo	zyo
sha	sya	ssh(i)	ss(i)
shu	syu	tch(i)	tt(i)
sho	syo	tts(u)	tt(u)
cha	tya		

Compare the charts in the following table (showing syllables of the National System) with those of the preceding table (showing syllables of the Hepburn System) and note the differences in spelling. The National System is employed mainly in railroad and highway signs.

Note that the same interrelationship exists between the charts of this table on the National System as between the charts of the table on the Hepburn System (on page 275).

TABLE II

SYLLABLES[1] OF THE NATIONAL SYSTEM IN MODERN JAPANESE

			0	1	2	3	4	5	6	7	8	9	10
Chart I	V O W E L S	1	a	ka	sa	ta	na	ha	ma	ya	ra	wa	n
		2	i	ki	*si*	*ti*	ni	hi	mi		ri		
		3	u	ku	su	*tu*	nu	*hu*	mu	yu	ru		
		4	e	ke	se	te	ne	he	me		re		
		5	o	ko	so	to	no	ho	mo	yo	ro		

Chart II		0	1	2	3	4	5	6	7	8	9	10
Chart II			ga	za	da		ba	pa			va	
			gi	*zi*	di		bi	pi			vi	
			gu	zu	du		bu	pu			vu	
			ge	ze	de		be	pe			ve	
			go	zo	do		bo	po			vo	

Chart III		0	1	2	3	4	5	6	7	8	9	10
Chart III	1		kya	*sya*	*tya*	nya	hya	mya		rya		
	3		kyu	*syu*	*tyu*	nyu	hyu	myu		ryu		
	5		kyo	*syo*	*tyo*	nyo	hyo	myo		ryo		

		0	1	2	3	4	5	6	7	8	9	10
	1		gya	*zya*			bya	pya				
	3		gyu	*zyu*			byu	pyu				
	5		gyo	*zyo*			byo	pyo				

Chart IV	-kk-	-ss-	-tt-	-pp-						

[1]Notice that in vertical column 5, the *h* of Chart I is converted to either *b* or *p* in Chart II. (See Section 4 of the Grammar, page 279). [2]Syllables in italics are spelled differently in the Hepburn system. See the lists of syllables on page 275 for a comparison.

2. SIMPLE VOWELS

a like the "a" in "father" but short and crisp.

e like the "ay" in "may" but without the final *y* sound.

i like the "e" in "keep" but still higher, short and crisp.

o like the "o" in "go" but without the final *u* sound.

u like the "u" in "put" but without rounding the lips.

Remember that *i* and *u* differ from the other vowels in that they tend to become "voiceless" or whispered (1) when they are surrounded by voiceless consonants (*h, k, p, s, t*), or (2) when they are preceded by a voiceless consonant and followed by a silence or pause (as at the end of a sentence). This is especially true when the syllable is not accented:

arimasu	there is
kitte	stamps

3. VOWEL CLUSTERS

a. Double Vowels

All simple vowels can appear in double[1] or "long" vowels. A double vowel is always pronounced twice as long as a simple vowel:

aa pronounced twice as long as single *a: haato* (heart)

ee pronounced twice as long as single *e: teeburu* (table)

ii pronounced twice as long as single *i: iin* (committee)

oo pronounced twice as long as a single *o: Tookyoo* (Tokyo)

---

[1]Double vowels can be indicated by writing the single vowel with a "macron" over it: e.g., *ã* (for *aa*).

uu pronounced twice as long as a single *u: nyuusu* (news)

b. Other Vowel Clusters

All simple vowels can also appear in combination with one or more other simple vowels to form a "vowel cluster." In such combinations, each of the vowels has equal weight and is pronounced so that it retains the sound it has as a simple vowel. Vowel clusters should *not* be pronounced like diphthongs, which combine two vowels to make a new sound.

au	*a* and *u* are both pronounced and given equal clarity and length.
ai	*a* and *i* are both pronounced and given equal clarity and length.

4. THE CONSONANTS

The letters *b, d, j, k, m, p, s, v,* and *y* in Japanese sound almost like the same letters in English. Pronounce the other consonants thus:

ch	as in "cheese."
f	by forcing the air out from between the lips; it appears only before *u*.
g	at the beginning of a word, somewhat like the "g" in the English word "go"; in the middle of a word, it resembles the "ng" in "singer."
h	like the "h" in "high," when it precedes *a, e, o;* like the "h" in "hue," when it comes before *i* or *y*.
n	as in "name" (but with the tip of the tongue touching the back of the teeth) when it precedes *a, e, o, u;* as in "onion" when it precedes *i*.

r	by placing the tip of the tongue near the back of the upper teeth and quickly bringing it down; it sometimes sounds like the "r" in a British version of "very" ("veddy").
sh	somewhat like the English "sh" in "sheep."
t	as in the English "to," but with the tip of the tongue touching the back of the upper teeth.
w	like the "w" in "want," but without rounding or protruding the lips; occurs only before *a*.
z	at the beginning of a word, like the *ds* in "beds;" in the middle of a word, like the *z* in "zero" (but some Japanese speakers do not make this a distinction; they use the two sounds interchangeably).

When a word begins with *ch, h, k, s, t,* or *ts,* and it joins with another word (which then *precedes* it) to make a new compound word, the initial letter or letters may undergo a change:

ch may become *j,* as it does in the change from *chie* [wisdom] to *warujie* [guile, wiles].

h may become *p* or *b,* as it does in the change from *hanashi* [story] to *mukashibanashi* [a story of the past].

k may become *g,* as it does in the change from *ken* (a counter for houses) to *sangen* [three houses].

s may become *z,* as it does in the change from *sen* [one thousand] to *sanzen* [three thousand].

t may become *d,* as it does in the change from *to* [door, windows] to *amado* [storm window, Japanese rain-window].

ts may become *z,* as it does in the change from *tsuki* [month] to *tsukizuki* [monthly].

5. THE DOUBLE CONSONANTS

When a double *p, t, k,* or *s* appears in a word, then the consonant sound becomes doubled in length. This same lengthening takes place when *tch* appears in a word.

kippu	tickets
kitte	postal stamps
itchoo	one city block

6. THE SYLLABIC *N*

The syllabic *n* differs from the ordinary *n* in several ways:

a. It always forms a full syllable by itself (that is, it is always held as long as one full syllable). It *never* joins with a vowel or another consonant to form a syllable. If a vowel follows the syllabic *n,* there is always a syllable boundary between the *n* and the vowel. For example, the word *gen'in* [cause] has four syllables—*ge-n-i-n*— since each of the syllabic *n*'s has the value of a full syllable.

b. The syllabic *n* seldom appears at the beginning of a word.

c. Its sound changes, depending on what follows it:

1. Before *n*, *ch*, *t*, and *d*, it is pronounced like
   the English "n" in "pen," but the sound is
   held longer.

ko**nn**a	this sort of
ha**n**choo	half a block
cha**n**to	properly
ko**n**do	this time

2. Before *m*, *p*, or *b*, it is pronounced like the
   English "m" but the sound is held longer.

SPELLING	PRONUNCIATION	MEANING
sa**n**mai	sammai	three sheets
shi**n**pai	shimpai	worry, anxiety
ka**n**ban	kamban	signboard

3. Before a vowel or a semi-vowel *(w, y)*, the
   syllabic *n* is pronounced somewhat like the
   English "ng" in "singer," but without fin-
   ishing the *g* sound, and the preceding vowel
   is often somewhat nasalized. Notice that an
   apostrophe is used when a vowel or *y* follows
   the syllabic *n*.

Na**n'**a	South Africa
ta**n'**i	unit
ho**n'**ya	bookstore
shi**n**wa	mythology

4. When the syllabic *n* precedes *k*, *g*, or *s*, or
   when it appears at the end of a word (that is,
   when it is followed by a pause), it is pronounced as in paragraph 3, above.

so**n**kei	respect
sa**n**gen	three houses
so**n**	loss
ka**n**sei	completion

7. CONTRACTIONS

a. The particle *de* [at, by means of] sometimes combines with the particle *wa* [as for] thus: *de* plus *wa* = *ja*.

Nihon ja yasui desu. This (thing) is cheap in Japan (but not here).

b. The *-te* form of the copula *de* (from *desu*) also can combine with the particle *wa* thus: *de* plus *wa* = *ja*.

Nihonjin ja arimasen. He is not a Japanese.

c. The *-te* form of a verb sometimes combines with the particle *wa* thus: *-te* plus *wa* = *cha*, or *-de* plus *wa* = *ja*.

Itcha ikemasen. You musn't go.
Yonja ikemasen. You musn't read it.

Some people consider such contractions to be in poor taste, but they are widely used, nevertheless.

8. ACCENT

Word accent in Japanese is indicated by lowering the pitch of the voice *after* the accented syllable.

Some words have, some do not have, an accent in Japanese. Accentless words are spoken with the voice pitch held even on all syllables of the word except the first; here the pitch is slightly lower. This is true regardless of the length of the word.

Certain words lose their accent when they are placed next to an accented word. Hence the accents are sometimes marked and sometimes not marked within the same sentence.

The inclusion or omission of accent is further determined by various subsidiary rules, not all of which are thoroughly understood at the present time. The student can learn much about the refinements of accentuation through listening to native Japanese speakers.

Notice that all accent marks are omitted from this Summary of Grammar.

9. INTONATION

a. **In a Declarative Sentence:**

There is a marked drop in the pitch of the voice on the last-voiced syllable.

b. **In a Direct Question:**

There may be a rising inflection on the last-voiced syllable. This rise in pitch is optional when the sentence ends with the question-particle *ka* or contains a question phrase such as *doko e* [where to]. When neither a question particle nor question word is used, the intonation described in paragraph A (above) is used.

c. **Suspension:**

The last-voiced syllable is spoken in approximately the same level tone as what precedes it.

10. THE NOUNS

a. Most nouns in a sentence are accompanied by one or two noun-particles[1] (i.e., *wa, ga, o, mo, no, ni, de, kara*) or by some form of the copula *desu* [it is]. Nouns are not declined.

[1]See the material on page 35 for particles used with nouns.

| *Nihon ni wa yama ga takusan arimasu.* | There are many mountains in Japan. |
| *Fujisan wa takai yama desu.* | Fuji is a high mountain. |

b. There are certain nouns, usually having to do with time, degree, or quantity, which may or may not appear with a particle. Such nouns may have the functions not only of nouns but also of adverbs, and may be used to modify predicates or entire clauses.

| *Kinoo ikimashita.* | I went there yesterday. |
| *Kinoo wa ikimasen deshita.* | I didn't go there yesterday. |

Here is a list of some more of these nouns:

maiasa	every morning
mainichi	every day
ima	present time, now
moto	former time, previously
sukoshi	a small amount, a little, some
takusan	a large amount, a great deal, plentifully, in a large quantity
hotondo	nearly all, almost completely
mada	as yet, still
zenzen	whole, completely (used with a negative predicate)
nakanaka	quite, considerably

c. Certain nouns normally occur only with the particles *na* or *ni*, and with the copula *desu*. These nouns are sometimes called "*na-ni-desu* nouns" or "copular nouns."

genki	vigor, good health
genki na	vigorous
genki ni	vigorously
genki desu	is vigorous

d. A noun beginning with a voiceless consonant changes that consonant to another (usually a voiced) consonant when it is suffixed to another noun to form a compound:

ORIGINAL INITIAL LETTER	CHANGES TO
ch	*j*
f	*p* (or) *b*
h	*p* (or) *b*
k	*g*
s	*z*
t	*d*
ts	*z*
fu*ne* boat	*ko**b**une* small boat
ku*ni* country	*yuki**g**uni* snow country
ta*mashii* soul	*yamato **d**amashii* the soul of Japan

e. Some nouns frequently take on a special function: i.e., they are used to relate or tie one part of a sentence to another, assuming a role comparable in the English language to that of a preposition, adverb, or conjunction. When so used, these nouns are always modified by a clause. They are sometimes classified as particles rather than as nouns. The list which follows contains some of the most widely used functional nouns:

NOUN	NOUN MEANING	FUNCTIONAL WORD MEANING
aida	duration, space; interval	during; as long as; while

ato site; place behind; time following; condition following after, subsequent to (usually preceded by the *-ta* form of a verb and followed by *de*)

baai occasion; situation in the event that, in case; when; should (something) happen

dake height; extent as much as

hazu notch (of an arrow) it (something) is "in the cards," it is expected that, it is supposed that (when followed by *desu*); it is not reasonable to expect that, it is hardly possible that (when followed by *wa* or *ga arimasen*)

hodo approximate degree to the extent of; not as ... as ... (usually followed by a negative predicate):

A wa B hodo yoku arimasen. A is not as good as B. the more ... the more ... (when preceded by a single verb in the present tense or a verb in the provisional form together with the same verb in the present):

Sono sake wa nomeba nomu hodo motto nomitaku narimasu.		The more you drink that sake, the more you want to drink.
hoo	side, direction, alternative direction	the use of this word denotes that a comparison is being made:
Kono hoo ga yasui desu.		This is cheaper.
Kusuri o nonda hoo ga ii desu.		It would be better (for you) to take some medicine.
ijoo (wa)	the above-mentioned	now that, since, inasmuch as, because of
kagiri	limits, bounds; maximum degree	as far as, so long as, as much as, provided that
kekka	result, outcome, consequence	with the result that, as a result of, because of
kiri	limit	nothing happened after
Nippon e itta kiri tayori ga arimasen.		There is no news from him since he went to Japan.
koto	fact; thing (abstract)	the act of doing . . . ; the act of having done . . . (makes a noun equivalent out of inflected words; used in many idiomatic expressions):

Hanasu koto wa dekimasen.		Talking is not permitted [possible]. I can't talk.
Hanashita koto wa arimasen.		I've never talked (with him). [The experience of having talked with him does not exist.]
mae	the front; prior time, former time	before, prior to [usually followed by *ni*]
mama	will (wish)	as it is (without doing anything further, without taking additional action); as it stands; exactly as; according to
mono	thing (tangible); person	the thing which; the one who; it's because (when it is used at the end of a sentence, usually in talk between women—a use similar to *kara* or *node*); that's the thing to do, you should, it is expected that (when preceded by a verb in the present form and followed by *desu*); used to do (when preceded

		by the *-ta* form of a verb and followed by *desu*)
nochi	the time after	after (used either with or without *ni* following it); subsequent to having done . . . (when it is preceded by the *-ta* form of a verb)
tabi	occasion, time	every time that
tame	sake	for the sake of; for the purpose of; because of
toki	time	(at the time) when
tokoro	place	just when, in the act of (when followed by *ni* or *de*); even if, no matter who, no matter what (when followed by *de*); to be on the point of (when preceded by the present form of a verb and followed by *desu*); to have just finished doing . . . (when preceded by the *-ta* form of a verb and followed by *desu*)

toori	the way, avenue	exactly as
tsumori	idea in mind	intend to, plan to (when preceded by the present tense of a verb and followed by *desu*); *(my)* notion [recollection] about it is that (something) was the case (when preceded by the *-ta* form of a verb and followed by *desu*)
uchi	the inside [the within]	while, during the time when
ue	top, surface, place over	on top of doing having done (something), upon doing . . . , besides (doing) . . . ; upon finishing, after (doing something), (when followed by *de*)
wake	reason, meaning, logic	that's the background of it, that's the story of it, that's what it is (when followed by *desu*);

it is hardly be-
lievable that
(something)
should happen
(or should have
happened) (when
followed by *ga
arimasen*).

f. Some nouns are converted into verbs when they
are used with *suru* or *dekiru*. The resultant
combinations mean, respectively, "do the action
of (something)" and "can do the action of
(something)." For instance:

shookai	introduction
shookai suru	to introduce
shookai dekiru	to be able to introduce, can introduce
ryokoo	travel
ryokoo suru	to travel
ryokoo dekiru	to be able to travel, can travel

g. The radical (i.e., the root plus *i* of some verbs)
can function as a noun:

yomu	to read,
yomi	reading; pronunciation
tsuru	to fish
tsuri	fishing

h. The stem of an adjective (i.e., the plain-present
minus the final *i*) can function as a noun:

akai (is) red   *aka* the color red

The stem of an adjective can also function as a
noun by adding *sa* or *mi*:

akai (is) red

fukai (is) deep

akasa redness

$\left\{\begin{array}{l}\textit{fukasa} \text{ depth (as a} \\ \quad \text{measure)} \\ \textit{fukami} \text{ depth (of} \\ \quad \text{thought)}\end{array}\right.$

i. Particles[1] used with nouns:

1. Following is a list of special particles used with nouns, and their functions:

ga marks an emphatic grammatical subject (see *mo,* below).

wa marks a sentence-topic which may either be the subject or object of the sentence, or a modifier.

no has two functions: (1) it links a noun to another noun or (2) converts a verb modifier into a noun modifier.

ni links a noun or noun equivalent (such as the stem or radical of a verb) to a verb, adjective, or copula.

o marks the thing acted on (see *mo,* below).

mo can be used instead of *ga* or *o* (see above) but carries the additional meaning of "that thing also."

e links a noun to a verb and marks the direction toward which an action is performed.

to does two things: (1) it links nouns together in a complete list (see *ya,* page 294) or (2) it marks the partner with whom the action is being performed.

[1]Note that Japanese is rich in these small words called "particles," which are used very frequently to show the grammatical relationship of one word to another within a sentence. Mastery of these particles is a key to rapid learning of Japanese. For particles used with verbs, see Section 18 of the Grammar, page 319.

ya links nouns together in an incomplete list (see *to,* page 293).

yori marks a noun or noun-equivalent as the standard against which a comparison is made.

2. Note that all of the following particles link a noun to a verb, adjective, or the copula. When one of these particles adds *no,* then the combination of the particle plus *no* can be used to link a noun to a noun:

kara marks a starting point in time or space. (See Lesson 10.)

made marks the ending point in time or space (See Lesson 10.)

de marks the means, way, or manner in which an action is performed.

bakari has two functions: (1) it can be used in place of (or sometimes together with) *ga* or *o* to carry the additional meaning of "nothing else," or (2) if it follows a number, it signifies that the number is only approximate.

dake can be used in place of or together with *ga* or *o* to carry the additional meaning of "that was the limit."

hodo can be used (1) to mark a thing against which a comparison is made and which is about the same in degree or extent as the thing compared, or (2) to mark a number which is only approximate.

kurai (or *gurai*) marks the approximate quantity, quality, or degree, and can often be used interchangeably with *hodo* (see above).

ka shows that (1) a statement is a question, or (2) it has the meaning of "either . . . or."

11. COUNTERS

"Counters" form a subclass of nouns often used adverbially to mean "to the extent of." There are several types:

a. Unit Counters

1. "Unit" counters name specifically what is being counted. The following unit counters are used with primary numbers: *ichi, ni, san* [one, two, three], etc.—and are suffixed to these numbers. Where an exception to the general rule occurs, it is shown.

COUNTER	MEANING	EXCEPTIONS
-jikan	hours	*yojikan* = four hours
-ji	o'clock	*yoji* = four o'clock
-fun (or *-pun*)	minutes	See also Grammar Section 4 for change of sound.
-byoo	seconds	*yonbyoo* = four seconds
-nichi	days	See also Lesson 27 for variations.
-shuukan	weeks	
-kagetsu	months	
-gatsu	name of the month	
-nen	years	
-sen	one-hundredth of a yen (Japanese currency)	

-en	yen (Japanese currency)
-sento	cent (U.S. currency)
-doru	dollar (U.S. currency)
-shiringu	shillings (British currency)
-pondo	pounds (unit of weight or of British currency)
-meetoru	meters
-kiro	kilometers, kilograms
-kiroguramu	kilograms
-kiromeetoru	kilometers
-mairu	miles
-inchi	inches
-sun	Japanese unit of measure (one-tenth of a *shaku* = about 1.2 inches)
-shaku	Japanese foot (ten *sun*)
-ken	Japanese unit of length equaling six *shaku*
-choo	sixty ken (about 119 yards); the length of a city block

-ri	Japanese mile (2.44 American miles)	
-do	times	
-peiji	pages; page number	
-gyoo	lines; line number	*yongyoo* = four lines, fourth line
-wari	one-tenth	
-kai	story (of a building)	

2. The following unit counters are used with secondary numbers (*hito-*, *futa-*, *mi-*, etc. They are usually used to count amounts less than seven).

-ban	nights
-heya	room
-ma	room

b. **Class Counters**

1. "Class counters" are used in a general rather than specific sense. The following class counters are used with primary numerals (*ichi, ni, san...*):

COUNTER	MEANING	EXAMPLES
-hiki (or *-biki*, or *-piki*)	animals, fish, insects	*ippiki, sánbiki, roppiki, jippiki*

-too	large, domesticated animals (such as horses, cows, dogs, cats)	
-wa (or *-ba*, or *-pa*)	birds	*sanba, roppa, jippa*
-satsu	bound volumes (of books and magazines)	
-mai	flat, thin things (such as sheets, newspapers, handkerchiefs)	
-hon (or *-pon*, or *-bon*)	thin, long things (such as pencils, tubes, sticks, matches, cigarettes)	*ippon, sanbon, roppon, jippon*
-ken (or *-gen*)	houses	*sangen*
-soo (or *-zoo*)	boats	*sanzoo*
-seki	ships	
-tsuu	documents, letters, telegrams	
-dai	vehicles (i.e., cars, wagons), machines such as typewriters, sewing machines	
-ki	planes and other aircraft	

-chaku	suits of clothes	
-soku (or *-zoku*)	pairs of things worn on the feet or legs (such as shoes, socks, stockings)	*sanzoku*
-ko	miscellaneous articles for which there is no specific counter	

2. The following class counters are used with secondary numerals (*hito-, futa-, mi-,* etc.):

-fukuro	bagful (of)
-hako	boxful (of)
-kumi	set, group, couple (of people)
-soroi	set, group
-iro	kind, variety
-kire	slices
-tsumami	pinch

12. PRONOUNS

All of the Japanese words that correspond to English pronouns are nouns. They take the same particles as other nouns and are modified by the same type of words, phrases, and clauses that are used to modify other nouns. Note that in Japanese there are more varieties of words that correspond to personal pronouns than there are in English.

A list of Japanese equivalents of personal pronouns and instructions for using them, follow:

a. **I, We**

SINGULAR	PLURAL	MEANING AND USAGE
watakushi	*watakushitachi*	I, we (used most widely)
watashi	*watashitachi*	I, we (slightly less formal than *watakushi* and consequently used less frequently)
boku	*bokutachi*	I, we (used by boys only: informal)
ore	*oretachi*	I, we (used by boys, but not in refined speech)

b. **You**

Avoid using any definite word for "you" as long as the sentence meaning is clear without it. If you cannot avoid using such a word, use the surname of the person you are addressing and add *-san* with the appropriate particle: (1) If you are speaking to a small child, use his given name or *botchan* (for a boy) or *ojoosan* (for a girl). (2) If you are speaking to a schoolteacher, a doctor, a dentist, a congressman (or member of the Japanese Diet), etc., use *sensei*[1] either preceded by or without the surname of the person you are

[1] *sensei:* sir [one who was born earlier]. *Yamada-sensei:* Mr. Yamada (said with great respect).

addressing. If you must employ the pronoun instead of the name, use *anata* [you, (sing.)], *anatagata* [you (pl.)], *anatasama* [you (sing., very formal)], or *mina sama* [you (pl., very formal)]. Many of the sentence examples in this course contain *anata* or *anatagata,* but it is well to remember that these should be replaced in actual conversation by the name of the person to whom you are speaking, whenever possible.

c. **He, She, They**

SINGULAR	PLURAL	MEANING AND USAGE
ano kata	*ano katagata*	he, she, they (polite)
ano hito	*ano hitotachi*	he, she (plain)
ano otoko no kata	*ano otoko no katagata*	he, they (polite: used only when it is necessary to indicate specifically "he (that man)" or "they (those men)"
ano otoko no hito	*ano otoko no hitotachi*	he, they (plain: same as above)
ano onna no kata	*ano onna no katagata*	she, they (polite: used only when there is need to indicate specifically "she" or "they" [feminine plural])

ano onna no hito	*ano onna no hitotachi*	she, they (plain: same as above)
kare	*karera*	he, they (most often used in translations from English or in sample sentences in texts; also used widely by post-World War II generations but not yet widely accepted as good usage
kanojo	*kanojora*	she, they (same as above)

d. **Possessives**

There are no possessive pronouns as such in Japanese. To form the possessive, combine a noun (used for the person referred to) with *no* [things of], as in the following examples:

watakushi no	my, mine
anato no (or the name of the person) plus *no*	your, yours
ano hito no	his, hers
watakushitachi no	our, ours
anatagata no } *minasan no* }	your, yours *(pl.)*
ano hito-tachi no	their, theirs

13. PRENOUNS

"Prenouns"—words such as *konna* [this sort of] or *sonna* [that sort of] precede a noun and modify its meaning. No particle is used to separate the prenoun and noun. Prenouns do not change their forms.

kono	this
sono	that
ano	that over there
dono	which
konna	this sort of
sonna	that sort of
anna	that sort of
donna	what sort of

14. *KO-SO-A-DO* WORDS

Some Japanese nouns and prenouns come in sets of four words which are usually pronounced alike except for the first syllable. These sets of words are called "ko-so-a-do words" because the first syllable is always one of the following four: *ko-*, *so-*, *a-*, or *do-*. Note that the word in such a group which begins with *do* is always a question word.

a. *ko-so-a-do* nouns

kore	this one
sore	that one[1]
are	that one over there[1]
dore	which one?
koko	this place
soko	that place
asoko[2]	that place over there
doko	which place? where?
kochira, kotchi	this way, this one (of two)

[1]See Lesson 17, page 80.
[2]An irregular form

sochira, sotchi	that way, that one (of two)
achira, atchi	that way, that one (of two)
dochira, dotchi	which way, which (of two)?

b. *Ko-so-a-do* prenouns

kono	this
sono	that
ano	that over there
dono	which?
konna	this sort of
sonna	that sort of (for something not far removed in feeling or time)
anna	that sort of (for something more remote in feeling or time)
donna	what sort of?

15. ADJECTIVES

Adjectives can end in *-ai*, *-ii*, *-ui*, or *-oi*, but never in *-ei*.

akai	(is) red
utsukushii	(is) beautiful
samui	(is) cold
kuroi	(is) black

Adjectives are inflected as follows:

a. Plain Forms

| PRESENT | *takai* | it is high |

PAST	*takakatta*	it was high
-*te* FORM	*takakute*	it is (was) high and . . .
INFINITIVE } ADVERBIAL }	*takaku*	{ is high and . . . highly
PROVISIONAL	*takakereba*	if it is high
CONDITIONAL	*takakattara*	if (when) it is (was) high
TENTATIVE	*takakaroo*	will probably be high

b. Polite Forms

PRESENT	*takai desu*	it is high
PAST	*takai deshita* } *takakatta desu* }	it was high
-*te* FORM	*takakute*	It is (was) high and . . .
INFINITIVE } ADVERBIAL }	*takaku*	{ it is (was) high and . . . highly
PROVISIONAL	*takakereba*	if it is high
CONDITIONAL	*takakattara*	if (when) it is (was) high
TENTATIVE	*takai deshoo*	it will probably be high

c. Extra-polite Forms

PRESENT	*otakai desu* } *otakoo gozaimasu* }	it is high
PAST	*otakai deshita* } *otakoo gozaimashita* }	it was high
-*te* FORM	*otakakute* *otakoo gozaimashite*	it is high and . . .

INFINITIVE ADVERBIAL	*otakaku*	{ it is high and . . . highly
PROVISIONAL	*otakakereba*	if it is high
CONDITIONAL	*otakoo gozaimashitara*	if (when) it is high
TENTATIVE	*otakoo gozaimashoo*	it will probably be high

16. COMPARISONS

There are several ways to show comparison:

a. Use *no hoo* [the side of] to show what is being compared:

Kyooto no hoo ga suki desu.	I like Kyoto better
Tookyoo no hoo ga samui desu.	Tokyo is colder [in climate].
Jidoosha de iku hoo ga ii desu.	It is better to go by car.

b. Use *yori* [than] to mark the standard against which a comparison is made:

Kyooto yori samui desu.	It is colder than Kyoto.
Kore wa sore yori takai desu.	This is more expensive than that.

c. Use both *no hoo* and *yori* in the same sentence to show that a comparison is being made:

Tookyoo no hoo ga Kyooto yori samui desu.	Tokyo is colder than Kyoto.
Yomu koto no hoo ga hanasu koto yori muzukashii desu.	Reading is more difficult than speaking.

d. Use *zutto* [by far the more] either with or without *no hoo* or *yori:*

Sono kisha no hoo ga kono kisha yori zutto hayai desu. *Sono kisha ga zutto hayai desu.*	That train is much faster (than this train).
Kore wa zutto yasashii desu.	This is much easier.

e. Use *motto* [still more] either with or without *no hoo* or *yori:*

Sore wa motto takai desu. *Sore wa kore yori motto takai desu.*	That is still more expensive (than this one).
Motto yukkuri hanashite kudasai.	Please speak more slowly.

f. Use *ichiban* [number one, most of all] or *mottomo* [the most] when comparing more than two things:

Ano hito ga ichiban takai desu. *Ano hito ga mottomo takai desu.*	He is the tallest.
Ichiban ii no o kudasai.	Give me the best kind.

g. Use *dochira* or *dotchi* [which of the two], or *dore* [which of more than two] when asking a question involving a comparison:

Nagoya to Kyooto de wa dochira ga chikai desu ka?	Which is nearer—Nagoya or Kyoto?

| *Nagoya to Kyooto to Hiroshima de wa dore ga ichiban tooi desu ka?* | Which is the farthest—Nagoya, Kyoto, or Hiroshima? |

h. Use *hodo* (to show approximate degree) and a negative predicate when making a comparison between two things that are not quite alike:

| *Nagoya wa Oosaka hodo tooku arimasen.* | Nagoya is not as far as Osaka. |
| *Tanaka-san wa Yamada-san hodo kanemochi ja arimasen.* | Mr. Tanaka is not as rich as Mr. Yamada. |

i. Use *hodo* also to describe situations resulting in extreme, intense, or severe effects:

| *Kimochi ga waruku naru hodo takusan tabemashita.* | I ate so much that I began to feel sick. |
| *Onaka ga itaku naru hodo waraimashita.* | I laughed so much that I began to get a stomachache. |

j. Use *no yoo ni* [in the likeness of, in the manner of] or *kurai* (or *gurai*) [more or less] when making a comparison between two things or situations that are pretty much alike:

| *Yamada-san wa Eigo ga Beikokujin no yoo ni yoku dekimasu.* | Mr. Yamada knows English as well as a native American. |
| *Yamada-san wa Eigo ga Beikokujin gurai dekimasu.* | Mr. Yamada knows English as well as [just like] a native American. |

17. THE CLASSES AND FORMS OF VERBS

a. Verb Classes

There are three classes of verbs in Japanese:

Class I—Consonant Verbs: includes all verbs except those in Class II and Class III.

Class II—Vowel Verbs: includes the majority of verbs which, in their plain present form terminate in -*eru* or -*iru*.

Class III—Irregular Verbs: *kuru* [come] and *suru* [do].

The stem (or root) of a *consonant* verb is that part left over after the final -*u* has been dropped from the plain present form. The stem always ends in a consonant except where there is another vowel before the final -*u*.

The stem of a *vowel* verb is that part remaining after the final -*ru* has been dropped from the plain present form. It always ends in either -*e* or -*i*.

The stem of the *irregular* verb *kuru* is *ki-*, and the stem of the irregular verb *suru* is *shi-*.

b. The Tenses

In Japanese, a verb form referred to as a "tense" actually describes the *mood* of the action or state.

1. The present tense (or -*u*-ending form) expresses an *incomplete* action or state and may have several English translations:

Hanashimasu.	I speak. I do speak. I will speak.
Tabemasu.	I eat. I do eat. I will eat.

2. The past tense (or *-ta* form), expresses a *completed* action or state. It too can have several English translations:

Hanashimashita.	I spoke. I have spoken.
Tabemashita.	I ate. I have eaten.

The plain form of the past tense is formed from the plain present as follows:

a. Consonant verbs

1. When the final syllable in the plain present is *-u, -tsu,* or *-ru,* drop it and add *-tta:*

PRESENT	PAST	
kau	*katta*	I bought
Tatsu.	*Tatta.*	I stood up.
Toru.	*Totta.*	I took it.

2. When the final syllable in the plain present is *-mu, 'nu,* or *-bu,* drop it and add *-nda:*

Nomu.	*Nonda.*	I drank it.
Shinu.	*Shinda.*	He died.
Yobu.	*Yonda.*	I called.

3. When the final syllable is *-ku* or *-gu,* drop it and add *-ita* in place of *-ku* and *-ida* in place of *-gu:*

kaku	*kaita*	I wrote
isogu	*isoida*	I hurried

4. When the final syllable is *-su,* drop it and add *-shita:*

Hanasu.	*Hanashita.*	I spoke.
Kasu.	*Kashita.*	I lent it.

b. For vowel verbs:

Drop the final syllable *-ru* and add *-ta:*

Taberu.	*Tabeta.*	I ate.
Miru.	*Mita.*	I saw it.

c. For irregular verbs:

Kuru.	*Kita.*	I came.
Suru.	*Shita.*	I did.

The polite form of the past tense is formed from the polite present (the *-masu* form) by replacing the final syllable *-su* with *-shita.*

POLITE PRESENT POLITE PAST

Ikimasu.	*Ikimashita.*	I went.
Tabemasu.	*Tabemashita.*	I ate.
Mimasu.	*Mimashita.*	I saw it.

3. The tentative (polite: *-mashoo;* plain: *-oo* or *-yoo*) expresses an action or state which is not certain, definite, or completed. It can have several English translations:

Yomimashoo.	I think I will read. Let's read.
Yomimashoo ka?	Shall we read?
Yonda deshoo.	I suppose he has read it.

The plain tentative is formed from the plain present as follows:

a. For consonant verbs:

Drop the final *-u* and add *-oo.*

PRESENT   TENTATIVE

Hanasu.	*Hanasoo.*	I think I'll speak. Let's talk.

Yomu.	*Yomoo.*	I think I'll read.
		Let's read.

b. For vowel verbs:

Drop the final *-ru* and add *-yoo.*

Taberu.	*Tabeyoo.*	I think I'll eat.
		Let's eat.
Miru.	*Miyoo.*	I think I'll see it.
		Let's see it.

The polite tentative is formed from the polite present by dropping the final *-su* and adding *-shoo.*

POLITE	POLITE
PRESENT	TENTATIVE

Hanashimasu.	*Hanashimashoo.*	I think I'll talk.
		Let's talk.
Tabemasu.	*Tabemashoo.*	I think I'll eat.
		Let's eat.

4. Formation of the gerund:[1]

a. The gerund is formed exactly like the plain past (see page 305) except that the final vowel is *-e.* A gerund actually has no tense; the "tense" feeling is determined by the "tense-mood," that is, the ending *(-u, -ta, -yoo),* of the terminal verb.

Kusuriya e itte kusuri o kaimashita.	I went to a drugstore and bought some medicine.

---

[1] The *-te* form

Normally, when there is more than one verb in a sentence, the gerund form is used for all but the last verb. The "radical" (for consonant verbs, made up of the stem plus *i;* for vowel verbs, the stem itself) is sometimes used instead of the *-te* form, but this is considered "bookish."

Kusuriya e itte kusuri o katte uchi e kaette sore o nonde sugu nemashita.	I went to the drugstore and bought some medicine and returned home and took it and went to bed right away.

b. The gerund is also used:

1. Adverbially: To modify a verb or adjective.

Isoide ikimashita.	He went hurriedly.
Naite hanashimashita.	He spoke in tears.
Itatte genki desu.	He is very well.

2. With *kudasai:* to form a request.

Kesa no shinbun o katte kudasai.	Please buy me this morning's paper.

3. With *imasu:* to form the progressive.

Hanashite imasu.	I am speaking.
Tabete imasu.	I am eating.

4. To form the "stative," which expresses the state resulting from a completed action, add *arimasu* after the *-te* form of an intransitive verb. The stative of a transitive verb is identical with the progressive in form, but not

in function. The idea of the stative is often translated by the passive, in English.

Te de kaite arimasu.	It's handwritten. [It is in the state of his having written it by hand.]

INDICATIVE
PLAIN PRESENT

CLASS I VERBS (CONSONANT VERBS)	CLASS II VERBS (VOWEL VERBS)	CLASS III VERBS (IRREGULAR VERBS)
hanasu	*taberu*	*suru*
speak	eat	do
will speak	will eat	will do

PLAIN PAST

hanashita	*tabeta*	*shita*
spoke	ate	did
have spoken	have eaten	has done

PLAIN GERUND[1]

hanashite	*tabete*	*shite*
speak and ...	eat and ...	do and ...
will speak and ...	will eat and ...	will do and ...
spoke and ...	ate and ...	did and ...

POLITE PRESENT

CLASS I VERBS	CLASS II VERBS	CLASS III VERBS
hanashimasu	*tabemasu*	*shimasu*
speak	eat	do
will speak	will eat	will do

[1]See the preceding section for additional meanings. The gerund must *always* precede another verb in the same sentence.

POLITE PAST

hanashimashita	*tabemashita*	*shimashita*
spoke	ate	did
have spoken	have eaten	have done

POLITE GERUND[1]

hanashimashite	*tabemashite*	*shimashite*
speak and . . .	eat and . . .	do and . . .
spoke and . . .	ate and . . .	did and . . .
has spoken	has eaten	has done
and . . .	and . . .	and . . .

PLAIN PRESENT NEGATIVE

CLASS I VERBS	CLASS II VERBS	CLASS III VERBS
hanasanai	*tabenai*	*shinai*
do not speak	do not eat	do not do
will not speak	will not eat	will not do

PLAIN PAST NEGATIVE

hanasanakatta	*tabenakatta*	*shinakatta*
did not speak	did not eat	did not do
have not	have not eaten	have not done
spoken		

PLAIN GERUND NEGATIVE[2]

hanasanaide	*tabenaide*	*shinaide*
do not speak	do not eat	do not do
and . . .	and . . .	and . . .

POLITE PRESENT NEGATIVE

hanashimasen	*tabemasen*	*shimasen*
do not speak	do not eat	do not do
will not speak	will not eat	will not do

POLITE PAST NEGATIVE

hanashimasen	*tabemasen*	*shimasen*
deshita	*deshita*	*deshita*

[1]The polite gerund is used in only the most formal conversations.
[2]The plain gerund negative is used in the same manner as the plain gerund. See the preceding section.

| did not speak | did not eat | did not do |
| have not spoken | have not eaten | have not done |

CONSTRUCTION OF INCREASING DEGREES OF POLITENESS

PLAIN: *hanasu*

POLITE: *hanashimasu*
ohanashi ni narimasu
hanasaremasu

VERY POLITE: *ohanashi kudasaimasu*
hanashite kudasaimasu

HUMBLE: *hanashimasu*
ohanashi mooshiagemasu
ohanashi sasete itadakimasu

Note that in the following groups, the "a" lines show the plain form of the verb and the "b" lines show the polite form.

PRESENT PROGRESSIVE

CLASS I VERBS	CLASS II VERBS	CLASS III VERBS
a. *hanashite iru*	*tabete iru*	*shite iru*
b. *hanashite imasu* he is speaking	*tabete imasu* he is eating	*shite imasu* he is doing

PAST PROGRESSIVE

CLASS I VERBS	CLASS II VERBS	CLASS III VERBS
a. *hanashite ita*	*tabete ita*	*shite ita*
b. *hanashite imashita* he was speaking	*tabete imashita* he was eating	*shite imashita* he was doing

PRESENT PROGRESSIVE NEGATIVE

a. *hanashite inai*   *tabete inai*   *shite inai*

b. *hanashite imasen*   *tabete imasen*   *shite imasen*
he is not speaking   he is not eating   he is not doing

PAST PROGRESSIVE NEGATIVE

a. *hanashite inakatta*   *tabete inakatta*   *shite inakatta*

b. *hanashite imasen deshita*   *tabete imasen deshita*   *shite imasen deshita*
he was not speaking   he was not eating   he was not doing

STATIVE

PRESENT STATIVE

CLASS I VERBS	CLASS II VERBS	CLASS III VERBS
a. *Hanashite aru.*	*Tabete aru.*	*Shite aru.*
b. *Hanashite arimasu.* The matter has already been mentioned to him. [The matter is in the state of my having spoken about it.]	*Tabete arimasu.* The meal is finished. [The meal is in the state of my having eaten it.]	*Shite arimasu.* It's done. [The work is in the state of my having done it.]

PAST STATIVE[1]

a. *Hanashite atta.*   *Tabete atta.*   *Shite atta.*

[1]Usually translated in English by the past perfect

b. *Hanashite* *Tabete* *Shite*
 arimashita. *arimashita.* *arimashita.*
 The matter The meal had The work had
 had been been eaten. been done.
 mentioned
 to him.

PRESENT STATIVE NEGATIVE

a. *Hanashite* *Tabete nai.* *Shite nai.*
 nai.
b. *Hanashite* *Tabete* *Shite arimasen.*
 arimasen. *arimasen.*
 The matter The meal is It is not done.
 has not not finished.
 been
 mentioned.

PAST STATIVE NEGATIVE

a. *Hanashite* *Tabete nakatta.* *Shite nakatta.*
 nakatta.
b. *Hanashite* *Tabete* *Shite arimasen*
 arimasen *arimasen* *deshita.*
 deshita. *deshita.*
 The matter It hadn't been
 hadn't The meal done.
 been hadn't been
 mentioned. finished.

PROVISIONAL AND CONDITIONAL

hatarakeba *tabereba* *sureba*
hataraitara *tabetara* *shitara*
hataraku to *taberu to* *suru to*
hataraku nara *taberu nara* *suru nara*
hataraite wa *tabete wa* *shite wa*
 if I work if I eat if I do

18. PARTICLES USED WITH VERBS

The following particles which are used with verbs can also be used with adjectives or the copula. (See also Section 10-I of the Grammar, page 293, for particles used with nouns.)

a. *bakari desu* =

1. (following a *-u* form) does nothing but (something); does only. . . .

Sotsugyoo o matsu bakari desu.	I am just waiting for graduation. (I have no more school work to do.)

2. (following a *-ta* form) has just done (something); did only (something):

Gohan o tabeta bakari desu.	I have just finished eating.

3. (following *-nai*) only does not do (something); is just short of; is merely doing (something)

b. *dake* = that is just about all; that is just about the extent of it; only; just:

Mita dake desu.	I just took a look at it.
Hanashi o suru dake desu.	I am just going to discuss it. (I won't make any decision yet.)

c. *ga* = but; in spite of that fact stated above (when preceded by either the plain or polite forms):

Ikimashita ga aemasen deshita.	I went (there) but I couldn't see him.

*Kaimashita ga mada
　tsukatte arimasen.*　　I have bought it but it
　　　　　　　　　　　hasn't been used.

d. *ka* =

　　1. a spoken question mark:

Kyoo wa oisogashii　　Are you busy today?
　desu ka?

　　2. . . . or . . . :

Kinoo deshita ka ototoi　Was it yesterday or was
　deshita?　　　　　　　it the day before
　　　　　　　　　　　　yesterday?

e. *kara* =

　　1. (following a *-te* form) after doing (some-
　　thing); since doing (something):

Mite kara kimemasu.　　I will decide after
　　　　　　　　　　　　taking [having taken]
　　　　　　　　　　　　a look at it.

　　2. (following any sentence-ending form— *-u,
　　-ta, -i*) and so, and therefore:

Omoi desu kara　　　　It's heavy so I will
　watakuski ga omochi　carry it.
　shimashoo.

f. *keredo(mo)*[1] = in spite of that fact stated before;
　　but; however; although:

Isoida keredo ma ni　　I hurried but couldn't
　aimasen deshita.　　　make it.

Yonda keredomo yoku　I read it but I didn't
　wakarimasen deshita.　understand it well.

g. *made* = up to the time of (something)'s happen-
　　ing; until; so far as:

Mainichi goji made　　Every day I work till
　hatarakimasu.　　　　five o'clock.

[1]The use of *mo* is optional.

Yamada-san ga kuru   I will stay here until
  made koko ni   Mr. Yamada gets
  orimasu.   here.

h. *na* =

  1. (following a present form) don't do (something); note that this is never used in refined speech; instead, *-naide kudasai* is used:

Hairu na!   Don't enter!
Hairanaide kudasai.   Please don't enter.

  2. (following a sentence-ending form) yeah, that's what it is (used only by men in colloquial speech):

Ii tenki da na!   What fine weather!
Genki da na!   You are in good shape!
     (You look fine!).

  3. (following a verb and used with *ka*) should I?; I wonder if I should? (used by men in colloquial speech):

Dekaykeyoo ka na?   Let's see. Shall we go
     now?

Eiga de mo miyoo ka   I guess I will see a
  na?   movie or something.

i. *-nagara* = (following an infinitive or radical, showing that two or more actions or states take place or exist concurrently) while; in the course of:

Arukinagara   Let's talk as we walk
  hanashimashoo.   (to that place).
Hatarakinagara   He is studying while
  benkyoo shite imasu.   working (he is
     supporting himself).

j. *nari* =

1. (when used in a parallel sequence) either...
or...; whether...or...:

Mizu nari ocha nari motte kite kudasai.	Please bring either water or tea (I don't care which).

2. (when *not* used in a parallel sequence) as soon as; the moment (something) has taken place:

Kao o miru nair nakihajimemashita.	He burst into tears the moment he saw me.

k. *ni* = the purpose of the "going" or "coming" that is expressed (when it follows the infinitive or radical of a verb):

Kaimono o si ni ikimashita.	He went shopping. [He went in order to shop.]

l. *node* = (following a sentence-ending form) and so; and therefore (note that the clause which follows has to be in the -*u* or *ta* form; -*masyoo* and -*te kudasai* are never used):

Amari tsukareta node sukoshi yasumitai desu.	I got very tired, so I would like to [take a] rest.
Okane o harawanakatta node okutte kimasen deshita.	I didn't send the money for it; that's why it didn't come.

m. *noni* =

1. and yet, but:

Yonda noni henji ga nai.	I called him but there was no answer.

2. although:

Itta noni awanakatta.   Although I went there, I didn't see him.

n. *to* =

1. (following a present form) whenever:

Hima da to sanpo shimasu.   Whenever I am free, I take a walk.

2. acts as an "end quote" when it precedes a verb meaning "say," "hear," "ask," "think," "believe":

Itsu kimasu ka to kikareta.   I was asked [as to] when I would be coming.

3. (when it follows a tentative and is in turn followed by *suru*) to be on the point of doing (something); to try to do (something):

Uchi o deyoo to suru tokoro e tomodachi ga kimashita.   Just as I was about to go out, a friend of mine came (to visit me).

o. *-tari . . . -tari suru* =

1. sometimes does (something); at other times does (something else):

Nihon to Amerika no aida o ittari kitari shite imasu.   He travels back and forth between Japan and the United States.

2. does (one thing) and (another):

Hito ga nottari oritari shite imasu.   Some people are getting on, some are getting off.

p. terminal particles:

1. *ne* = isn't it? doesn't it?

Erai hito desu ne?	He is a great man, isn't he?

2. *sa* = sure it is so (used only by men):

Shitte iru sa!	Of course I know it.

3. *wa, wa yo* = a diminutive used only by women:

Sanji ni denwa o kakeru wa (yo).[1]	I will phone you at three.

4. *yo* = an exclamatory particle:

Kyoo wa okyakusan ga aru yo!	We are going to have a visitor today.

5. *zo* = an emphatic particle used only by men (slang):

Naguru zo!	I'll hit you!

19. NEGATIVES

a. Used with Verbs

1. Plain forms

   a. Plain negative present—formed from the stem of a consonant verb plus the suffix *-anai*, or the stem of a vowel verb plus *-nai:*

Kaku.	I write.
Kakanai.	I don't write.
Taberu.	I eat.
Tabenai.	I don't eat.

[1] The use of *yo* is optional.

Notice that a verb like *kau* [buy] or *warau* [laugh], whose plain present ends in two vowels, appends an extra *w* before adding *-anai:*

Kawanai.	I don't buy.
Warawanai.	He doesn't laugh.

    b. Plain negative past—formed from the stem of the negative present plus *-katta* (like the plain negative past of an adjective):

Kaita.	I wrote.
Kakanakatta.	I didn't write.

    c. Plain negative tentative:

        1. For a consonant verb, use the plain present plus *-mai.*

        2. For a vowel verb, use the stem plus *-mai.*

        3. For the irregular verbs, use *komai* and *shimai.*

Kakoo.	I think I'll write it.
Kakumai.	I don't think I'll write it.
Tabeyoo.	I think I'll eat.
Tabemai.	I don't think I'll eat.

b. Used with a Copula
    1. Plain forms:

. . . *da*	It is . . .
. . . *de aru*	It is (formal, bookish) . . .
. . . *ja nai*	It is not . . .
. . . *de wa nai*	It is not . . .
. . . *datta*	It was . . .
. . . *ja nakatta* . . . *de wa nakatta* }	It was not . . .

. . . *daroo*	It may probably be . . .
. . . *de nai daroo*	It is most probably not . . .

2. Polite forms:

. . . *desu*	It is . . .
. . . *ja arimasen*	It is not . . .
. . . *deshita*	It was . . .
. . . *ja arimasen deshita*	It wasn't . . .
. . . *deshoo*	It may probably be . . .
. . . *ja nai deshoo*	It is most probably not . . .

c. **Used with Adjectives**

1. Plain forms—formed from the stem of the adjective plus *-ku* plus *-nai:*

Takai.	It is expensive.
Takakunai.	It is not expensive.
Takakatta.	It was expensive.
Takakunakatta.	It wasn't expensive.
Takakaroo.	It may be expensive.
Takakunakaroo.	It is most probably not expensive.

2. Polite—formed from the stem of the verb plus *-ku arimasen:*

Takai desu.	It is expensive.
Takaku arimasen.	It is not expensive.
Takai deshita.	It was expensive.
Takaku arimasen deshita *Takakunakatta desu.*	It was not expensive.
Takai deshoo.	It is probably expensive.
Takakunai deshoo.	It is most probably not expensive.

d. **Other negative expressions** (used with negative verbs, the copula, or adjectives):

hotondo	hardly
zenzen	not (at all)
hitotsu mo	nothing
dare mo	no one
doko mo	nowhere
itsu mo	at no time
dochira mo	neither . . . nor
kesshite	never

20. WORD ORDER

There are two very important rules to remember for word order in declarative sentences:

a. A predicate word (the copula, verb, or adjective used as a predicate) is placed at the *end* of the clause or sentence except when a sentence-ending particle such as *ka* (the question-mark particle) or *ne* [isn't it? doesn't it?] is used, in which case the predicate word is placed *immediately before* such a particle.

b. A modifier *always precedes the word or clause it modifies:*

1. An adjective or adjectival phrase (a noun plus *no*) always precedes the noun it modifies;

2. A prenoun always precedes the noun;

3. An adverb or adverbial phrase always precedes the adjective, adverb, verb, or copula it modifies;

4. A modifying clause always precedes the noun it modifies.

For example:

akai booshi	a red hat
ano hito	that person
ano hito no booshi	that person's hat; her (his) hat
ano hito no akai booshi	that person's red hat; her red hat
ookina booshi	a big hat
ano hito no ookina akai booshi	that person's big red hat
katta booshi	the hat she bought
kinoo katta booshi	the hat she bought yesterday
kinoo Matsuya de katta booshi	the hat she bought at Matsuya's yesterday
ano hito ga kinoo no gogo Matsuya de katta booshi	the hat which she bought at Matsuya's yesterday afternoon
ano hito ga kinoo no gogo Matsuya de katta ookina akai booshi	that big red hat which she bought at Matsuya's yesterday afternoon
ano hito ga kinoo no gogo watakushi to issho no itte Matsuya de katta ookina akai booshi	that big red hat which she bought yesterday afternoon with me at Matsuya's

21. QUESTIONS

The word order for questions is the same as for declarative sentences. The question particle *ka* may or may not be added at the end to show that a question is being asked. For instance:

When *ka* is used, it is not necessary to use the rising intonation that is customary for a question in English;

the intonation may remain that of a declarative sentence even though a question is being asked. However, when a question is being asked and *ka* is not used, the rising intonation must be employed, and the last syllable is pronounced with a distinct rise in pitch. (See Lesson 13, page 67.)

Ikimasu.	I am going.
Ikimasu?	Are you going?
Ikimasu ka?	Are you going?

See the following section for other words that are used in formulating questions.

22. QUESTION WORDS

There are several words that are used to form questions. Study the chart at the end of this section to help you grasp more easily what the words are and how they are used.

QUESTION WORDS	MEANING	NOTES
nan, nani[1]	what thing? what? how many?	*nan* is usually used before a word beginning with *d*, *n*, *s*, *sh*, and *t*; *nani* is used everywhere else. The meaning "how many?" applies only when the word is used before a counter.
nannin	how many persons?	

[1] Notice that this is a noun in Japanese.

ikutsu[1]	what number? how many?	The answer must be a number.
iku-	how many . . . ?	A prefix used only with a counter.
itsu[1]	what time? when?	When used adverbially, it may sometimes be used without a particle.

Itsu kimashita ka?	When did it arrive?
Itsu kara hajimarimasu ka?	When does it begin?
Itsu ga ii desu ka?	When would it be good for you?

dare[1]	which person? who?	*dare no:* whose? *dare ni:* to whom? *dare kara:* from whom: *dare to:* with whom?
dore[1]	which thing? which?	Used when there is a choice of more than two.
dochira[1]	which of these two? which direction? which place (polite)?	Used when there is a choice of only two.

---

[1]Notice that this is a noun in Japanese.

dochira e		where to?
dochira kara		where from?
dotchi	see above	A variant for the first meaning of *dochira*.
doko[1]	which place? where?	
Doko ni arimasu ka?		Where is it?
Doko de tabemashita ka?		Where did you eat?
Doko kara kimashita ka?		Where did you come from?
Doko ga itai desu ka?		Where does it hurt?
dono	which	A prenoun used when there is a choice of *more than* two. Use *dochira no* when there is a choice of *only* two.
donna	what sort of?	A prenoun used when you are interested in the kind or type of thing being discussed.
doo	how? in what manner?	An adverb.
ikaga	how (polite)?	An adverb; same as *doo* (above) but used in refined speech.

[1]Notice that this is a noun in Japanese.

23. SOMETHING, EVERYTHING, NOTHING, ANYTHING

Each of the question words appearing in the first column of this chart undergoes a change in meaning when it is used together with one of the particles appearing in the other columns. The new meaning is shown for each combination.

QUESTION WORD	+ ka	+ mo (used with affirmative) predicate	+ mo (used with negative predicate	+ de mo	+ -te mo
nani, nan = what	nani ka = something or other	nani mo ka mo = everything	nani mo = nothing	nan de mo = anything	nani . . . te mo = whatsoever
dore = which one	dore ka = one or the other; any-one	dore mo = all, any	dore mo = no one, not any-one, not a one	dore de mo = whichever it may be; any-one at all	dore . . . te mo = whichsoever

QUESTION WORD	+ ka	+ mo (used with affirmative) predicate	+ mo (used with negative) predicate	+ de mo	+ -te mo
dochira = which of the two	dochira ka = either one	dochira mo = both	dochira mo = not either one, neither one	dochira de mo = whichever it may be, either one	dochira . . . te mo = whichever
dotchi, doko = which of the two	dotchi ka = either one	dotchi mo = both	dotchi mo = not either one, neither one	dotchi de mo = whichever it may be, either one	dotchi . . . te mo = whichever
doko = which place	doko ka = some-where or other	doko mo = everywhere; all places	doko mo = not anywhere, no-where	doko de mo = wherever it may be, any place at all	doko . . . te mo = wherever

QUESTION WORD	+ ka	+ mo (used with affirmative) predicate	+ mo (used with negative) predicate	+ de mo	+ -te mo
donata = which person (polite)	*donata ka* = somebody	*donata mo* = everybody	*donata mo* = not anybody, nobody	*donata de mo* = whoever it may be, anybody at all	*donata . . . te mo* = whoever
itsu = what time	*itsu ka* = sometime or other	*itsu mo* = always	*itsu mo* = not anytime, never	*itsu de mo* = whenever it may be; anytime at all	*itsu . . . te mo* = whenever
doo = how	*doo ka* = somehow or other; please, by some means or other	*doo mo* = in every way, very	*doo mo* = somehow; not; in no way	*doo de mo* = however it may be; anyway at all	*doo . . . te mo* = however, one does in whatever way ever way

QUESTION WORD	+ ka	+ mo (used with affirmative) predicate	+ mo (used with negative) predicate	+ de mo	+ -te mo
dooshite = why	dooshite ka = somehow or other, for some unknown reason	dooshite mo = by all means, under any circumstances	dooshite mo = somehow or other... not; however one tries... not	dooshite de mo = by all means; at all costs	—
ikutsu = how many	ikutsu ka = some number, several	ikutsu mo = any number	ikutsu mo = not many, no great number, not much to speak of	ikutsu de mo = however many it may be; any number at all	ikutsu... te mo = however many one may
ikura = how much	ikura ka = some amount	ikura mo = any amount; ever so much	ikura mo = not much; no great amount	ikura de mo = whatever amount it may be	ikura... te mo = however much it may be one may

24. EVEN IF, EVEN THOUGH

a. Affirmative

Use *-te* plus *mo:*

Ame ga futte mo ikimasu.	I'll [still] go, even if it rains.
Takakute mo kaimasu.	I'll [still] buy it even if it's expensive.

b. Negative

Use *-nakute* plus *mo:*

Ame ga yamanakute mo ikimasu.	I will go [anyhow] even if it doesn't stop raining.
Yasukunakute mo kamaimasen.	I don't care even if it's not cheap.

c. Permission

Use *-te mo ii desu* for "you may [you have my permission to]"; use *-nakute mo ii desu* for "you don't have to [you have my permission not to; even if you don't, it is all right with me]":

Itte mo ii desu.	You may go.
Ikanakuto mo ii desu.	You don't have to go.

d. No matter how, No matter who, No matter how much

Use a question word plus *-te mo:*

Donna ni yasukute mo kaitaku arimasen.	I don't want to buy it no matter how cheap it is.
Dare ga shite mo kekka wa onaji desu.	No matter who does it, the result will be the same.

Ikura yonde mo imi ga wakarimasen deshita.	I couldn't understand it no matter how many times I read it.

25. HEARSAY

To express the ideas, "I hear that . . ." or "They say that . . ." in Japanese:

a. **For the Affirmative.** Use any sentence-ending form of a verb or an adjective plus *soo desu:*

Kyoo wa Yamada-san ga kuru soo desu.	I hear that Mr. Yamada is coming to visit us today.
Sapporo de wa yuki ga futta soo desu.	I hear that it snowed in Sapporo.
Takai soo desu.	I understand (that) it's expensive.

b. **For the Negative.** Use any sentence-ending form of a verb or an adjective in the negative plus *soo desu:*

Rajio no tenki yohoo de wa kyoo wa ame wa furanai soo desu.	According to the weather forecast it's not going to rain today.
Yamada-san wa konakatta soo desu.	I hear that Mr. Yamada didn't come.
Takakunai soo desu.	I hear (that) it's not expensive.

26. SEEMING

You can express the idea of "it seems" or "it seems to me that . . ." in several ways in Japanese:

a. **For the Affirmative**

  1. Use a sentence-ending form plus *yoo desu:*

Moo shitte iru yoo desu.	It seems to me that he already knows it.
Ano hito wa Amerika e kaetta yoo desu.	It seems that he has gone back to the United States.

2. Use a sentence-ending form plus *rashii desu:*

Moo shitte iru rashii desu.	It seems to me that he already knows it.
Ano hito wa Amerika e kaetta rashii desu.	It seems that he has gone back to the United States.

3. Use the stem of an adjective plus *-soo desu:*

Kurushisoo desu.	It seems that he is finding it painful.

b. **For the Negative**
  1. Use a sentence-ending form in the negative plus *yoo desu:*

Mada shiranai yoo desu.	It seems that he is unaware of this.
Ana hito wa Nihon ni konakatta yoo desu.	Apparently [it seems that] he didn't come to Japan.

2. Use a sentence-ending form in the negative plus *rashii desu:*

Mada shiranai rashii desu.	It seems that he is unaware of this.
Ana hito wa e Nihon konakatta rashii desu.	Apparently [it seems that] he didn't come to Japan.

3. Use the stem of a negative adjective plus
-*sasoo desu:*

Kurushikunasasoo desu.	He is apparently [it seems that he is] not finding it painful.

27. IMMINENCE

To express the idea "it appears that . . . will soon happen":

a. **For the Affirmative**

Use the radical of the verb plus -*soo desu:*

Ame ga furisoo desu ne.	It looks like rain, doesn't it?
Yamada-san wa yame-soo desu.	It looks as if Mr. Yamada is ready to quit.

b. **For the Negative**

Use the radical of a verb plus -*soo ja arimasen:*

Ame wa furisoo ja arimasen.	It doesn't look as though it will rain soon.
Nedan wa yasuku narisoo ja arimasen.	It doesn't look as though the price is going down.

28. OBLIGATION

To convey the idea of obligation or impulsion (expressed in English by "should," "must," "ought to," "have to"):

a. **For the Affirmative**

1. Use the negative provisional of a verb or an adjective plus *narimasen* or *ikemasen* [if you don't do it, it won't do; if not (something), it won't do]; or

2. Use the negative *-te* form plus *wa* plus *nari-masen* or *ikemasen*:[1]

Ikanakereba
narimasen.
Ikanakereba ikemasen.   I should (must, have to,
Ikanakute wa   ought to) go.
narimasen.
Ikanakute wa ikemasen.

Yokunakereba
narimasen.
Yokunakereba
ikemasen.   It should (must, has to,
Yokunakute wa   ought to) be good.
narimasen.
Yokunakute wa
ikemasen.

b. **For the Negative**

1. Use the *-te* form plus *wa* plus *narimasen* or *ikemasen* [if you do (something), it won't do; if it is (something), it won't do]:

Itte wa narimasen.   I should not (must not,
Itte wa ikemasen.   ought not to) go.

c. *Beki desu* [should], *beki ja arimasen* [should not]

The use of *beki* for "should" is relatively new in spoken Japanese and some people still do not accept it.

1. For the affirmative, use the plain present of a verb plus *beki desu*:

Iku beki desu.   I should (must, have to,
                           ought to) go.
Iku beki deshita.   I should have gone.

---

[1] Notice the use of a double negative.

2. For the negative, use the plain present of a verb plus *beki ja arimasen:*

Iku beki ja arimasen.   I should not go.
Iku beki ja arimasen   I shouldn't have gone.
  deshita.

3. For warning or prohibition (seen in public signs only), the plain present of a verb is used with *bekarazu* [don't][1]:

Hairu bekarazu!   No admission!
Tooru bekarazu!   No trespassing!
Sawaru bekarazu!   Don't touch!

29. PERMITTING AND PROHIBITING

To express the granting of permission, use *-te* plus *mo* plus *ii desu* [you may, it's all right to]:

Kaitakereba katte mo ii   If you want to buy it,
  desu.   you may (buy it).
Uchi e motte kaette mo   You may take it home if
  ii desu.   you wish.

To forbid or prohibit some action, use *-te wa narimasen* or *-te wa ikemasen* [you may not, you must not]:

Sonna mono wa katte   You must not buy such a
  wa ikemasen.   thing (as that).
Uchi e motte kaette wa
  ikemasen.   You can't take it home
Uchi e motte kaette wa   with you.
  narimasen.

---

[1]*Bekarazu* is a form left over from classical Japanese.

30. ALTERNATIVES

In statements setting forth a choice of alternatives, use:

a. **-tari ... -tari shimasu** (the *-ta* form plus *ri* followed by the *-ta* form plus *ri suru*):

Kyoo wa ame ga futtari yandari shite imasu.	Today it has been raining off and on.
Ano hito wa chikagoro gakkoo e ittari ikanakattari shimasu.	He has been irregular recently in (his) attendance at school.
Nichiyoobi no gogo wa shinbun o yondari terebi o mitari shimasu.	On Sunday afternoons I spend my time doing such things as reading newspapers and watching television.
Hito ga detari haittari shite imasu.	People are going in and out.

b. **-tari shimasu** (a single *-tari* followed by *shimasu*):

Eiga e ittari shimashita.	Among the various things (I did), I went to the movies. I spent my time going to the movies and doing things like that.
Miyagemono o kattari shimashita.	I hunted for souvenirs and did (other) things like that.

31. THE THREE P'S: PASSIVE, POTENTIAL, AND POLITE

A verb made up of its stem plus *-areru* or *-rareru* may be any one of the following: (1) passive, (2) potential, or (3) polite. (Used *-areru* with a consonant verb and *-rareru* with a vowel verb.) The exact meaning of such a verb is determined by the context in which it is used.

a. Passive

Watakushi wa junsa ni namae o kikaremashita.

I was asked my name by a policeman.

b. Potential

Nihon no eiga wa Amerika de mo miraremasu.

Japanese movies can be seen in the United States too. [One can see a Japanese movie in America too.]

c. Polite

Itoo-sensei wa kinoo Amerika kara kaeraremashita.

My teacher, Mr. Ito, came back from the United States yesterday.

The passive of some Japanese verbs—most particularly the passive forms of intransitive verbs—means "(something) happened when it wasn't wanted," or "I underwent (something)," or "I suffered from the interference of (something)":

Kisha no naka de kodomo ni nakarete komarimashita.

We were embarrased by our baby, who cried continuously while riding on a train.

Ame ni furarete sukkari nurete shimaimashita.

We were drenched by the rain.

32. CAUSATIVE

To form the causative of a verb, add *-aseru* to the stem of a consonant verb and *-saseru* to the stem of a vowel verb. The causative forms of the irregular verbs are: (for *kuru*) *kosaseru,* and (for *suru*) *saseru.*

Causative verbs may be used to express the thought that:

    a. X *causes* (makes, forces) Y to do (something), or

    b. x *allows* (permits, lets) Y to do (something).

Notice that in each instance the element Y is marked by the particle *ni.*

Tanaka-san wa Yamada-san ni denpoo o utasemashita.	Mr. Tanaka had Mr. Yamada send a telegram.
Kodomo ni kimono o kisasete kudasai.	Please have the children put on their clothes.
Kyoo wa itsu mo yori ichijikan hayaku kaerasete itadakitai desu.	I would like to have your permission to go home one hour earlier than usual. [I would like to have you make me go home . . .]

When a combination of a causative and a passive ending is used, the causative ending always comes first.

*Ik**aserare**mashita.*	I was made to go.
*Tabes**aserare**mashita.*	I was made to eat it.

33. DESIDERATIVES

The desiderative is the grammatical term for verbal expressions that signify a desire to do something.

a. To say, "I want to do (something)," use stem of the verb plus *-itai* or *-tai*. Add *-itai* to the stem of a consonant verb and *-tai* to the stem of a vowel verb. The corresponding forms for the irregular verbs are *kitai* [want to come] for *kuru* and *shitai* want to do [for *suru*]:

Kyoo wa kaimono ni ikitai desu.	I want to go shopping today.
Ima wa nani mo tabetaku arimasen.	I don't want to eat anything now.

b. To express the idea, "one shows that he wants to do (something)," add *-itagaru* to the stem of a consonant verb and *-tagaru* to the stem of a vowel verb. The corresponding forms for the irregular verbs are *kitagaru* (for *kuru*) and *shitagaru* (for *suru*):

Kodomo ga soto e ikitagatte imasu.	The children can't wait to go outside.
Uchi no kodomo wa sono kusuri o nomitagarimasen.	Our child doesn't like to take that medicine. [Our child shows that he doesn't like to take that medicine.]

c. Use the stem of an adjective plus *-garu* to express the meaning that "someone[1] shows outwardly that he feels . . .":

Samugarimashita.	He showed that he felt cold.
Hoshigarimashita.	He showed that he wanted to have it.

d. To say, "I want you to do (something) for me," use the *-te* form plus *itadakitai desu:*

[1] Usually not the speaker

Kono tegami o Eigo ni yakushite itadakitai desu.	I would like you to translate this letter into English for me.
Kore o katte itadakai desu.	I would like you to buy this for me.

A variant of this expression is *-te choodai,* usually used by children when speaking to other children, or among adults in an intimate, informal, or relaxed situation.

Katte choodai.	Buy it for me.
Sore o totte choodai.	Pick it up for me.

34. TO DO (SOMETHING) FOR . . .

a. To say, "He does (something) for me," in the polite form, use *-te kudasaimasu;* in the plain form, use *-te kuremasu:*

Sonokoto wa Yamada-san ga shirasete kudasaimashita.	Mr. Yamada was kind enough to inform me about it.
Shirasete kudasai.	Please let me know.
Ani ga katte kuremashita.	My older brother bought it for me.

b. Use *-te agemasu* to say, "I do (something) for you (him, her)," in the polite form; use *-te yaru* for the plain form:

Sore wa anata ni katte ageta no desu.	I bought it for you.
Anata ni katte agemashoo.	I'll buy it for you.
Kodomo ni katte yarimashita.	I bought it for our child.

c. Use -te itadakimasu to say, "I always have him do (something)," in the polite form, and -te moraimasu in the plain form:

yamada-san ni katte itadakimashita.	I had Mr. Yamada buy it for me.
Tomodachi ni yakushite moraimashita.	I had a friend of mine translate it for me.
Yamada-san ni yakushite itadaite kudasai.	Please have it translated by Mr. Yamada.

35. MAY, PERHAPS, PROBABLY

To say that "something may (might) happen," add ka mo shiremasen after the -u or -ta ending of a verb or copula, and to the -i or -ta ending of an adjective.

Ame ga furu ka mo shiremasen.	It may rain (but I can't tell for sure).
Ame wa furanai ka mo shiremasen.	It may not rain (but I can't tell for sure).
Yuube ame ga futta ka mo shiremasen.	It may have rained last night (but I can't be sure about it).

36. IF AND WHEN

a. **The Use of to**

1. Use to between two clauses to show that the second clause follows as a natural result of the first clause. The particle to in such a case comes at the end of the "if" or "when" clause:

Ame ga furu to anmari hito ga takusan kimasen.	When it rains, not too many people come.
Kippu ga nai to hairemasen.	If you don't have tickets, you can't get in. [If there isn't a ticket . . .]

Atàrashii to takai desu.   When it's new, it's
                               expensive.

2. Note that the predicate before *to* is *always* in
   the present form regardless of the tense of the
   rest of the sentence:

Hima da to sanpo   Whenever I had time, I
   shimashita.   took a walk.

3. The predicate before *to* usually appears in the
   plain present form. When *to* is used for "if"
   or "when," the predicate of the main clause
   (the one following the clause ending in *to*)
   must be in the *-u* or *-ta* form; it can *never* end
   in *-masyoo* or *-te kudasai.*

b. **The Use of -tara**

To introduce a condition or a supposition, add
-ra to the *-ta* form of a verb, adjective, or
copula:

Ame ga futtara   If it rains, I won't go.
   ikimasen.
Denpoo ga kitara   If you get a telegram,
   denwa o kakete   please phone me.
   kudasai.
Anmari samukattara   If it's too cold (for
   mado o shimete   you), please shut the
   kudasai.   window.
Nihonjin dattara dare   Anybody who is a
   de mo ii desu.   native Japanese will
                              do. [If it's a native
                              Japanese, anybody
                              will do.]

c. **The Use of *nara***

Use *nara* with a noun or a sentence-ending form
of a verb or adjective to express "if":

Byooki nara yasumu hoo ga ii desu.	If you are sick, you had better rest.
Shiranai nara oshiete agemasu.	If you don't know, I'll teach you.
Yasui nara kaimasu.	If it is inexpensive, I'll buy it.

d. **The use of *eba*, *-reba*, or *-kereba***

This form—*-eba* or *-reba* for a verb, *-kereba* for an adjective—is used only for unconfirmed situations:

Ame ga fureba ikimasen.	If it rains, I won't go.
Ame ga furanakereba ikimasu.	If it doesn't rain, I will go.
Mireba sugu wakarimasu.	If I take a look at it, I can readily identify it.
Takakereba kaimasen.	If it's expensive, I won't buy it.

e. **The Use of *-te wa***

This expression for "if" is most often found in an expression denoting "must" (i.e., "if you don't do . . . , it won't do"):

Okane ga nakute wa kaemasen.	If you have no money, you can't buy it.
Yoku benkyoo shinakute wa ikemasen.	If you don't study hard (you must!), it won't do.

37. WHETHER . . . OR . . . , IF . . . OR . . .

a. **The Uses of *ka***

1. Use *ka . . . ka* in a sentence conveying the meaning "whether or not":

Okane ga aru ka nai ka shirimasen.	I don't know if he has money or not.

Takai ka yasui ka　　I don't know if it is
　shirimasen.　　　　expensive or not.

2. Use *ka doo ka* to express "if . . . or":

Okane ga aru ka doo ka　　I don't know if he has
　shirimasen.　　　　　　money or not.
Takai ka doo ka　　　　I don't know if it's
　shirimasen.　　　　　expensive or not.
　　　　　　　　　　　[. . . if it's expensive
　　　　　　　　　　　or what.]

Iku ka doo ka　　　　I don't know whether
　shirimasen.　　　　he is going or not.

3. Use *ka* in a sentence having the sense of
　　"either . . . or":

Suiyoobi ka Mokuyoobi　　He will come on
　ni kimasu.　　　　　　Wednesday or else on
　　　　　　　　　　　Thursday.

Yoshida-san ka mata wa　　Please have either Mr.
　Kida-san ni kite　　　　Yoshida or Mr. Kida
　moratte kudasai.　　　come.

38. NOUN-MAKERS

Certain nouns which appear at the end of a clause
convert that entire clause into a noun equivalent. For
example:

a. *no* = the one (the time, the person, the place);
　　the act of:

Kesa hayaku uchi e　　The person who phoned
　denwa o kaketa no wa　us early this morning
　Tanaka-san deshita.　was Mr. Tanaka.
Kinoo mita no wa　　　The one we saw
　Amerika no eiga　　　yesterday was an
　deshita.　　　　　　American movie.

Kyooto e itta no wa Shigatsu deshita.	It was in April that we went to Kyoto. [The time when we went to Kyoto was April.]
Mainichi yoru osoku made hataraku no wa karada ni warui desu.	Working late night after night is bad for your health.

b. *koto* = the act of; the experience of:

Hokkaido e itta koto ga arimasu.	I have been to Hokkaido. [The experience of having gone to Hokkaido exists.]
Nihongo wa hanasu koto wa dekimasu ga yomu koto wa dekimasen.	I can speak but I can't read Japanese.

39. IN ORDER TO

a. To say that "one goes or comes in order to do (something),"

    1. Use the radical plus *ni* plus a verb of locomotion such as *ikimasu* or *kimasu:*

Mi ni ikimasu.	I am going there to see it.
Gohan or tabe ni ikimashita.	He went to eat.
Amerika no shinbun o yomi ni kimashita.	I came to read American newspapers.

    2. Use a noun describing an action, plus *ni* plus a verb of locomotion:

Kaimono ni ikimashita.	He went out to shop [for shopping].

Ryokoo ni dekakemashita.	He set out on a journey.

b. To say that "one does (something) for the purpose of doing (something other than going or coming),"

1. A present-tense verb plus the noun-maker *no* plus *ni* plus a verb:

Kono megane wa hon o yomu no ni tsukaimasu.	I use these glasses for reading books.
Kono basu wa shitamachi e iku no ni benri desu.	This bus is convenient for going downtown.

2. Use *tame ni* plus a verb:

Jidoosha o kau tame ni okane o karimashita.	I borrowed some money to buy a car.
Tomodachi o miokuru tame ni eki e ikimashita.	He went to the railroad station to see a friend off.

40. REQUESTS, COMMANDS

There are several ways to express a request, command, or wish in Japanese. Use:

a. *-te kudasai* = **please do** (something); do (something)

1. For the affirmative:

Hayaku kite kudasai.	Please come early. Come early.
Yukkuri hanashite kudasai.	Please speak slowly.

2. For the negative:

Hayaku konaide kudasai.	Please don't come early.

Yukkuri hanasanaide kudasai.

Please don't speak slowly.

b. *o kudasai* = please give me

Juuen no kitte o kudasai.

Give me a ten-yen stamp, please.

Mizu o kudasai.

Please give me some water.

c. *ga hoshii desu* = I want to have (preceded by the noun showing the thing desired)

Puroguramu ga hoshii desu.

I would like a program.

Sake wa hoshiku arimasen.

I don't want any sake.

d. *-te itadakitai (no) desu (ga)*[1] = I would like to ask you to

Kore o yonde itadakitai desu.

I would like to ask you to read this for me (but do you have time or would it interfere, etc.).

Eigo de kaite itadakitai no desu ga.

Would you mind writing (may I trouble you to write) this in English?

e. *yoo ni shite kudasai* = be careful (not) to, try to,

Kono tegami wa hayaku dasu yoo ni shite kudasai.

Please make every effort to send this mail out early.

Kore wa otosanai yoo ni shite kudasai.

Please be careful not to drop this.

---

[1]The use of *no* and *ga* is optional in this construction.

f. **The Imperative of a Verb**

Each verb has a form called the "imperative" which is constructed by adding *-e* to the stem of a consonant verb and *-ro* to the stem of a vowel verb. The imperative of the irregular verbs is *koi* for *kuru* [come] and *shiro* for *suru* [do].

Ike!	Go!
Miro!	Look at it!

Take·note, however, that the imperative (except for *kudasai,* the imperative of *kudasaru,* whose use is illustrated above) is used *only* in "rough" speech, and *should not* be used in everyday conversation.

41. ADVERBIAL EXPRESSIONS

a. **Formation of Adverbial Expressions**

1. Many adverbs are formed by adding *-ku* to the stem (the plain present minus *-i*) of adjectives:

ADJECTIVE		ADVERB	
takai	expensive	*takaku*	expensively
yasui	cheap	*yasuku*	cheaply
yasashii	easy	*yasashiku*	easily
karui	light	*karuku*	lightly

2. Some adverbial expressions are formed from *na-ni-desu* nouns by using *ni* following the noun (see Section 10 of the Grammar, page 285):

ADJECTIVAL PHRASE		ADVERBIAL PHRASE	
kantan na	simple	*kantan ni*	simply
benri na	convenient	*benri ni*	conveniently
tokubetsu na	special	*tokubetsu ni*	especially
joozu na	skillful	*joozu ni*	skillfully

b. **Comparison of Adverbial Expressions**

Adverbial expressions can be compared like adjectives (see page 306):

POSITIVE	COMPARATIVE	SUPERLATIVE
takaku = expensively	*motto takaku* = more expensively	*ichiban takaku* = most expensively

c. **Adverbial Expressions of Place**

Use *ni* when the verb is *arimasu* [there], *imasu* [be at a place] or *sunde imasu*. Use *de* for most other cases.

koko ni, koko de	here
soba ni, soba de	at the side, near
mae ni, mae de	before, in front
ushiro ni, ushiro de	behind
ue ni, ue de	on top
shita ni, shita de	underneath
naka ni, naka de	inside
soto ni, soto de	outside
doko ni, doko de mo	everywhere (with an affirmative verb)
doko ni, doko de mo	nowhere (with a negative verb)
tooku ni, tooku de	far
chikaku ni, chikaku de	near
doko ni, doko de	where
doko e	to which place
soko ni, soko de	there (nearby)
asoko ni, asoko de	there (far off)

d. Adverbial Expressions of Time

kyoo	today
ashita, asu, myoonichi	tomorrow
kinoo, skaujitsu	yesterday
ototoi, issakujitsu	the day before yesterday
asatte, myoogonichi	the day after tomorrow
ima	now
sono toki	then
mae ni	before
moto	once, formerly
hayaku	early
sugu	soon, presently
osoku	late
tokidoki	often, from time to time
itsu mo	always
nagai aida	for a long time
. . . tari . . . tari shimasu	now . . . now, sometimes . . . sometimes (See Section 31 of the Grammar)
mada	as yet, still
moo	already *(with an affirmative)*
moo	no longer *(with a negative)*

e. Adverbial Expressions of Manner

yoku	well, frequently; studiously; hard
waruku	ill, badly
konna ni	thus, so
onaji yoo ni	similarly
hantai ni	otherwise, conversely
issho ni	together
taihen	much, very

yorokonde	willingly
toku ni	especially
waza to	on purpose, expressly

f. Adverbial Expressions of Quantity or Degree

takusan	much, many
juubun (ni)[1]	enough
sukoshi	little
motto	more
hidoku	extremely, excessively
amari, anmari	too, too much, too many
sonna ni	so much, so many

42. THE TRADITIONAL WRITING SYSTEM

The traditional Japanese writing system contains four types of symbols which are usually used together:

1. One set of forty-six phonetic symbols called *hiragana;*

2. One set of forty-six phonetic symbols called *katakana;*

3. 1850 ideographic symbols called *kanji;* and

4. The letters of the English (or Roman) alphabet, called *Roomaji,* together with the Arabic numerals, which are called *arabiya suuji* or *san'yoo suuji.*

Each of the symbols in *haragana* and *katakana* represents *one syllable,* and each of the forty-six basic syllables of the Japanese language is written with a single symbol, whether in *hiragana* or *katakana* (see Tables IV and VIII, which follow), *Hiragana* symbols are considered to be standard, and are most

[1]The use of *ni* is optional.

widely used. Katakana symbols are used primarily for (a) writing "loan" words (words derived from Western languages), and (b) to give special emphasis to certain words within a sentence, in much the same way that italics are used in English.

a. The Hiragana Symbols

Study the chart of *hiragana* symbols on pages 360–362. Compare it with Chart I of Table I on page 275. Note that the *sound* or *syllable* for each symbol appears in the corresponding square of that chart. For instance, at the point of intersection of vertical and horizontal columns 1 in the chart below, the symbol stands for *ka*.

SPECIAL NOTES FOR THE *HIRAGANA* SYMBOLS

1. Note that the first vertical row of symbols (headed "O"), shows the symbols for the *vowel-syllables only.* In all of the other columns (except the last), each consonant-plus-vowel combination has a new symbol as each stands for a different syllable.

2. Note too that there are *two* symbols for the vowel-syllable *o* (here separated by a diagonal line). The one on the right of the diagonal line (を) is used *only* to write the particle *o* (the thing acted on, or the direct object); it is *never* used to represent anything else.

3. Some symbols have a dual function:

   a. The symbol for *ha* (は) is also used to write the particle *wa* [as for]. The symbol for *wa* which appears at the juncture of vertical column 9 and horizontal column 1 is never used to write the particle *wa* but is used to write the syllable *wa* in all other cases. For instance, わたくしは = *watakushi wa*.

b. The symbol used for *he* (︿) is also used to write the particle *e* [to, toward]. The symbol for the vowel *e* (え) (which appears in the 0 column) is used to write all other *e*'s.

4. Write syllables other than the forty-six basic syllables covered in the above table as follows:

a. Syllables listed in Chart II of Table I (see page 275), are written using the basic symbols plus a diacritical mark (" or °) on the upper right shoulder of each symbol, as in Table VI, on page 362.

The following table shows the number of strokes that are necessary to write each of the *hiragana* symbols. In each chart within the table, the first vertical column shows the completed symbol; the following columns show the strokes that make the symbol. Match these left-hand columns against the symbols in Table IV to read the symbols. The charts are numbered to correspond with the vertical columns in Table IV.

b. Syllables that have a *y* in the middle, i.e., *kya, kyu, kyo, gya, gyu, gyo*, etc., are written with special combinations of two syllables (see Table VII, page 362). This is true also of the syllables *cha, chu, cho, sha, shu, sho, ja, ju, jo*. Thus, in writing *kya*, you combine the symbol for *ki* with the symbol for *ya*. Note that in forming these special combinations, the symbols for *ki, shi, chi, ni, hi, mi*, and *ri* are used as if they were symbols just for the initial consonant, and not for the

Table IV

THE *HIRAGANA* SYMBOLS

CONSONANTS

		0	1	2	3	4	5	6	7	8	9	10
		vowel	k	s	t	n	h[1]	m	y	r	w	n
v	1. a	あ	か	さ	た	な	は	ま	や	ら	わ	ん
o	2. i	い	き	し	ち	に	ひ	み		り		
w	3. u	う	く	す	つ	ぬ	ふ	む	ゆ	る		
e	4. e	え	け	せ	て	ね	へ	め		れ		
l s	5. o*	お	こ	そ	と	の	ほ	も	よ	ろ		

TABLE V

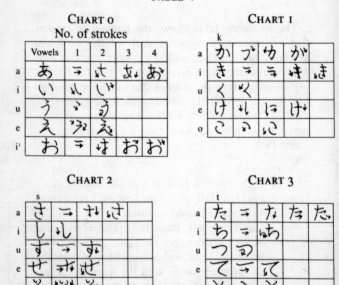

CHART 0

No. of strokes

Vowels	1	2	3	4
a	あ			
i	い			
u	う			
e	え			
i[1]	お			

CHART 1

k

a	か			
i	き			
u	く			
e	け			
o	こ			

CHART 2

s

a	さ			
i	し			
u	す			
e	せ			
o	そ			

CHART 3

t

a	た			
i	ち			
u	つ			
e	て			
o	と			

[1]Remember that a word beginning with *h* may change its initial letter to either *b* or *p*. See Section 4 of the Grammar.

CHART 4

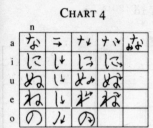

CHART 5

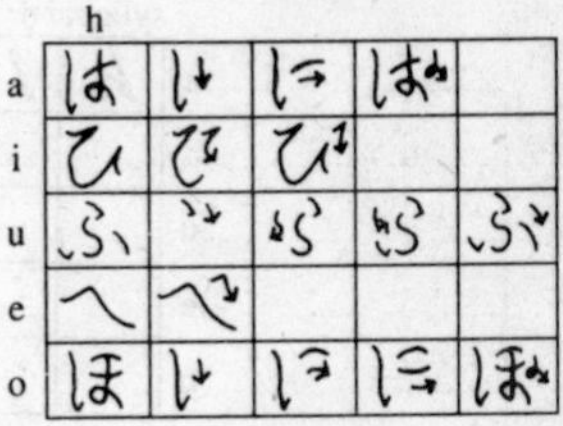

CHART 6

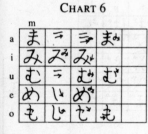

CHART 7

CHART 8

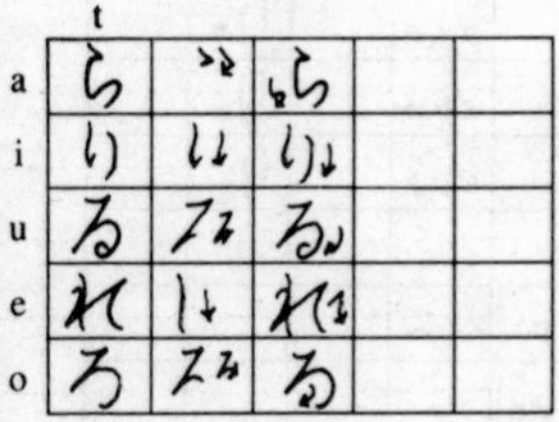

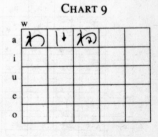

CHART 9

CHART 10

syllabic n

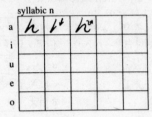

a	ん	ん゛	ん゜		
i					
u					
e					
o					

TABLE VI

	1	2	3		5'	9
	g	z/j	d	b	p	v
1-a	が	ざ	だ	ば	ぱ	う゛ぁ
2-i	ぎ	じ		び	ぴ	う゛ぃ
3-u	ぐ	ず		ぶ	ぷ	う゛
4-e	べ	ぜ	で	べ	ぺ	う゛ぇ
5-o	ご	ぞ	ど	ぼ	ぽ	う゛ぉ

TABLE VII

COMPLETE LIST OF THE SPECIAL COMBINATIONS

	1	2	3	4	5	6	7	8	9
	k	sh	ch	n	h	m		r	
1.	きゃ	しゃ	ちゃ	にゃ	ひゃ	みゃ		りゃ	
3.	きゅ	しゅ	ちゅ	にゅ	ひゅ	みゅ		りゅ	
5.	きょ	しょ	ちょ	にょ	ひょ	みょ		りょ	

	1	2	3	4	5	6	7	8	9
	g	j			b	p			
1.	ぎゃ	じゃ			びゃ	ぴゃ			
3.	ぎゅ	じゅ			びゅ	ぴゅ			
5.	ぎょ	じょ			びょ	ぴょ			

consonant-plus-vowel syllable. And so, to write *kya,* you would use the symbol for *ki* (き), which here would represent the consonant *k,* plus the symbol for *ya.* Remember, too, that the second symbol in a special combination must always be one of the following three: *ya* (や), *yu* (ゆ), or *yo* (よ), and this second member of the combination is usually written smaller than the first, and is usually placed slightly right of the center in a text written from top to bottom. Study Table VII for examples of these special combinations, and compare with Chart III, Table I, for sound values.

c. The syllables *va, vi, vu, ve,* and *vo,* which occur only in words introduced into Japanese fairly recently from Western languages, are written respectively (ゔぁ , ゔぃ , ゔ , ゔぇ , ゔぉ) in *hiragana.* More frequently, they are written in katakana, as follows:(ヴァ , ヴィ , ヴ , ヴェ , ヴォ). Some Japanese do not use these syllables; in place of them they use the symbols for *ba, bi, bu, be,* and *bo,* respectively. Thus, *va* becomes *ba* and *vaiorin* [violin] becomes *baiorin.*

d. To write a double consonant in Japanese, you *always* use the symbol for *tsu* (つ) for the first letter, *regardless of the sound that is being doubled,* whether *kk, ss, ssh, tt, tch, tts,* or *pp.* Note that the symbol for *tsu,* when it is used in this way, is frequently written smaller than usual and placed to the right of center in a text that is written from top to bottom. In a text written horizontally from left to right, however, the symbol for *tsu* is placed either a little above or below the center. Study the examples below. See how the *tsu* symbol is written in place of the first letter in a doubled consonant which appears here in bold-face type:

Chotto	ちょっと	a little
Kekkon	けっこん	marriage
Isshuukan	いっしゅうかん	one week
Ippun	いっぷん	one minute

e. There are two ways to write a double vowel:

1. When the double vowel appears at the beginning of a word, it is expressed by writing the symbol for the corresponding vowel-syllable, twice;

2. When it appears following a consonant, the first letter of the double vowel is written as part of the consonant-plus-vowel symbol (see Table IV, page 360), and the second letter of the double vowel is expressed by the use of the vowel symbol. (See the examples which follow):

aa (a-a)	ああ	Oh!
okaasan (*o-ka-a-san*)	おばあさん	mother
oishii (*o-i-shi-i*)	おいしい	it is delicious
kuuki (*ku-u-ki*)	くうき	air
neesan (*ne-e-san*)	ねえさん	older sister

There is one exception to this rule: to write *oo*, you almost always use the symbol for the vowel-syllable *u* in place of the second *o*, as illustrated below.

kooshoo (ko-**o**-sho-**o**)	こうしょう	negotiation
Tookyoo (to-**o**-kyo-**o**)	とうきょう	Tokyo
moo (mo-**o**)	もう	more, not any more (with a negative)
doozo (do-**o**-zo)	どうぞ	please
doozoo (do-**o**-zo-**o**)	どうぞう	bronze statue

b. **The Katakana Symbols**

All the rules used for writing in *hiragana* apply to *katakana* as well. (See the introductory material to Section 42 of the Grammar, page 357.) However, instead of the round and cursive lines employed in *hiragana*, relatively straight and angular lines are used in writing *katakana* symbols.

The following table shows the number of strokes that are necessary to write each of the *katagana* symbols. In some cases, arrows show the direction in which the strokes should be made. In each chart within the table, the first vertical column shows the completed symbol; the following columns show the strokes necessary to make the symbol. Match these left-hand columns against the symbols in Table VIII to read the symbols. The charts are numbered to correspond with the vertical columns in Table VIII.

TABLE VIII

THE *KATAKANA* SYMBOLS
CONSONANTS

	0	1	2	3	4	5	6	7	8	9	10
	vowel	k	s	t	n	h	m	y	r	w	n**
1. a	ア	カ	サ	タ	ナ	ハ	マ	ヤ	ラ	ワ	ン
2. i	イ	キ	シ	チ	ニ	ヒ	ミ		リ		
3. u	ウ	ク	ス	ツ	ヌ	フ	ム	ユ	ル		
4. e	エ	ケ	セ	テ	ネ	ヘ	メ		レ		
5. o*	オ	コ	ソ	ト	ノ	ホ	モ	ヨ	ロ		

TABLE IX

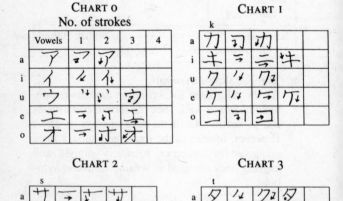

CHART 0 — No. of strokes

CHART 1

CHART 2

CHART 3

*Note that in *katakana*, as in *hiragana*, there are two symbols for *o*, separated here by a diagonal line. See the Special Notes for the Hiragana symbols on page 358.

**Syllabic *n*

CHART 4

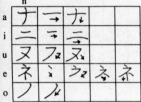

CHART 5

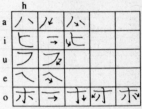

CHART 6

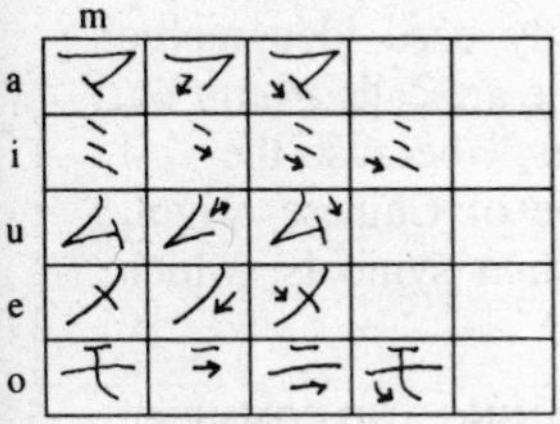

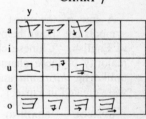

CHART 7

CHART 8

CHART 9

CHART 10

syllabic n

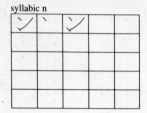

c. Ideographic Symbols

A few of the most frequently used ideographic symbols are shown below. These are called *kanji* or, in English, "Chinese characters," because the vast majority of these characters are of Chinese origin, unlike the *hiragana* and *katakana* symbols, which were created in Japan.

SYMBOL	READING	MEANING AND COMMENT
1. 日	*hi* *nichi* *bi* *jitsu*	the sun; a prototype was a stylized picture of the sun: ☉ . This symbol also is used to write *-nichi* in *mainichi* [everyday], *nichi* and *-bi* in *Nichiyoobi* [Sunday], and it occurs in many other words pertaining to the sun, day, day of the week, etc. Write this figure in the order shown by the arrows:

2. 月　*tsuki*　the moon; a stylized pic-
　　gatsu　ture of the moon; its
　　getsu　prototype was more
　　　　　like a crescent: 🌙
　　　　　This symbol is also
　　　　　used for many other
　　　　　words pertaining to the
　　　　　moon, such as month
　　　　　(as a duration of time)
　　　　　or name of the month,
　　　　　etc. The order of writ-
　　　　　ing is: ↓) 刀丿 ㄇ 月

SYMBOL	READING	
3. 木	*ki*	a tree; a picture of a tree;
	moku	its proto-type had the
	boku	branches and roots
		more pictorially
		drawn: 朩

The order of writing is:
一 十 才 木

4. ⌐ー　*hitotsu*　one: "one-ness" is de-
　　ichi　picted by one line,
　　　　　"two" is 二 ,
　　　　　"three" is 三 , but
　　　　　beyond three it is not
　　　　　this simple
　　　　　The stroke is written
　　　　　from left to right: ⇁

LETTER WRITING

Formerly, letters were written in accordance with
rather rigid forms, but today such forms are seldom
used except in formal announcements of weddings,
deaths, and the like. Instead, ordinary personal correspondence is written without adhering to any particu-
lar form, except that, at the beginning, it is quite
common to discuss the weather at the time of writing.

This section gives examples of both formal (or business) letters and informal (personal) correspondence.

FORMAL

a. Salutation

1. In a formal letter, it is customary to begin with one of the following highly stylized salutations:

   a. *Haikei:* corresponds to "Gentlemen," "Dear Sir(s)," or "Dear Madam" [I humbly state . . .].

   b. *Kinkei:* corresponds to "Gentlemen," "Dear Sir(s)," Dear Madam" [I reverently state . . .].

   c. *Haifuku* (used only in reply to a letter): "Gentlemen," "Dear Sir(s)," "Dear Madam" [I reply humbly . . .].

2. The addressee's name does not appear until the very end of the letter, where it is written in the following order:

   a. The family name,

   b. The given name, and

   c. The proper honorific (the most common and useful of which is *-sama,* a formal variation of *-san* [Mr., Mrs., Miss]. (See also the section on Complimentary Closings, below.)

3. When a letter in Japanese is written in the English alphabet, it customarily follows the form for an English letter; thus, the addressee's name is used with the honorific *-sama,* and the formal salutation word (see Item 1, above) is omitted.

b. **Complimentary Close**

1. First, use one of the following stylized closing remarks:

   a. *Mazu wa oshirase made.* = Just to inform you (of) the above.

   b. *Maze wa goaisatsu made.* = Just to extend my greetings to you.

   c. *Toriaezu gohenji made.* = Just to answer your letter in a hurry.

2. Then add one of the following complimentary closings:

   a. *Keigu.* = Respectfully yours. [I have respectfully stated.]

   b. *Soosoo.* = Sincerely yours. [In a hurry. Hurriedly.]

   c. *Kashiko.* = Sincerely yours. [In awe (used by women only).]

3. After signing your name, place the addressee's name with the proper honorific on a separate line, either flush with the left margin or slightly indented:

   a. *Yamada Yoshio-sama* = Mr. Yoshio Yamada

   b. *Yamada Yoshio sensei*[1] = Mr. Yoshio Yamada (used for a minister, priest, doctor, schoolteacher, congressman, etc.)

   c. *Yamada Yoshio-dono* = Mr. Yoshio Yamada *(used in official letters).*

   d. *Yamada Yoshio Shichoo-dono* = (Mr.) Mayor Yoshio Yamada (used for writing to someone we would address as "the

---

[1]*Sensei,* unlike *-san* or *-sama,* may be used by itself as a term of address (somewhat like our word "sir"), and consequently is not always appended to the name as a suffix.

Honorable"—i.e., a distinguished office-holder: consists of the addressee's name plus his official title plus the honorific *-dono* or *-sama*)

c. **Examples**

Now study the construction of the letters which follow.

BUSINESS LETTERS

Peter Paine[1]
Marunouchi Hotel
Chiyoda-ku, Tookyoo
Shoowa 61 nen[2]
9 gatsu 25 nichi

Japan Quarterly
Asahi Shinbun Sha
Yuurakuchoo, Chiyoda-ku
Tookyoo

Japan Quarterly ichinenbun no koodokuryoo to shite nisen yonhyaku en no kogawase o ookuri itashinasu. Ouketori kudasai.

Piitaa Pein
(Peter Paine)[3]

---

[1]It is customary to retain the English name of the writer in the Japanese heading.
[2]*Shoowa* 61 *nem* = the sixty-first year of the Era of Showa, corresponding to the year 1986.
[3]Normally, the English name would be signed as in the parentheses.

Marunouchi Hotel
Chiyoda-ku, Tokyo
September 25, 1986

Japan Quarterly
Asahi Shinbun Sha
Yūraku-cho, Chiyoda-ku
Tokyo

Gentlemen:[1]

Enclosed you will find a money order for ¥2,400 for a year's subscription to your magazine *Japan Quarterly.*

Very truly yours,
Peter Paine
Sakata Shookai, Ltd.
2, 4-choome, Ginza
Chuuooku, Tookyoo
Shoowa 61 nen
8 gatsu 16 nichi

Tanaka Shookai
3, 1-chome, Yuurakuchoo
Chiyoda-ku, Tookyoo
Haifuku:

Otoiawase no shinamono wa saru 8 gatsu 13 nichi ni machigainaku kozutsumi de hassoo itashimashita.

Mazu wa oshirase made.
Sakata Yukio

Sakata Shōkai, Ltd.
2, 4-chome, Ginza
Chūō-ku, Tokyo
August 16, 1986

[1]In Japanese, it is not necessary to use such a salutation.

Tanaka Shōkai
3, 1-chome, Yūrakuchō
Chiyoda-ku, Tokyo
Gentlemen:

In reply to your recent letter, we wish to advise you that the merchandise was mailed to you parcel-post on August 13.

> Very truly yours,
> Yukio Sakata

INFORMAL

a. **Salutation and Content**
   1. Do not use one of the formal salutations described in the preceding section on formal letters.
   2. It is customary to mention the recent weather and climate in your locality.
   3. Inquire into the health of the person to whom you are writing and his family.
   4. Go into whatever other topics you want to bring up.

b. **Close**
   1. Don't use any of the complimentary closing remarks described in Item B-2 of the preceding section on formal letters.
   2. Instead, close with a stylized remark such as:
      a. *Dewa mata.* = Well, then again.
      b. *Gokigen yoo.* = Wishing you good health.
      c. *Okarada o odaiji ni.* = Keep well. Take good care of yourself.
      d. *Minasan ni yoroshiku.* Regards to everyone.

3. Sign your name on a new line.
4. Place the addressee's name on another line, either flush with the left margin or slightly indented.

c. **Examples**
   Study the informal letter and thank-you note which follow.

INFORMAL LETTER

Shoowa 61 nen
3 gatsu 15 nichi

Azusa sama:

Otegami ureshiku haiken shimashita.

Minasama ogenki no yoo de nani yori ni omoimasu.

Sate watakushidomo no Kyooto hoomen no koto desu ga Shigatsu no hajime ni jikkoo suru koto ni shimashita. Nishuukan taizai no yotei desu. Minasama ni ome ni kakareru no o tanoshimi ni shite imasu.

Kanai no Irene mo issho ni mairimasu. Shoobai no hoo mo okagesama de umaku itte imasu. Kore ga tsuzuite kureru to ii to omoimasu. Chotto muri na chuumon ka mo shiremasen ga otaku mo Shigatsu ni haittara sukoshi te o nuite issho ni ikuraka asoberu yoo ni shimasen ka.

Konoaida Nomura kun ni attara kimi wa doo shite iru daroo to itte imashita. Kare mo shigoto wa umaku itte iru rashii desu.

Daiji na koto o wasureru tokoro deshita ga Gurando Hotel ni heya o yoyaku shite moraemasen ka? Shigatsu itsuka kara desu. Onegai shimasu.

Ja kyoo wa kore de shitsurei shimasu. Otayori o matte imasu. Okusan ni yoroshiku.

Jakku
(Jack)

March 5, 1986

Dear Azusa:

I was very happy to receive your last letter. I'm glad to hear that all of you are well.

First of all, I've some good news for you. I expect to spend two weeks in Kyoto at the beginning of April and I'm looking forward to seeing you and your family.

My wife, Irene, is coming with me; she's delighted to be able to meet your wife at long last. Business is pretty good right now. Let's hope it keeps up. Try not to be too busy during the month of April so that we can have some time together. I suppose that's a little difficult for a busy man like you.

The other day Nomura asked about you. His business is going well.

I almost forgot the most important thing. Can you reserve a room for me at the Grand Hotel for April fifth? You'll be doing me a great favor.

I'll stop writing now. I hope to hear from you soon. My best regards to your wife.

Yours,
Jack

THANK-YOU NOTE

Yamada on-okusama,

Kono tabi wa taisoo rippa na okurimono o choodai itashimashite atsuku atsuku orei mooshiagemasu. Hanga ni wa watakushi mo higoro kyoomi o motte ori sono ue ni kondo itadakimashita no wa kyakuma ni kakete yoku choowa itashimasu no de hontoo ni yorokonde orimasu. Arigatoo gozaimashita.

Mazu wa on-rei made.

Robaato Sumisu
Robert Smith

Dear Mrs. Yamada,

I should like to thank you for your delightful present. The wood-block print is beautiful and matches the other things in my living room perfectly.

Thank you ever so much.

(Sincerely yours,)[1]
Robert Smith

ADDRESSING AN ENVELOPE

For a letter using the English alphabet:

Peter Paine
3 Oiwakecho
Bunkyoku, Tokyo

Tanaka Taroo Sama
Kyooto Daigaku Igakubu
Kyooto

In Japanese writing and using a Japanese envelope:

[1]Note that in Japanese there is no formal closing in a note of this kind.

	Cassette	Record		
Advanced ($11.95)			record $15.95	□ 010852
French	□ 558866	□ 558874	manual $3.00	□ 512831
Spanish	□ 558831	□ 55884X	Shorthand	
			cassette $15.95	□ 542528
			record $15.95	□ 010860
For Foreign-Speaking, Who Wish to Learn			Book I $3.00	□ 512718
English ($15.95)			Book II $3.00	□ 512726
	Cassette	Record	Better Speech	
English for French	□ 50202X	□ 508192	cassette $15.95	□ 542455
English for Spanish	□ 558793	□ 558807	record $15.95	□ 001373
English for Italian	□ 513234	□ 502003	correct speech $3.00	□ 512505
English for German	□ 513226	□ 501996	correct usage $3.00	□ 512513
English for Portuguese		□ 508206		
English for Chinese	□ 508176	□ 508184	**Living Language Videocassette**	
			Program ($39.95)	
			French (60 minutes)	□ VHS 555549
Children's Courses ($15.95)				□ Beta 555611
French	□ 542463	□ 001357	Spanish (77 minutes)	□ VHS 555557
Spanish	□ 542471	□ 001365		□ Beta 55562X
			German	□ VHS 560151
			(90 minutes)	□ Beta 560143
Business Skills				
Keyboard Typing				
cassette $15.95		□ 542536		

Order Here
LIVING LANGUAGE, Dept. 849
34 Engelhard Avenue, Avenel, N.J. 07001

YES—rush me the LIVING LANGUAGE COURSES® I've checked.

Name (Please Print) _____

Address _____

City _____ State _____ Zip _____

_____ Courses @ $15.95			
_____ Courses @ $11.95			
_____ Manuals/Dictionaries @ $3.95			
_____ Books @ $3.00			
_____ Videocassettes @ $39.95			
	N.Y. and N.J. Residents add Sales Tax		
	Shipping & Handling Charge _____ Items @ $1.85 Each		
TOTAL ITEMS ORDERED	**Total Amount Due**		

□ Check or Money Order Enclosed Made Payable to Crown Publishers, Inc.
(No cash or stamps, please)

Charge   □ MasterCard   □ Visa   □ American Express

Account Number (include all digits)

Card Expires | | | | MO   YR

Signature _____